Children's Literature

Volume 4

Volume 4

Annual of
The Modern Language Association
Seminar on Children's Literature and
The Children's Literature
Association

Temple University Press

Philadelphia

Children's Literature

EDITOR-IN-CHIEF:
  FRANCELIA BUTLER

CO-EDITORS:
  BENNETT A. BROCKMAN and WILLIAM E. SHEIDLEY

BOOK REVIEW EDITOR: Ross Miller
ADVISORY BOARD: Nancy Chambers, Martin Gardner, William T.
  Moynihan, Peter F. Neumeyer, William Rosen
CONSULTING EDITORS: Jan Bakker, Marcella Booth, Rachel
  Fordyce, Narayan Kutty, Meradith McMunn, Thomas J. Roberts,
  Barbara Rosen
SPECIAL CONSULTANTS: Charity Chang, Edward G. Fisher, Corine
  T. Norgaard
CONSULTANTS FOR THE CHILDREN'S LITERATURE ASSOCIATION:
  Anne Devereux Jordan, Jon C. Scott
EDITORIAL ASSISTANTS: Colleen McMahon, Ellen Rochford, Joan
  Somes, Karon Harris

Editorial correspondence should be addressed to:
  Editors, *Children's Literature*
  Department of English, U–25
  University of Connecticut
  Storrs, Connecticut 06268

Manuscripts submitted should conform to the second edition of the
MLA Style Sheet. An original and one copy are requested.
Manuscripts should be accompanied by a self-addressed envelope
and postage.

Temple University Press, Philadelphia   19122
© 1975 by Francelia Butler. All rights reserved
Published 1975
Printed in the United States of America

International Standard Book Number: 0-87722-042-5 cloth; 0-87722-076-X paper
Library of Congress Catalog Card Number: 75-21550 mc 78-2585
Cover illustration: "The Tale-Teller" by Masafumi Takeuchi

Contents

Reviews

Varia

Children's Literature
Volume 4

The Editor's High Chair
Including an Interview with Madame Indira Gandhi

The breakdown of belief in truth and goodness has reached such proportions that it is accepted as normal in much literature, including that written for children. Children's stories often tell about going to a grocery store or a department store. How many of them mention that, when mother makes her purchase (often with the child watching) and writes the check, she must show her driver's license, then be photographed and even fingerprinted, and that the parcel she carries is carefully stapled shut to prevent her from dropping any stolen merchandise into it?

Teachers are represented as telling stories to children in a kind of idiot vacuum. How many people realize that some insight into these stories would help the children and that few teachers are given insight through graduate courses in the humanities? No one has a doctoral degree from a program in children's literature in the humanities, and it is likely to take a great struggle even to get a well-established course in the subject listed in a graduate school catalog.

If, as many people feel, the humanities, like the churches, are dying, it is because some academic humanists dislike facing real issues and habitually take a bland, Chamber of Commerce attitude toward the needs of the students to whose well-being they should be dedicated. A professor who gives complicated exegeses of literature parroted from books of criticism may wink at cheating, perhaps because he himself has cheated. Small wonder, in a world of tiny cheats and careful skirting of the problem in literature, that when students write their own stories, cheating is not considered serious. For example, when a class was assigned the writing of fables, several of them wrote fables something like this one:

A mouse steals a little bit of cheese each day from a woman's kitchen. Then one day, he manages to drag away a whole chunk of cheddar. Missing the chunk, the lady of the house sets a trap and catches the mouse. Moral: It's O.K. to cheat a little bit, but don't do it on a large scale or you're likely to be caught.

When children grow up with this attitude, then the fingerprinting, the photographing, the stapling are necessary. Professors of English should strive to relate literature to such situations here and now, to relate it to life.

3

Those who scorn children's literature fail to realize that, because of its simplicity, it is most difficult to teach, and its teaching should be an honored profession. It comes near to the hearts and psyches of all of us. Few people quote Milton, but many quote snatches of Mother Goose. Even Shakespeare, in the most serious part of *King Lear,* found it necessary to use parts of several rhymes later known as "Mother Goose rhymes," including "Fie, foh, and fum, / I smell the blood of a British man," "Pillicock sat on Pillicock-hill," and "Sleepest or wakest thou, jolly shepherd? / Thy sheep be in the corn." It was in this simple poetry that he could fuse the beauty and the horror of the world, as he did in his own verse: "Full fathom five thy father lies; / Of his bones are coral made."

The neglect by humanists of the study of the literature of the future generation is not limited to the United States. In fact, more tolerance is shown to children's literature here than in Europe or in the Far East. In the summer of 1974, I went to India to interview Mme Indira Gandhi on the current state of children's literature there. An account of that interview follows:

In mid-April, Professor Narayan Kutty, who teaches children's literature at Eastern Connecticut State College, suggested that because of the interest her father, Nehru, had in children's literature, I should try to arrange an interview with Mme Gandhi during a research trip to Southeast Asia later that spring. Accordingly, on April 26, I wrote her. Since I was about to leave the country and was not sure when I would arrive in New Delhi, I wrote that I would ring her office on arrival.

When I reached New Delhi, I made connections with her office and was given an appointment at 3:30 on June 19. I was told to go to gate six, the Venue office in the Secretarial Complex, South Block. My friend Mary Ann MacDougall, Professor of Educational Statistics at the University of Virginia, was also granted permission to interview Mme Gandhi.

We took a cab to the great mall, which is bordered by striking buildings of beige and red stone, a combination of Indian and English architecture, a magnificent, mystical sight stretching almost beyond the comprehension, like buildings in a fairy tale. The temperature was well over 100°. On the lawn near the Venue office, two men in white were lazily switching with twigs a white bull pulling a lawn mower.

At the entrance of gate six, a servant in white sat squirting a hose on the rough rattan curtains of the entrance way. Water was running under the wooden slats which had been placed over the floor. Some of the spray touched me lightly, and it was refreshing. Inside the door, in an office, sat several men and one or two guards. No guns were visible, however. When I announced that we had an appointment with Mme Gandhi, one of the men escorted us both to the second floor to a spacious, Victorian-type waiting room decorated in shades of green, with a domed painted ceiling depicting stages in Indian life in the 1920s.

Mary Ann and I sat very quietly. I think we were wondering if the room was bugged. After about twenty minutes, we were escorted to the outer office of the Prime Minister. Here, two men were seated at desks and two others were waiting, presumably for Mme Gandhi. The Prime Minister's Secretary came out of a side door, and introduced himself. He asked what other important people I had seen on my trip, and I told him, "Only important monuments." He advised us both not to leave New Delhi without seeing the Old Fort, where the land has been excavated, revealing evidence of several civilizations in the strata.

At that point, the door opened and there stood Mme Gandhi. I was struck immediately by how small she looked compared with my image of her, which was drawn from newspaper pictures. She wore a light cotton sari with a small figured design in moss green. The border was green and she had thonged green shoes on her bare feet. She wore no makeup, no jewelry. All this I saw at a glance and forgot about as soon as I looked at her directly. Her eyes are dark and intent and she kept her chin tilted slightly upward—a regal woman.

I found myself saying, "Mme Gandhi, I'd like you to meet my friend, Professor Mary Ann MacDougall," and Mme. Gandhi said, "How do you do?" and then walked to her desk for a moment. We followed along, but she suggested that we chat in another area of the large room, where there were chairs, a sofa, and a coffee table. We remained standing until she joined us. After she sat down, we sat in chairs on each side of her.

First, I presented her with the most recent issue of *Children's Literature* (Volume 3), and then began the questioning. I gave her a copy of the questions, so that she could easily follow along—an unnecessary precaution, of course, since she speaks fluent English, having been educated in England and in Switzerland. It was necessary to give her a preamble to each question, however, so that she would fully understand what it was about. The questions follow, as well as the replies:

Ques. Enrollments in literature courses in the Humanities are down all over the United States, except in a few subjects, notably children's literature. Students in philosophy, psychology, anthropology, sociology, as well as the languages are electing children's literature—perhaps out of concern for those who must live after them as well as for themselves. Now, some of the best scholars in the Humanities are beginning to show an interest in the subject. They are being forced to meet student demand. Up to now, scholars in the Liberal Arts have had contempt for children's literature as too trivial for their consideration. The same situation prevails in Europe.

Do you know of any evidence that philosophers, psychologists, and literary scholars in Indian universities are interested in a careful study of the literature of the future generation?

Ans. None at all. The usual pattern is moralizing to children and talking down to them.

Ques. One of the evidences of the new, deep interest in the subject can be seen in an article by James Hillman, who gave the Terry lectures at Yale following Jung, Dewey, Erich Fromm, and other such eminent psychologists. Hillman is Editor of Spring Publications of the Jung Institute, Zurich. He argues that every child between the ages of five and twelve should be introduced to the folktales of his own culture, so that fragments of archetypes in his subconscious can surface and form patterns in a process of preventive psychotherapy. He bases his conclusions on some thirty years' clinical experience. No one knows how it works, but story itself, especially in the ancient legends, has a soothing effect, helps to heal.

Might, for example, the Indian tales—Mahabharata and Ramayana—have the same effect on Indian children?

Ans. Perhaps. Not at the expensive schools, where they are really not taught, but one gets these tales in many ways besides literature—at festivals, and so on. At ordinary schools, they learn the old tales that provide a link with the past.

Ques. An Indian scholar in America says many children in India today are left in a vacuum. They cannot wholly accept the old folk values of self-sacrifice and self-effacement, because the values are in conflict with the Western values of self-fulfillment, particularly in a materialistic way. Do you think this is true?

Ans. No. I think this is a superficial judgment. I don't believe there is that much difference between the values of the East and the West. Everyone admires someone who is self-sacrificing. Any conflict here is more apparent than real. The real conflict is between the old and the new in India.

Ques. Is there any attempt on the part of philosophers and psychologists in the humanities to make a fusion or synthesis of these values for the benefit of young people, not as a directive to writers, but to create an intellectual climate in which they can function more freely?

Ans. No. As I said, there is not that great a difference between the

Eastern and Western philosophies of life. There is materialism in Ramayana, for that matter. Greater respect is given to renouncement, but the average person is not expected to give everything up. The real confusion is between the old and the new India. India is a poor country, but apathetic resignation is gone. Where once people were very poor, now they see things which create a frustration. The greater conflict is between the young educated people and parents who are illiterate. The young are alienated from their parents, who are not educated in the real sense of the word. We have an uneducated father who is an authority figure—head of a communal family. It is the old India against the new —not a clash of values.

Ques. C. S. Lewis, famous religious philosopher at Oxford, said that if he wanted to write anything really deep, he wrote a children's book. (Perhaps, because of the limpid simplicity, one can see into the depths of things, as in the Psalms, Aesop's Fables, Christ's parables, Plato's dialogues.) Oxford University has been fortunate in having many great writers who respected children's literature, among them C. S. Lewis, Lewis Carroll, John Ruskin, J. R. R. Tolkien, and W. H. Auden, who wrote criticism of children's books. In the United States, few great writers go into the field, and books often tend to be propagandistic, one-idea books suggesting success if one behaves in a certain way. Indeed, in the West, the whole field of children's literature seems to have developed from the Puritan attempt to threaten children with hell if they did not behave in a certain way. It is not surprising, since the Puritans were of the merchant class, that the field has developed along commercial lines, the main emphasis now being more subtle—to promise children success if they behave in acceptable ways. No doubt this has discouraged great writers from entering the field. I have heard that in India, too, the best writers tend to leave the field alone. Is this a fair statement? Are there any recent efforts to attract great writers to the field?

Ans. So far as I know, no great writers in India are attracted to the field and there is no effort to attract them to it.

Ques. Dr. James Hillman has also indicated that all repression, including that of women, goes back to the child. I believe that one of the main reasons scholars in the humanities in the United States look down on children's literature is that they relate it to women, who bear children and also bear much of the responsibility for the early education of children—mothers, primary teachers, librarians in children's rooms. Might the problem of the neglect of children's literature in India on the part of scholars in the humanities be due in part to the classical relationship of women with children? Of course, one possible explanation for the neglect of the field may be that its very simplicity makes it difficult to teach without a complex exegesis. (At this point, Mme Gandhi paused and smiled. She saw that I was trying to trap her into a "women's lib" statement. Then, with a twinkle in her eye . . .)

Ans. Perhaps association of women with the field is the reason for the neglect. . . . Let's say it's an interesting question which deserves further study.

Ques. Undoubtedly, you are often asked what stories you read as a child or were told to you. Who were your storytellers and which stories did you enjoy most?

Ans. The servants and a grandmother knew the old tales and told them to me. When I was six or eight, I read *Winnie-the-Pooh, Alice in Wonderland,* the Grimms' Tales, and the Indian classics.

Ques. No American books?

Ans. No American books. I discovered them much later.

Professor MacDougall then asked some questions:

Ques. I have noted with interest the significant contributions of the Children's Book Trust in India and the International Children's Competition in encouraging the writing of essays, stories, and poems. Is there a parallel concern here to preserve and share culture between the diversity of Indian peoples, with respect to the role of the family in the educational process?

Ans. Indirectly. Foreign exchange programs help—living in other homes. There are no special programs for acculturation or socialization, no concerted programs for reading. I am trying to get a film program going. One can say so much in a film. But we have several million children to educate.

Ques. What educational programs do you perceive as being the most successful in equalizing the academic training among the many social, economic, and cultural groups?

Ans. Recreational programs. Preschool in New Delhi and the cities.

Ques. How does the family perceive the educational process?

Ans. The family want their children to have an education.

At this point, since we had been promised fifteen minutes and had stayed twenty-five minutes, we felt that we should go. We thanked Mme Gandhi for her time, and we walked to the door, she to her desk to deposit the copy of *Children's Literature.* To my surprise, she then hurried after us. At the door, she extended her hand and wished us both a pleasant journey.

Several things about the experience astonished me. One was that in spite of the fact that I was carrying a large handbag stuffed with a powder can, a flashlight, and other metal objects that would have been an airport checker's nightmare, there was no security check of any kind. Another was the directness and, at the same time, the informality with which Mme Gandhi answered questions.

Small wonder that everyone we came in contact with in New Delhi loved her—the waiters, the shopkeepers, the cab drivers (who said she rode a cab to work; that cab, with her in it, no doubt became a coach and four). They pointed out her modest pumpkin-colored home to us. At the Hotel Claridge desk, I discovered by accident when I tried to cash a check that mentioning I had come to New Delhi to see her had magical powers—far more effective than showing a credit card. She was indeed the Good Witch Indira and I had a feeling that perhaps I could make a wish any time and she might materialize to have tea with us.

But next day the whole incident was put in perspective. Mary Ann and I were riding in a cab in Kashmir, an area where Mme Gandhi was in some danger. Suddenly, a soldier jumped in our car and ordered the driver to take him to a certain point along the road. He then ordered him to park. At that point, we noticed that soldiers were stationed along the road. I asked what the trouble was.

"The Prime Minister, Mme Gandhi, will pass here within the hour," he said importantly.

We let him out and tried to go on, but were stopped. After a quarter of an hour or so, jeeps passed, carrying men with machine guns. Then a black Mercedes, men with guns on top of it, sped by. In the back seat in one corner, was a small woman.

"She's wearing a coral sari today," I observed.

On reaching home, I discovered that some American scholars doubted whether Mme Gandhi really knew the situation with respect to children's literature in India. I therefore addressed letters to two persons in India whose opinions would be wholly informed. The first was Mohini Rao, Editor of Children's Books and Director of the National Book Trust. (The Trust has a project known as Nehru Bal Pustakalaya— Nehru Library for Children—for publishing children's books. Each book in the series is published in thirteen languages simultaneously.) I also sent a letter to Sharada Nayak, Secretary of the Educational Resources Center in Delhi of The University of the State of New York—a cooperative undertaking to develop materials for teaching and study about India in American schools, colleges, and universities. I asked each woman independently to comment on the same questions I had asked Mme Gandhi. Their replies were strikingly similar to hers.

First, Mohini Rao wrote as follows:

Children's literature in India actually started getting attention and encouragement only after Independence. Prior to that, we were dependent to a great extent on books imported from England. Original writers for children in Indian languages did not receive much encouragement.

Although now there is a clamor for better and more books for children and more attention is being given to this question both at the governmental and private level, it is not a subject which interests universities. Scholars of literature, philosophy, or psychology do not treat this subject as part of the Humanities.

Some eminent Indian writers like Tagore have written for children. Tagore's brother, Abanindra Nath Tagore, the great painter, also wrote for children. Satyajit Ray, the world-famous film producer, brings out a quarterly magazine for children and he himself does all the illustrations for it.

Here in India children's literature is not associated more with women than with men, although my experience as an editor has revealed that women do have a better aptitude for writing for children. They are more warm, direct, and unpretentious.

Stories in the Indian epics, Ramayana and Mahabharata, do have archetypes, and I think there is a lot of substance in James Hillman's suggestion. Although no one has yet made a study of Ramayana and Mahabharata from this point of view, I do feel that they have a similar role in India to that of Grimms' fairy tales in the West. Ramayana and Mahabharata are mythological writings and their main characters are supernatural both in their good and evil deeds. Since these are revered books, their appeal naturally is different from that of other common folk stories.

Sharada Nayak replied as follows:

So far as I am aware, there are no scholars in Indian universities who are doing any work on children's literature. Among Indian novelists writing in English who have taken an interest in children's literature and who are writing for children, there are Mulk Rak Anand and Ruskin Bond. The former, however, is better known as a novelist of adult fiction.

Published children's literature is largely derived from the epics, myths and legends of India, part of the vast oral tradition. Though a child hears these stories from mother and grandmother, he also sees them performed in the folk theatre, puppet shows, and in the movies. There is this unifying element in all of India's diversity. I would agree with James Hillman's idea that these mythological stories have the role he describes.

It would seem from the views of these eminent persons that, just as in the United States, India has a long way to go before the study of children's literature is given the serious attention it deserves. Besides the information on the state of children's literature in India obtained from the interviews referred to above, this issue contains an article on contemporary children's literature in India by Kamal Sheoran of the Children's Book Trust, New Delhi. Indeed, this is an annual with an international flavor, for there are also prints of Chinese children with literary folk relationships, articles on children and literature in medieval France and England, on Romanian folk literature, and on children's literature now in Canada.

The big news is that beginning with this volume, *Children's Literature* is being published by Temple University Press. The Press is a pioneer, then, in this exciting field: the first university press ever to publish a journal of children's literature. The Press recognizes that children's literature is perhaps the most baffling, the most complex of all literatures. Most of it is written by adults trying to recall their childhood and attempting to communicate with parents and children—that is, with a dual audience of children and adults. In this sense, the literature has a kinship with that of the Middle Ages, and medievalists are often drawn to the field.

Ideally, humanists are concerned with the humane, and if they are specialists in the field of literature, they are naturally interested in literature in relation to people. If they are interested in children's literature, they are concerned not only with the aesthetic qualities of literary form, language, and structure, but also with the appeal and the appropriateness of the works for children.

Since, after all, that is what humanism is all about, most humanists in the field are scholars who love children enough to want to give them something beyond the written-to-order stories in which various lessons are pointedly enfolded—tolerance towards homosexuality, the need for recycling bottles, how to accept a new baby in the house, and so on. The idea is to search out and to study literature which children can live by rather than books that they can exist by. This series of annuals is designed for all those who share these views of the importance of the literature of those who must live after us.

—Francelia Butler

Articles

On Not Writing for Children*

P. L. Travers

"On Not Writing for Children"—what an odd title for a lecture, you will say, especially from one whose books are largely read by children! But I hope they are also read by grownups, as you will see by what I'm going to say. I think that grownups are a very important part of children's literature, so called. I'm not sure that I believe in children's literature, but as I go on, you'll see why. Well, you know, I'm not writing for children. This seems to suggest that there exists some particular reason for the fact that I don't write for children, and that I am proposing to explain it: a sort of secret recipe that, with luck, can be divulged.

But if there is a secret, I am not going to divulge it, not because I will not, but because I cannot. I cannot tell you how it's done. There is something in me that hesitates to inquire too closely into this business of writing; fear perhaps that if one discovered the "how" of it, the way it's done, one might be tempted to make use of it and let it become mechanical. There is something in me that could go on writing and writing, book after book about Mary Poppins; and maybe I will do that, but if I know how to do it, I shan't be able to do it at all. To me it is a mystery, and I think it should remain a mystery. Some of you will know, perhaps, that one of the most annoying aspects of a character in a book of mine is that she never explains. There is a Chinese ideogram called *pai* that has, I am told, two different meanings, depending on the context. One is "explain," but the other one is "in vain." How can I add anything to that? It is in vain to explain that the Chinese know better than we, even though they are doing all those terrible things to Confucius.

And yet I feel bound to clarify this feeling I have. No, it is stronger than a feeling—this conviction I have, that very few people write for children.

Not long ago, an American journalist, Clifton Fadiman, a well-known writer and collector of children's books, asked me for (and I quote) "your general ideas on literature for children, your aims and purposes and what led you to the field." Well, this flummoxed me. I hadn't any ideas, general or specific, on literature for children and I hadn't set out with

*Transcription of a paper read by P. L. Travers at the University of Connecticut, March 26, 1974. Copyright © P. L. Travers, 1975. All rights reserved.

15

aims or purposes. I couldn't say that anything I had done was intended or invented. It simply happened. Furthermore, I told him that I was not at all sure that I was in his field, even though many children throughout the world have been kind enough to read my books. I said it was a strong belief of mine that I didn't write for children at all, that the idea simply didn't enter my head. I am bound to assume, and I told him this, that there is such a field. I hear about it so often, but I wonder if it is a valid one or whether it has not been created less by writers than by publishers and booksellers—and perhaps indeed by people who teach Children's Literature. I am always astonished when I see books labeled "For from 5 to 7" or "From 9 to 12" because who is to know what child will be moved by what book and at what age? Who is to be the judge? I'm not one; I can't tell.

Nothing I had written before Mary Poppins had anything to do with children and I have always assumed, when I thought about it at all, that she had come out of the same well of nothingness (and by nothingness, I mean no-thing-ness) as the poetry, myth, and legend that had absorbed me all my writing life. If I had been told while I was working on the book that I was doing it for children, I think I would have been terrified. How would I have had the effrontery to attempt such a thing? For, if for children, the question immediately arises, "for what children?" That word "children" is a large blanket; it covers, as with grownups, every kind of being that exists. Was I writing for the children in Japan, where Mary Poppins is required reading in the English language schools and universities, telling a race of people who have no staircases in their homes about somebody who slid up the bannisters? For the children in Africa, who read it in Swahili, and who have never even seen an umbrella, much less used one? Or to come to those nearer my own world, was I writing for the boy who wrote to me with such noble anger when he came to the end of the third book where Mary Poppins goes away forever, "Madum (he spelt it M-A-D-U-M), you have sent Mary Poppins away. Madum, I will never forgive you. You have made the children cry." Well, what a reproach! What a picture! The children weeping in the world and I alone responsible! The labels "From 5 to 7" or "9 to 12" can have no relation to such a letter. It came straight out of the human heart, a heart that, no matter what its age, was capable of pain. That boy had already begun to know what sorrow was and he reproached me for his knowledge.

Or was I writing for the children in Trinidad, a group of whom asked me to talk to them when I was in the library at Port of Spain? It was they, however, who did the talking, telling me more about the books than

I could ever have known. But I noticed that the smallest child, a little dark plum-colored boy, was silent. Had he read the book? I asked. Yes. Then what was it he liked about Mary Poppins? He shook his head sombrely. "I don't like her," he said. Well, this immediatedly charmed me. Praise is something you feel shy of trusting, but blame—ah, blame is where you learn your lessons. "No?" I asked with interest, hoping to hear the reason why. But then the solemn face suddenly broke, like a cracked melon, into a smile. His eyes shone with his secret joke. "I don't like her, I love her." Well, what an answer, what a declaration! Was I writing, could I even dream of writing, for creatures who understood so much and in particular for this one child, hardly more than six years old, who already knew and could strictly evaluate the shades of feeling between liking and loving? This was an extraordinary thing to happen.

Or for that other child who was asked to write an essay on his favorite subject or his favorite book? It was short, just five or six lines, but his teacher thought so well of it that she kindly sent it to me. It said, "The Lord is the Father of all things and Mary Poppins is the Mother of all things and they are married, or has been married, and they are both a miracle." Well, I find that moment of uncertainty in the "has been married" very touching and I think I see the reasoning behind it. The Lord doesn't figure in any of the books—He's never mentioned. Clearly, therefore, at some stage, he and Mary Poppins must have agreed to part. I like to think that this was not due to any fundamental incompatability but rather that the pair came to an amicable agreement to function in different spheres. Now, could I dare, could I presume to write for such a child? Perhaps, indeed, it was he who was writing for me, teaching me what to look for in my own work. For a writer is, after all, only half his book. The other half is the reader and from the reader the writer learns. He has to learn his lessons as the reader.

Then there was the boy of sixteen who called to me from an upper room in my house and earnestly asked me to make him a promise. With some hesitation, I agreed, uncertain where it would lead me. And what do you think the promise was? "You must never, never be clever," he said. "I have just been reading *Mary Poppins* again and I have come to the conclusion that it could only have been written by a lunatic." Well! I have never had thoughts of being clever, so I accepted the epithet lunatic as I believe he meant it, as a sort of praise. And here, again, a reader had given me a clue. Moonstruck! A writer needs to be moonstruck, which is to say absorbed in, lost in, and in love with his own material. Perhaps that's part of the secret—to be in love with one's own material, to be moonstruck by it.

If I go back to my own childhood—no, not back but if I, as it were, turn sideways and consulted—wasn't it James Joyce who said, "My childhood bends beside me"? If I go back or if I turn sideways, I am once again confronted with the question of who writes for children. We had very few books in our family nursery. There were all the Beatrix Potters, the Nesbits, and the two Alices which I loved then and still love, for there is nothing in them that I have left behind or rejected as belonging specifically to childhood. What was worth reading then is worth reading now. And of course, there were the fairy tales and row upon row of Dickens and Scott, which I inched through simply because they were something to read and I was a reading child. There was also, now I come to think of it, Strewel Peter, which is nowadays thought to be cruel. Probably none of you has heard of Strewel Peter, but it's a very old book, far older than I am—went back into my mother's childhood. But nothing in him frightened me. My parents, I knew, would never let me be drowned in ink or have my thumb cut off by the Great Long Red-Legged Scissors Man. And it is worth asking here, I think, why we grown-ups have become so squeamish that we bowdlerize, blot out, gut, and retell the old stories for fear that truth with its terror and beauty should burst upon the children. Perhaps it is because we have lived through a period of such horror and violence that we tremble at the thought of inflicting facts upon the young. But children have strong stomachs. They can be trusted with what is true.

I once bowdlerized a book for a child, a child very dear to me. It was *Black Beauty*. Do you know that *Black Beauty* is the best seller in the world other than the Bible? It's an extraordinary thing to think of. Well, there's a part where Ginger, Black Beauty's friend, is to be killed. I quickly foresaw this and made up the story that Ginger was sent to a buttercup field to end his days in happiness, and it went down very well. Then I went away and my sister was left to read *Black Beauty* again to this child who adored it. And when I came back, I found a stony face to greet me, and I said, "Aren't you pleased to see me?"

"No," he said, "I'm not."

"Why, what have I done?"

"You've lied to me. Ginger is dead!"

"Oh," I said, "I've always tried not to lie to you, but I thought you wouldn't be able to bear it, so I put it into a buttercup field."

He said to me with tears in his voice, "Of course I could have beared it, you should have trusted me."

You should trust the children; they can stand more than we can.

As a child, I had a strong stomach myself. For, as well as the then unbowdlerized fairy tales, I had a great affection for a book that I found on my father's shelf called *Twelve Deathbed Scenes*. I read it so often that I knew it by heart, each death being more lugubrious and more edifying than the one before it. I used to long to die—on condition, of course, that I came alive the next minute to see if I, too, could pass away with equal misery and grandeur. Now, I wonder about the author of that book. Nobody in his lifetime could have accused him of being a writer for children. He would not have made such a claim himself. And yet, in a sense, he was writing for children since one loving reader of ten years old was keeping his memory green.

It was the same with my mother's novels. Every afternoon, when she fell asleep, I would slip into her room, avidly read for half an hour, and sneak away just as she was waking. Those books fascinated me, not because they were so interesting but because they were so dull. They dealt exclusively with one subject, which seemed to be a kind of loving. But love, to me, was what the sea is to a fish, something you swim in while you are going about the important affairs of life. To the characters in these books, love was something strange and special. They pursued it avidly while leading what to my mind was a completely stationary existence. They never played games, never read a book, no teeth were ever brushed, no one was reminded to wash his hands, and if they ever went to bed it was never explicitly stated. I looked forward to those stolen half-hours as, I suppose, a drunkard does to a drinking bout. It was not so much pleasure as a kind of enthrallment. I was ensnared, as by a snake-charmer, by such a distorted view of life. But what of the authors? Did they, in their pursuit of love, see themselves as writers for children? Surely not, surely not. Yet for one child indeed they were.

Who, then, writes for children? Who, I wonder? One can, of course, point to the dedication pages as proof positive that somebody does. One thinks of Beatrix Potter's Noel and Hilary Lofting's children. But I wonder if such names are not really a sort of smoke screen. A dedication, after all, is not a starting point, but rather a last grand flourish. You do not write a book for this or that person. You offer it to him when it is finished. Nothing will persuade me, in spite of all his poetic protestations, that Lewis Carroll wrote his books for Alice, or indeed for any child. Alice was the occasion but not the cause of his long, involved, many-leveled confabulations with the curious inner world of Charles Lutwidge Dodgson. Of course, when it was all over, when he had safely committed it to paper, he could afford a benignant smile and the assurance that it had been done for children. But do you really believe that? I don't.

It is also possible that these dedicatory names may be a form of unconscious appeasement, perhaps even of self-protection. A writer can excuse himself to society for having invented the pushme-pullyou animal with a head at both ends, which you will remember happens in Dr. Dolittle, by saying with an off-hand laugh, "After all, it's for children." And if a man happens to find himself in the company of a white rabbit, elegantly waistcoated and wearing a watch, scurrying down a rabbit hole and afraid of being late for the party, he does well to clap a child's name on the book. He may then well hope to get off lightly.

But in the long run, truth will out, as it did when Beatrix Potter declared, "I write to please myself!"—a statement as grand and absolute in its own way as Galileo's legendary "Nevertheless, it moves." There is, if you notice, a special flavor, a smack of inner self-delight, about the things people write to please themselves. Think of Milne, think of Tolkien, think of Laura Ingalls Wilder—those books not written for children, but that children nevertheless read.

For a long time I thought that this assertion, "I write to please myself," backed up by C. S. Lewis' statement that a book that is written solely for children is by definition a bad book, were the last words on the subject of writing or *not* writing for children. But the more I brooded, the more I saw that, as far as I was concerned, neither of these comments was the complete answer. And then, by chance, I turned on the television one evening and found Maruice Sendak being interviewed about his book, *Where the Wild Things Are*. All the usual irrelevant questions were being flung at him—Do you like children, have you children of your own? Ridiculous questions for anybody who has written a book. And to my astonishment I heard my own voice calling to him in the empty room. "You have *been* a child. Tell them that!" And his screen image, after a short pause, said simply and with dignity, "I have been a child." Well, it was magical. He couldn't possibly have heard me and yet, distant in space but at the same moment of time, we had both come to the same point. "I have been a child."

Now, I don't at all mean by this that the people who write, how shall I put it, the books that children read, are doing it for the child they were. Nothing so nostalgic, nothing so self-indulgent, nothing so sentimental. But isn't there, here, a kind of clue? To be aware of having been a child! Many people forget this; but who are we but the child we were? We have been wounded, scarred, and dirtied over, but are still essentially that child. Essence cannot change; to be aware of and in touch with this fact is to have the whole long body of one's life at one's disposal, complete and unfragmented. You do not chop off a section of your imaginative substance and make a book specifically for children; for if you are honest you have, in fact, no idea where childhood ends and maturity begins. It is all endless and all one. And from time to time, without intention or invention, this whole body of stuff, each part constantly cross-fertilizing every other, sends up—what is the right word?—intimations. And the best you can do, if you are lucky, is to be there to jot them down. This being there, this being present to catch them, is important; otherwise they are lost. Your role is that of the necessary lunatic who remains attentive and in readiness, unselfconscious, unconcerned, all disbelief suspended, even when frogs turn into princes, and nursemaids, against all gravity, slide up the bannisters. You have, indeed, to be aware that on a certain level, not immediately accessible, perhaps, but one that one derides at one's peril—on a certain level the frog is lawfully a prince and the transcending of the laws of gravity—up the bannisters or up the glass mountain, it really makes no difference—is the proper task of the hero. And heroes and their concomitant villains are the very stuff of this kind of literature.

Now these matters, I submit, have nothing to do with the labels "From 5 to 7" or "From 9 to 12"; they have nothing to do with age at all, unless they refer to all ages. Nor have they anything to do with that other label, "Literature for Children," which suggests that this is something different from literature in general, something that pens off both child and author from the main stream of writing. This seems to me hard both on children and on literature. For if it is literature indeed, it can't help being all one river and you put into it, according to age, a small foot or a large one. When mine was a small foot, I seem to remember that I was grateful for books that did not speak to my childishness, books that treated me with respect, that spread out the story just as it was, Grimm's Fairy Tales, for instance, and left me to deal with it as I could. If they moralized, I was not offended. I let them do it because of the story. If they tried to explain, I humored them, again for the sake of the story. Book and reader communed together, each accepting the other. So, remembering my own experience as a reader, could I, as a writer, speak to a child by way of his childishness?

Childlikeness—ah, that's a different matter. It is a quality that can be found in child and grown-up alike. It has nothing to do with age. Not very long ago, a woman journalist came to see me and told me how she had read *Mary Poppins* to her child very quietly so as not to disturb the father, who was working in the same room. And night after night, with increasing irascibility, he protested against this quietness. He was not being disturbed, he said, and begged her not to mumble. If there was one thing he detested, he said, it was the sound of somebody mumbling. And at the end of a week of such protestations, when he was going away for a night, he took the child aside and whispered, "Listen carefully to the story and when I come back you can tell me all that has happened." He, himself, had been listening all the time.

Well, I have a feeling of affection for that father for I think there was something in him that would agree with me, if I put it to him, that what is real, is real for everyone, not *only* but *also* for children. And he would not, I think, think me frivolous if I suggested that the country where the fox and the hare say goodnight to each other, this country is the place we are all seeking, child and grown-up alike. We are looking for miracles, looking for meaning. We want the fox not to eat the hare, we want the opposites reconciled. Child and grown-up alike, we want it. And I hope *you* will not think me frivolous when I say that it is not only children but many grown-ups, lunatic grown-ups if you will, who in their own inner world are concerned at the Sleeping Beauty's sleep and long for her to be wakened.

And here it is worth while remembering, since we are discussing Not Writing for Children, that neither the Sleeping Beauty nor Rumpelstiltz-kin was really written for children. In fact, none of the fundamental fairy stories was ever written at all. They all arose spontaneously from the folk and were transmitted orally from generation to generation to unlettered listeners of all ages. It was not until the nineteenth century, when the collectors set them down in print, that the children purloined them and made them their own. They were the perquisites of the grown-ups and the children simply took them. I remember a poem of Walter de la Mare's which begins, "I'll sing you a song of the world's little children magic has stolen away." Well, I could sing you a song of the world's magic the children have stolen away. For in the long run it is children themselves who decide what they want. They put out their hands and abstract a treasure from all sorts of likely and unlikely places, as I have tried to show. So, confronted with this hoard of stolen riches, the question of who writes or who does not write for children becomes small and, in fact, irrelevant. For every book is a message, and if children happen to receive and like it, they will appropriate it to themselves no matter what the author may say nor what label he gives himself. And those who, against all odds, and I'm one of them, protest that they do not write for children cannot help being aware of this fact and are, I assure you, grateful.

That's all I have to say.

Children at Play

An Album of Twelve Leaves

Reproduced below is an album of twelve figural studies of children dating from the late nineteenth and early twentieth centuries. They are done in the traditional Chinese format of the round fan. (The folding fan was introduced from Japan during the Ming Dynasty, 1368–1644.) Each painting is twelve by fourteen inches and is mounted on a rectangular backing. The reproductions are from photographs supplied by Professor T. C. Lai, who has also supplied material for some of the captions.

The medium used is essentially brush and ink with color limited to filling in areas already defined by line; minimal shading is found in some faces and rocks. A single artist did all the leaves, and various versions of his nicknames appear in the signatures found on each leaf along with his seals, although the abbreviated form of these signatures makes it difficult to identify the artist. Other seals belong to subsequent owners of the set.

The use of children as subject matter in a high art format such as this represents a minor genre which first appeared in the work of court artists. The subject reflects the deep-seated concern in China with the continuation of family lines, and in later centuries pictures of this kind were presented as wedding gifts, both as an inducement to and as a promise of the begetting of numerous offspring. Of great interest in many of these leaves is the depiction of activities and positions that were considered at least as much the province of adults as of children, a reflection of a tendency in traditional Chinese culture not to differentiate childish from adult concerns. In literature, for instance, serious subjects such as history, philosophy, and poetry were considered proper for presentation to child and adult alike, while tales of fantasy, magic, heroism, and derring-do were also popular with all ages. But the former were viewed as a written genre, while the latter were presented by storytellers in impromptu street performances. Thus, in China, an oral tradition remained strong long after fully matured literacy was achieved.

In painting, serious subjects and landscape predominated as subject matter, but visual depictions of the lighter side of life did appear, as is the case here, with children playing the roles.

—*Stephen Wilkinson*

Children playing cymbals, gong, drums, and long horn. The group at right is in cold-weather clothing though the scene is indoors. Note the table with candlestick, cups, and a tray of refreshments behind them. A painting of bamboo mounted with silk brocade hangs on the rear wall.

Children parading with lighted lanterns. A practice associated with the night of the full moon of the eighth lunar month, when lanterns of differing shapes such as the fish, butterfly, and various blossoms seen above were employed. Note the pull toy on the left, which is in the shape of the Taoist god of longevity with his distinctive bulging head and rustic crosier. The rock with large holes on the far left is a particularly prized specimen in garden decoration. This type is named T'ai Hu (Lake Tai) after the site where it is found.

Goldfish viewing. A common pastime among the gentry, who collected prized specimens. The pose of the child asleep on a banana leaf is taken from earlier painted depictions of ladies of spectacular beauty.

A ball game. The children are able to kick, bounce, and throw the ball in this game.

Children playing with firecrackers. An activity associated with the lunar New Year's celebration, when the first act of the New Year was to set off firecrackers on one's doorstep to
ward off evil spirits for the coming twelve months. Note the addition of a martial note in the
presence of a miniature fortress on which one child is placing a flag.

Children performing the Dragon Dance. On festive occasions teams of men would dance
through the streets covered by dragon costumes. Each dragon would be led by a figure such
as the child carrying an oversized ball symbolizing a pearl. It was his job to set the pace and
direct the progress of the men whose sight was impeded by the skin of the dragon costume.

Children pitching coins. A line is drawn at the far end and the coin is thrown at the sloping board, from which it bounces toward the line. The winner is the one whose coin lands closest to the line without overshooting it. Note the garden rock and bamboo. Bamboo was a popular plant in gardens, for, in the pliancy which enabled it to withstand the onslaught of wind and heavy weather, it was held to symbolize the staying power of a good scholar-official.

Children holding a cricket fight. The catching, grooming, and fighting of crickets was a popular pastime, by no means confined to the young.

Children playing blind-man's buff. Note the table and stools on the veranda. These, along with the volumes in cloth-covered cardboard cases and the jar holding writing brushes just to the left of the post on the left side, were for the use of the scholarly master of the house.

Children playing "the eagle trying to catch a chick." The boy with his back to us plays the eagle while the boy at the front of the line is the mother hen protecting her brood.

Children flying kites. Kite flying is indulged in by Chinese of all ages, particularly at the celebration of the ninth day of the ninth month, when they are let loose. A long flight foretells a good fortune.

Children feeding pet birds. The birds are normally kept on long strings, though they are allowed to fly free from time to time. Collecting birds was popular among the upper classes.

Manabozho of the North Central Woodlands

Hero of Folk Tale or of Myth?

Alethea K. Helbig

The American Indians had a rich literary tradition in their myths and tales which were once the living, viable center of their culture. Among the Menomini:

> It [was] customary for an old man to begin in the fall, and, giving a section every evening, spin out his stock of myths until early spring. These myths [were not to] be told except for a payment of tobacco. They [were not to] be told in summer time, and he who [violated] this rule [would] surely have snakes, toads, and all manner of nasty crawling things sleep with him.[1]

Since the "old man" who spun out his myths no longer lives, we are forced to depend on written collections made first by explorers and travelers and later by anthropologists and folklorists for our sources for these tales. The primary focus of these early collectors was on the life and customs of the Indians rather than upon their stories as stories. While everyone considers it legitimate and valuable to look at these tales from the anthropological viewpoint, or even from the psychological or historical or some other scholarly viewpoint, few people have taken them seriously as literature. This is partly because they were first written down as informative records, without much regard for the stylistic or dramatic elements that are important in the written development of an imaginative story.

Recently, however, authorities such as Coffin, Marriott and Rachlin, and Clark have pointed out that these tales can also be studied as literature.[2] When one considers them as literature, one discovers that they are full of comedy, drama, and suspense, and therefore give the reader the kind of pleasure that comes from reading good stories. In addition, they do what any good piece of literature does: they broaden the reader's view of life by giving him imaginative insights into the meanings of human experience. We have never had the problem of whether or not we should take seriously the stories we inherited from the Greeks. This is true partly because they came to us in an acceptable literary form and partly because much of our cultural heritage is derived from the Greek. It is only recently that we have come to respect the culture of the American Indians. Although the stories of the Indians were probably intended for an adult audience—like the myths and tales of other people—they also appeal to children because they are imaginative and dramatic and are, therefore, good stories.

On the North American continent there were many different tribes, each having hundreds of tales with many different protagonists. One of the most important of these was Manabozho. The tales of this figure had a wide appeal among the North Central Woodland Indians, who occupied the forested area from the Ohio River to Hudson Bay and from the Albany River to the Mississippi. Since most of the tales are short and uncomplicated, stories of wonder and magic about the adventures of Manabozho, monsters, and animals, one function of which was to amuse, Manabozho would seem to be a hero of folktale. The longer and more developed stories of his cycle, however, reveal him as a semidivine being who performs great deeds, sometimes at considerable cost to himself, in order to help people and who shows by his own example how people should and should not live. Therefore, even though there are many folktale aspects evident in the cycle of Manabozho, he is nevertheless primarily a heroic figure and belongs to the realm of myth and heroic tale.

Since Manabozho was a trickster, one of that kind of hero particularly prevalent among the American Indians, his essential characteristic was that he was both evil and beneficent, combining the contradictory qualities of villain and savior, rogue and benefactor, destroyer and creator, simpleton and culture hero. And because Manabozho is a knavish sort, playing tricks on people and sometimes being tricked in return, there is a great deal of humor in the tales. Frequently, the situations in which Manabozho finds himself are absurd, and the humor becomes highly comic and even farcical. He dives and swims with some ducks on a wager to see who can stay under water the longest, but he closes his eyes and, instead of proceeding toward the goal stake, swims in circles, finally striking his head on a rock and knocking himself senseless. Sometimes the fun in the adventure develops because Manabozho is highly inquisitive and cannot control his curiosity. Once he wonders what it is like inside a dried-out buffalo skull, so he changes himself into an ant and crawls inside. Then, forgetting himself in his pleasure at rummaging around in there, he changes back into his human form. His head gets stuck inside the skull, and unable to see where he is going, he bumps into animals and bangs into trees until by chance he stumbles over a rock and, falling down, cracks the skull open. So Manabozho is often a simpleton, and his ridiculous antics are amusing to contemplate. A narrator recorded by Bloomfield summed up the entertainment function of the Manabozho tales in this way: "The reason he [Manabozho] did those things was that mortal men might always laugh, whenever the story of him is told, as long as there is an earth, as generation after generation continues to live here on earth."[3]

But Manabozho's stories are not always comic; there is more than buffoonery in them. They are also didactic stories in which the morals to be conveyed are made palatable by the comedy and the dramatic suspense. Since his legends served as a means of perpetuating the tribal ways of life, they have a great deal to communicate about the things the Woodland people valued. They demonstrate vices to be deplored, such as pride, disobedience, rashness, just plain silliness, greed, and carelessness, and they exalt, among others, the virtues of prudence, self-control, being one's self, doing things in a way appropriate to one's own life style, and not judging by appearances.

Since the Indians believed that it is a virtue to be yourself, the "borrowed plumes" theme occurs in a number of forms. Manabozho attempts to fly with the birds, but he plummets to the ground. When he admires the beaver's tail, which makes an interesting "plinking" sound on the ice in the winter, the beaver pins a tail of some sort on Manabozho. But no matter how hard he tries, he cannot make his tail go "plink! plink!" He only looks ridiculous.

On the whole, Manabozho is a careless sort, lacking in prudence, foresight, and self-control. Intemperate in his eating habits, he tends to overeat until, unable to move or defend himself, he can only lie and wait for his stomach to go down. A colossal blunderer, he often overreacts and loses his head. In one story, he hears some spooky noises after dark as he is walking home from fishing. Dropping his catch, he races home to the safety of his lodge, where his grandmother, with whom he lives, tells him that the noises were made by owls in order to get his fish. They had counted, correctly, on frightening him with their hoots. In such tales, Manabozho is a simpleton whose comic adventures illustrate vividly what will happen if one does not practice certain virtues: one will get into trouble and feel ridiculous because of one's stupid and irrational behavior. The tales caution against being boastful and against being wasteful. They warn against being so naive that one is easily tricked or taken advantage of, as Manabozho often takes advantage of the creatures around him, and against associating with bad people and consequently getting into trouble. But to cooperate with one's fellows, to use one's common sense, to live with moderation, to look ahead and consider possible courses of action—these are lessons implicitly conveyed by the tales of Manabozho. These were virtues the people of the Woodlands valued and wanted future generations to value.

Although many of Manabozho's stories are accounts of adventure and magic such as one finds in folk tales, stories which entertain and which sometimes also convey moral values, many other tales are serious in their dramatic tone and are full of suspense and conflict. In these stories Manabozho is not a rogue and buffoon; he functions as a heroic figure. He appears as a leader and a demigod who serves as the culture hero who creates and regulates the world. He is of miraculous birth, the son of a virgin and the West Wind. Raised by his grandmother, he wars with monsters and performs heroic and extraordinary deeds, undergoing a catastrophe like that of Jonah and a deluge like Noah's. Responsible for cultural necessities, such as fire, and other phenomena, he wanders about the recreated earth perpetrating tricks and being tricked. In later life, he develops into a wise man and prophet of whom advice and boons are sought. Eventually, he rejoins the company of the divine order.

Manabozho seems to have been a force for good from a very early age. Growing up under the care of his grandmother, he soon reveals the qualities of great size, strength, wisdom, and courage by which he is able to achieve worthy ends, and for which he is later remembered and admired. His father, the West Wind, informs Manabozho in his early youth that it is his destiny to use his great strength and keen wit to do good for people and to make the earth safe for them by killing monsters and evil spirits and by providing people with the means of living easier and better lives. His father says that if he makes the world a good place, his fame will last forever, and people will never stop telling stories of his deeds. He further promises his son that after Manabozho's work on earth is finished there will be a place for him in the North with his elder brother, the North Wind, and that he will take up residence there as a mighty wind spirit. In his youth, then, Manabozho learns from his father that a divine plan is operating in his life.

Manabozho soon undertakes a series of tasks in accordance with his father's command to improve the world. He slays numerous monsters and destroys many evil spirits, often risking his life to carry out the divine orders. He also fulfills his culture-hero role when he recreates the world after the flood. In the new world, Manabozho acts as a regulator and transformer, bringing about many features of the landscape and of animal and vegetable life. According to Schoolcraft, an early nineteenth century collector, "there is scarcely a prominent lake, mountain, precipice, or stream in the northern part of America, which is not hallowed in Indian story by his fabled deeds."[4] He is responsible for many natural phenomena such as the islands in the Straits of Mackinac. He causes ducks to have flat backs, gives the snowshoe rabbits their flat, yellowish feet, the woodpeckers their red heads, and the woodchucks their grey coats. In a late story which shows the influence of white culture, he comes out the winner in an argument with Paul Bunyan about whether or not all the pine trees should be lumbered off, and that is why there are large pine forests growing in the northern woodlands yet today. Moreover, he gives the Indians many good and useful gifts. He fixes the seasons and puts the moon in the sky. He invents lances, hatchets, and arrow points and gives them to the Indians. He names the plants—including the medicinal herbs—so that people can identify them, and he teaches them their uses. He instructs the Indians in how to make maple sugar. He gives them fire so they can keep warm and cook their food. He is responsible for their having corn. He institutes the special religious rites and chants of the Medicine Lodge so that people can be cured of their illnesses. In order that the earth might not become overpopulated and life be extremely hard for all, he decrees that people should die, and he puts one of his brothers in charge of the place of the dead. And the tales go on and on, presenting Manabozho as the kind teacher and helper of his people and as a powerful regulator in nature.

The stories do not say how long Manabozho lives on earth. As he grows older, he loses his reputation as a culture hero and buffoon and becomes more of a magician and wise man. He moves somewhere far away, perhaps to the North or East, where people journey to make requests of him. The humblest and least selfish petitions are always most pleasing to him, and in his wisdom he grants those he considers most worthy. There is a tale of how he punishes an arrogant and selfish request for everlasting life by changing the young man who sought it into a tall rock, which some say is Sugar Loaf Rock on Mackinac Island in northern Michigan. Eventually, he is taken by his father to the far north to assume the position he has been promised among the winds. In his younger days, Manabozho was often arrogant, proud, and foolish. But he matures in mind as well as in body and so becomes worthy of making judgments concerning others and of rewarding or punishing the kind of behavior in which he had once engaged. In Manabozho all the exceptional and extraordinary qualities of man and divinity are combined, and his primary task is to serve as a divine guide and role figure. He has come not only to make the world a better place physically, but also to improve the quality of life by showing people by his own example how they should and should not live.

As we have them today, the stories of Manabozho cut across the border between folk tale and myth, incorporating elements of both and producing a highly complex literary character. Although the substance of the two kinds of tales is much intermingled, the mythological tales form a sort of framework for the folk tales and are much more serious in tone. Combined with the folk tales, they complete the picture of Manabozho as one "foreordained by a power greater than himself to suffer and play pranks" in order to make the world a good place for people and to show them how to live.[5] The stories show folktale qualities in that they were highly entertaining and fast moving, good always for a laugh or a scare or a vicarious adventure, no matter how often they were told. But in addition, the stories provided a vehicle by which basic cultural values could be acted out in story form by the primary Woodland heroic figure.

In the combination of heroic and trickster features displayed by Manabozho lives a character who appealed to the Indians in the old days, and who still has enough universal interest to appeal to people today. Just as the stories of Prometheus or Persephone or Baucis and Philemon give imaginative replies to some of the basic human questions answered by the myths or reveal to us something of the attitudes of the Greeks toward men and gods, so do the stories of Manabozho give us valuable glimpses of Indian life in America. In the same way that children and young people are given myths of other cultures to read and study for what they can gain from them as literature, they can be expected to enjoy and appreciate the exciting stories of Manabozho. In addition to deriving pleasure from reading and hearing these tales, they can acquire a limited but nevertheless valuable insight into Indian life and values. By so doing, they will be extending their own view of the world and understanding of life.

NOTES

1. Alanson Skinner and John V. Satterlee, "Folklore of the Menomini Indians," *Anthropological Papers of the American Museum of Natural History,* XIII, part 3 (New York, 1915), 235.

2. Tristram P. Coffin, *Indian Tales of North America* (Philadelphia: American Folklore Society, 1961); Alice Marriott and Carol K. Rachlin, *American Indian Mythology* (New York: Crowell, 1968); Ella E. Clark, *Indian Legends of the Pacific Northwest* (Berkeley: University of California Press, 1966).

3. Leonard Bloomfield, *Menomini Texts* (New York: Publications of the American Ethnological Society, 1928), p. 213.

4. Mentor L. Williams, ed., *Schoolcraft's Indian Legends* (East Lansing: Michigan State University Press, 1956), p. 79.

5. Walter James Hoffman, "The Menomini Indians," *Bureau of American Ethnology,* Annual Report 14 (Washington, D.C.: Smithsonian Institution, 1896), p. 236.

A Symposium on Children and Literature in the Middle Ages*

1. The Literacy of Medieval Children

William Robert McMunn

Before turning to the literacy of medieval children, I would like to state a few preliminary definitions as a general introduction. All of us on the panel agree that "children's literature" did not exist in the Middle Ages. During the medieval period, there was no literary genre designed expressly for the entertainment of children. Instead, all literature was for people of all ages.

Hence, we must distinguish carefully between three related but essentially different concepts—children's literature, child characters in literature, and childhood as a social institution. Children's literature is literature designed primarily for the entertainment of children, as opposed to adults. There were many didactic works written for medieval students, but even the most entertaining of these, such as Ælfric's *Colloquy,* in which different characters describe in Latin their occupational duties, subordinate entertainment to instruction. Child characters occur frequently in modern children's literature, but they also occur in literature written for a general audience of children and adults. The presence of child characters does not prove that a work containing them is children's literature, nor does the absence of child characters prove that the work would not appeal to children. All societies recognize that infancy is a different phase of life from adulthood, but not all societies have recognized childhood, that period between infancy and adulthood, as a separate phase of life with a distinctive psychology and social role. Some scholars, as we shall hear from Dr. Barstow, have maintained that there was, in effect, no separate phase of life in medieval society that would correspond to childhood as we know it today. The existence of a separate genre of literature for children would be good evidence for believing that the society which produced that literature recognized such a separation.

*Presented to the MLA Seminar on Children's Literature, Chicago, December 28, 1973.

But the absence of children's literature in the Middle Ages does not necessarily prove that childhood as we know it did not exist then. However, the nonexistence of medieval children's literature is certainly compatible with the thesis that children in the Middle Ages were thought to be simply miniature adults. To learn more about whether the concept of childhood existed in the Middle Ages, we naturally turn to literature. The social roles played by child characters in medieval literature can give us valuable evidence concerning the social roles played by real children in medieval society. Mrs. McMunn and Dr. Brockman will discuss this for medieval France and England, respectively.

The relationships among these three concepts—children's literature, children in literature, and the role of childhood in society—should be kept in mind during all of our discussion this afternoon.

It is commonly believed that most children, and indeed most adults, were illiterate during the Middle Ages, unless they belonged to the clerical orders. Hence, it is often assumed that children had no access to the written literature of the period, though of course they would have heard the orally recited legends and heroic tales, and the stories of religious edification, that were available to all.

The frequent allusions to this oral literature during the Middle Ages demonstrate that oral literature must have been an important medium of entertainment and instruction then, just as it has been since the invention of language. No child characters are explicitly present at Hrothgar's feast in *Beowulf,* but Germanic and Anglo-Saxon children must have heard stories like the tragic episode of the sons of Finn, told by the *scop* on that occasion.[1] Such exciting stories embodied and transmitted the code of personal loyalty that was a dominant social and ethical force in ancient and medieval Germania. More direct evidence of the availability of oral literature to medieval children is given by the biographer of the ninth-century English King Alfred the Great. He tells us that young Alfred listened "day and night" to the oral recitation of Old English heroic poems and memorized them; even before he learned to read, he won a book as a prize from his mother by memorizing its contents before his brothers could do so.[2] Although the illiterate child was fascinated as much by the ornamental initial letter of the book as by its literary content, his mother's gift must have contributed to the love of books and learning which eventually led King Alfred to institute great reforms in English education, and even to translate important Latin works into the vernacular himself so that more of his subjects could read them.

The oral tradition for children and adults remained strong through the Middle Ages. In the twelfth century Wace wrote in Anglo-Norman that he had heard minstrels in his youth who sang "how William long ago blinded Osmunt and dug out the eyes of Count Riulf and how he caused Ansketil to be slain by trickery, and Balzo of Spain to be guarded with a shield."[3] Many other examples could be given.

In addition to this rich heritage of oral literature, we have reason to believe that written literature could also be experienced by many children and adults of the secular classes as well as the clergy. The earliest schools in Europe after the collapse of the Western Roman Empire continued in the tradition of the classical Latin educational system. Though they were primarily for the education of the clergy, there were nearly always some secular pupils, even at the monastery schools. Classical and medieval schools admitted pupils about the age of six or seven and trained them to read and write Latin, emphasizing Latin grammar, the composition of Latin verses, and rhetorical exercises like those which Dr. Riggio will discuss. Greek had been commonly taught in the late classical period, but its use in the schools declined in the fourth and fifth centuries, so that it was known only rarely to Western medieval readers, even among the clergy.[4]

In the fourth century Jerome had advocated instruction for young students in a variety of pagan authors, in addition to Christian works. He believed that women as well as men should be literate, and he personally tutored a number of upper-class women, and later corresponded with his female disciples on various learned subjects.[5]

The spread of Christianity to northern Europe brought with it literacy and the establishment of schools for the teaching of Latin. Latin continued to be the primary language of literacy, but it was natural that in non-Latin-speaking countries works in the vernacular language were written down and read.

After a period of educational decline in France, when it was said that even high-ranking churchmen were sometimes functionally illiterate, Charlemagne in the eighth century brought together a group of famous scholars and teachers for the purpose of reforming the Frankish educational institutions. Chief among these educators was Alcuin, a Northumbrian Englishman who was educated at the flourishing monastery school at York.[6] During the period of Charlemagne's educational reforms, some Frankish bishops decreed that in every village and on every estate priests should arrange for schools to which any Christian father might send his children without paying a fee.[7] True universal education did not become an actuality, but under Charlemagne there apparently was widespread education for literacy across a fairly broad spectrum of social classes.

Similarly, in ninth-century England, after he had fought the invading Danes to a standstill, King Alfred attempted to restore his kingdom's devastated educational system by decreeing that the sons of English freemen should be taught to read English and that those who wanted to continue their education should be taught Latin as well.[8] Alfred also inaugurated a program of translation so that those who could not read Latin could read the most important books in their native language.

In the eleventh century the Italian St. John is said by his biographer to have refused to take any pleasure from the salacious stories of profane authors that were so fascinating to his schoolmates.[9] Although this sort of diatribe against non-Christian writings was conventional, it does imply that there was sufficient literacy to make the danger of such stories seem real to the pious.

The Third Lateran Council in 1179 advocated the establishment of Church-sponsored schools for the education not only of clerks but also of poor students whose parents could not afford to send them to school.[10]

During the later Middle Ages literacy became more and more widespread throughout the classes of society. The most nearly universal literacy in medieval Europe occurred in Iceland, where literacy was common among all classes of freemen. A thirteenth-century work from Norway contains practical advice for the budding merchant in the form of a dialogue between father and son. This practical handbook, obviously meant to be read by middle-class young people, urges the would-be merchant to study lawbooks, especially the Bjarkey code, in order to win the lawsuits that will arise in the course of business. Furthermore, the young man is advised to learn "all the languages, first of all Latin and French" and not to neglect his native tongue.[11]

In the later Middle Ages, children first had some training from their mothers or nurses. Then about the age of six or seven they went to school to learn the ABCs, some psalms, and how to read and write, often in Latin as well as in their vernacular. They read classical and medieval works of poetry, history, biography, and hagiography, as well as works on science and magic. Sometimes good intentions outstripped accomplishment. A thirteenth-century French fabliau amusingly refers to a "very wise" father's instruction of his son. As soon as the child was of an age to do "bad things," the father wanted to teach him "good sense" so he "had books brought to show the boy," as if the books had some magical power.[12]

But even a joke like this points to the spread of education beyond the nobility and the clergy. Medieval parents wanted their children to become literate, and it is recorded that in fourteenth-century England some villeins were willing to pay a fine in addition to the cost of education itself for having sent their sons to school without their lord's permission.[13]

With the increasing body of readers who could read in their native language but not in Latin, translations from Latin and works composed directly in the vernacular became more and more frequent. In the twelfth century, Marie de France chose to versify some Breton lais that she had heard, rather than translate one more work from Latin into French, since so many others had already done so.[14] In the twelfth and thirteenth centuries, child characters in French and English romances are frequently said to know how to read and write in Latin and the vernacular.

Finally, in the courtesy books of fourteenth- and fifteenth-century France and England, we have proof of widespread literacy among the young people of the upper and middle secular classes. These books were used to teach youths by precept and example what to read, how to dress, how to behave in polite society, and how to avoid illicit sexual advances. The courtesy books are obviously meant to be read by young men and women, who must have been literate in order to make use of them.[15]

Thus, although the proportion of medieval children and adults who were literate was by no means constant, it is clear that literacy in the Middle Ages was not the exclusive property of the nobility and the church. Throughout the Middle Ages, and increasingly in the later centuries of the period, a large number of medieval children of all classes could read and enjoy the writings that were available to them.

NOTES

1. *Beowulf and the Fight at Finnsburg,* ed. Friedrich Klaeber (3rd ed.; Boston: D. C. Heath, 1950), ll. 1063–159.

2. *Educational Charters and Documents, 598–1909,* ed. Arthur F. Leach (Cambridge: Cambridge University Press, 1911), pp. 24–27.

3. Wace, *Roman de Rou,* ed. H. Andresen (2 vols.; Heilbronn, 1878–79), Vol. I, ll. 1361–67, trans. Urban Tigner Holmes, Jr., "Norman Literature and Wace," *Medieval Secular Literature,* ed. William Matthews (Berkeley and Los Angeles: University of California Press, 1965), p. 63.

4. M. L. W. Laistner, *Thought and Letters in Western Europe, A.D. 500 to 900* (2nd ed.; Ithaca: Cornell University Press, 1957), pp. 34–44.

5. Laistner, pp. 47–48.

6. Laistner, pp. 192–205.

7. Laistner, pp. 202–3.

8. Alfred's preface to the West Saxon version of Gregory's *Pastoral Care,* ed. Henry Sweet, *Anglo-Saxon Reader* (14th ed., rev. C. T. Onions; Oxford: Oxford University Press, 1959), pp. 4–6; also in *Educational Charters,* pp. 22–25.

9. James Westfall Thompson, *The Literacy of the Laity in the Middle Ages,* (University of California Publications in Education no. 9, 1939; reprinted, New York: Burt Franklin, 1963), p. 64.

10. *Educational Charters,* pp. 122–23.

11. *The King's Mirror,* trans. L. M. Larson (New York: The American-Scandinavian Foundation, 1917), excerpted in *The Portable Medieval Reader,* ed. James B. Ross and Mary M. McLaughlin (New York: Viking Press, 1949), p. 146.

12. *Nouveau recueil de Fabliaux et Contes inédits des poètes français des XIIe, XIIIe, XIVe et XVe siècles,* ed. M. Meon (Paris, 1823), I, 364, 11, as quoted by Ferdinand Fellinger, *Das Kind in der altfranzösischen Literatur* (Göttingen: Vandenhoeck & Ruprecht, 1908), p. 128. I am grateful to Professor Keith Sinclair for bringing Fellinger's book, a mine of pertinent information, to my attention.

13. Lynn Thorndike, "Elementary and Secondary Education in the Middle Ages," *Speculum,* XV (1940), 403.

14. Marie de France, "Prologue," *Lais,* ed. A. Ewert (Oxford: Blackwell, 1944), pp. 1–2.

15. Several such books are conveniently collected in *Early English Meals and Manners,* ed. Frederick J. Furnivall (Early English Text Society, extra ser. no. 3, 1868; reprinted., London: Oxford University Press, 1932), and *A Fifteenth-Century Courtesy Book,* ed. R. W. Chambers (Early English Text Society, original ser. no. 148, 1914; reprinted., London: Oxford University Press, 1937).

2. The Concept of the Child in the Middle Ages

The Ariès Thesis

Allen M. Barstow

It is doubtful whether any literature was written solely for children in the Middle Ages, but it is quite plausible to say that all vernacular fiction was directed toward an audience that contained children. The adult lifespan was half what it is today, a fact which, combined with the inclusion of children in the audience, leads us to conclude that the average age of such an audience must have been considerably lower than it is in the case of modern adult literature.

Further study of this important problem is hindered by unanswered questions of historical semantics. Our concept of the terms *child* and *childhood* is inevitably colored by our cultural formation, to such an extent that we dare not with impunity attribute our modern notions of these terms to the medieval world.

Until recently, social historians have not given much scholarly attention to the semantic questions, but in 1960 the French demographer Philippe Ariès set forth some clear, albeit controversial, theories concerning the history of the concepts of "child" and "family." *L'Enfant et la vie familiale sous l'Ancien Regime* (Paris: Plon, 1960) was rendered into English as *Centuries of Childhood: A Social History of Family Life* (New York: Knopf, 1962; Vintage Giant Paperback, 1967). Filling a void with authoritative statements based on extensive research, Ariès' work has become required reading in this country for historians of education and child psychology as well as for scholars of children's literature, but medievalists have not yet declared themselves on his thesis of medieval social development.

Ariès traces the evolution of the child and the family from the late Middle Ages to the revolution, principally in France, but with frequent references to England and other countries of western Europe. Our interest is with his conclusions concerning the medieval period, which is his point of departure for explaining later developments.

It behooves us to begin with an attempt to define what is meant by *child*. In the Middle Ages, as in more recent times, the concept is not closely limited in terms of age, for the most frequently used designations for children (in whatever language) may be applied to anyone from birth to majority. This does not agree with the classical tradition, in which man's life was frequently divided into septennates: infancy, childhood, adolescence, and youth (which was the middle age and therefore the prime of life), followed by senescence, old age, and senility. Ariès uses the lack of linguistic precision in the Middle Ages to support his argument that there was at that time no distinction between different levels of childhood.

Lack of arithmetical precision is, of course, a salient trait of the medieval mind, but it can be demonstrated that society did indeed recognize the traditional ages of non-adults. Ariès himself offers abundant proof that infancy was a distinct concept in medieval society, for all the evidence indicates that until the age of seven the infant was reared by his mother or by a mother-substitute. He was then sent into the world of men. Ariès assumes that there was no form of instruction during infancy, an age during which the offspring did not count and was simply ignored by adults.

Ariès notes the paucity of children in the iconography of the tenth through thirteenth centuries. In the few cases in which infants are depicted, they are almost invariably portrayed as little men—that is, with the features, the expression, and even the musculature of full-grown men. In this early period of iconography, says Ariès, there is no trace of the sentimentally inspired aesthetic which later developed around infancy. The latter is first seen in the thirteenth century in baby-like renditions of the Christ child and soon spread to depictions of angels and the soul. Not until the fifteenth century, however, does Ariès detect the presence of lay children in iconography.

He concludes that in the early Middle Ages, by which he means the twelfth through the fourteenth centuries, there was a lack of sensitivity to children. He argues that, since infant mortality was very high indeed and surviving children would leave the home at the age of seven, parents were inured to the loss of infants one way or the other. He cites several authors, all postmedieval, to show that even the death of an infant, although regrettable, was not cause for excessive sorrow.

This insensitivity to infants went hand in hand with a complete lack of family life as we know it. The function of the medieval family was procreation and the transmission of name and property, but the family was not a vital social unit. The essential social units were the community of lower-class workers on one hand and the well-to-do household on the other. For the poor, the dwelling was a hovel which served only as a protection from the elements. Life was public, and its focus was the communal street, which is frequently depicted in late medieval art. Nor was the large household a family in the modern sense, for it consisted not only of parents and their children, but also relatives, guests, apprentices, and servants. Their lives were intermingled to such an extent that there was no privacy, and hence no domesticity. To be sure, the family existed, as did infants, but Ariès concludes that neither existed as a concept in medieval society.

We have thus far spoken mostly of infancy, but Ariès is even more concerned with the second age of life, childhood proper, or in this case that which replaced childhood. At about the age of seven, the little boy was sent by his father to be an apprentice in the house of a relative, a patron, or a prominent acquaintance. Here he performed domestic tasks and helped the head of the household in his trade. It was thus through practical experience and by direct contact with the adult world that he learned the art of living.

After infancy, the child participated fully in every aspect of adult society, donning adult clothes, engaging in the games and recreation of adults, and participating in adult social intercourse. This society, unlike our own, was polymorphous in that it was characterized by open access to and free intermingling with people of all classes and ages. After infancy, according to this thesis, there was thus no distinction of the child or adolescent from adults, no awareness of any essential differences between age groups.

After this insensitivity of the Middle Ages, according to Ariès, came towards the end of the fifteenth century an awareness of the child as droll, a source of amusement, and this is the first time that we can speak of a concept of the child. But soon this attitude was replaced by a more Christian notion, that of the child as an innocent soul, full of potential for moral and spiritual growth, but particularly vulnerable to temptation and evil influence. Henceforth the child would be regarded as a tender plant to be carefully protected and nurtured.

The need for protection inspired a radically new form of initiation into the adult world. Society replaced apprenticeship with a system involving increasingly longer periods of formal education. The child was cloistered in a school, preferably a boarding school, in which he was severely disciplined and received theoretical and moral training, using texts which were written or adapted for the young. The pedagogical use of child psychology dates from the fifteenth century, and Ariès cites particularly the theologian Jean Gerson and his successor Robert D'Estouteville. This new concept of childhood culminated in the English boarding schools and the French colleges, the latter under the direction of newly established teaching orders—Jesuits, Oratorians, and Jansenists.

Returning now to the thesis concerning medieval society, we may recapitulate with a formula: youth equals infancy (under maternal care) plus childhood (or rather apprenticeship) in the adult world. Except during infancy, there were no physical, social, or cultural barriers between classes or age groups. Life was public and collective, not private and intimate. The apprentice was not distinguished from adults, while the family did not exist as a social concept. These are serious charges indeed, and since Ariès does not display familiarity with vernacular literature, we must examine very closely indeed his conclusion that the medieval world was insensitive to infants and unaware of apprentices or children as distinct from adults.

3. The Schooling of the Poet

*Christian Influences and Latin Rhetoric
in the Early Middle Ages*

Milla B. Riggio

Every literature teacher in any culture must at some point answer the question: What should I teach and when and how should I teach it? Perhaps the most difficult dimension of this question lies in the problem of how to deal with the past, how to teach children and young adults to respond to or to comprehend literature written in traditions with which they are no longer naturally familiar. How, for instance, can one effectively explain the complex symbolical reaches of biblical and classical allusion in a novel like *Moby Dick* to students who have never heard of Elijah and do not understand the value of naming the four winds? No amount of factual glossing will ever recreate the interweaving of traditions, that steady presence of biblical and classical hero, that enlarges the maniacal character of Captain—or is it King—Ahab.

One of our essential problems is how to teach literature grounded in a daily reading of the Bible to students who do not read the Bible. The first Christian teachers faced a similar, though somewhat inverted, problem. During the third, fourth, and fifth centuries in the Latin world, especially Gaul, Italy, and northern Africa, the secular educational order passed slowly into its inevitable demise. Despite the Emperor Julian's edict of 362 against Christian teachers, churchmen gradually replaced non-Christians in the important positions of secular authority, including that of rhetor, the highest post in the rhetorical schools. As this change was made, Christian teachers had to find methods of absorbing an incongruous past. But then, unlike now, it was the Bible which determined the conditions and assumptions of the present against which the past was to be judged and into which it was to be assimilated.

It would be easy to suggest that the problems in the rhetorical schools during the politically chaotic third, fourth, fifth, and sixth centuries were simply those of two clashing cultures—a pagan past giving way to Christianity. However, the situation was more complicated than that formula suggests. The structure of the school system itself was increasingly precarious. Until they passed out of existence in the early sixth century in Gaul, an area that has been called "more Roman than Rome,"[1] the rhetorical schools maintained the traditional two-part structure, comprised at the first level of a school of grammar and on the secondary level of a school of rhetoric. However, though structurally similar to late classical schools, these early medieval schools of rhetoric suffered from a loss of direction and purpose. Initially, they had been the training grounds for young orators and public figures. With the loss of the forum as the major arena of public life, the schools were forced to shift their emphases and methods. The old curriculum, strained and altered to meet new conditions, could scarcely provide a steady sense of continuity with the classical pagan past.

Moreover, the early Christians were not on the whole a culturally alien group in Greek and Latin society. Though the early church was itself far from unified, representing the merger of Eastern, Middle Eastern, and

Western influences, of mystery cults and rival religions, early Christians in the Greek and Latin world were fully part of Greek and Latin culture. As they became accepted and even powerful in that society, they shared in the existing education. Jerome in the fourth and Augustine in the early fifth century were but two of the many prominent Christians who studied and taught in the rhetorical schools. Frequent conversions further blurred the line between pagan and Christian. One of Jerome's teachers, the prominent rhetorician Gaius Marius Victorinus, was a pagan when he taught Jerome but a Christian at his death. Culturally, socially, even historically, early Christian roots were embedded in Graeco-Roman traditions. Even first-century biblical exegetes, such as Philo of Alexandria, were more at home with Plato than with Genesis and Exodus. Beneath the struggle for control of social, political, and religious institutions which was waged in the early Middle Ages, there ran a deep channel of continuity between Latin pagans and Latin Christians.

It seems obvious to us now that from the beginning Christian doctrine was based on the Hellenization of Hebraic mythology, theology, and history. However, it was more difficult for early Christians to acknowledge their own most natural traditions. For while their cultural background and their very process of education was largely that of the Graeco-Roman world,[2] the documents which formed the basis of their religious teachings were the Semitic books of the Old Testament. These contained mythical, literary, and historical perspectives which were often at odds with those established in the Greek and Latin world. Hebraic symbols were naturally meaningful to the early Christian only when they paralleled those of Graeco-Roman culture. And the vast genealogies of Hebrew history were virtually meaningless to the Greek or Roman Christian; after all, the Hebrew span of history did not include Greece or Rome. Early Christians in the Greek and Roman cultures found themselves ironically forced to accept as sacred truth a world history in which they were not even included.

Obviously, elaborate methods of interpretation and a thorough process of assimilation were essential. Throughout the early centuries of Christianity, teachers everywhere in the Greek and Latin world wrestled to reconcile the Hebraic with the classical; various shifts were made to facilitate that assimilation. In the hands of such exegetes as Philo of Alexandria, for instance, even the Hebrew genealogies took on allegorical significance.[3] The Hebrew historical scheme was expanded to include the history of Greece and Rome, the origins of which were customarily placed shortly after the flood.[4]

These particular cultural and religious conditions created an almost schizophrenic, certainly paradoxical, unwillingness either to keep or to let go of the past. On the one hand, Christians of the third, fourth, and fifth centuries were forced to disdain pagan authors because their writings projected social and religious ideals repugnant to Christian teachers. However, such attacks were made against an inescapable literary and educational heritage. For, on the other hand, though the Hebrew documents could be interpreted as the most valid mythical or even historical accounts of the world's process, they did not provide the necessary models for training young students. Reading works in their own language was essential to learning that language.

Attitudes toward the past were also complicated by the cultural chaos of the present. A natural reverence for the grandeur of the Roman past warred continuously and strongly with the impulse to assert God's Word as supreme. Such reverence, illustrated by and combined with the rigorous, steadily losing effort to maintain the language of the past, made it impossible for all but the narrowest Christian teachers simply to discard classical writers. Learned men such as Jerome and, earlier, Tertullian who denounced classical works were rejecting their own educational and literary heritage, a process which was only too obviously painful for them. The paradox for all well-educated, intelligent Christian teachers was that of Jerome and Tertullian: the past which must be denounced on theological grounds was crucial to the training of the young. The biggest problem of early Christian education was how to solve this paradox—how to maintain the past while also losing it.

Christian responses to this paradox were various and often contradictory. There are, for instance, clear signs that distinctions were made between the reading habits of young students and those of older, more mature Christians. Pagan studies denounced as adult reading were regarded by some prominent churchmen, including Gregory the Great, Clement of Alexandria, Origen, and Eusebius of Caesarea, as necessary preparation for a thorough education.[5] Even St. Augustine, though only hesitantly sanctioning pagan authors, distinguished between the imagination of the young and that of the more mature.[6] And while condemning pagan education, Augustine, like Jerome and Tertullian before him, clearly reflects the value of such teaching. Though the distinction between the imagination of the young and that of the more mature Christian was frequently made, it was more customary to emphasize new methods of narrating biblical stories than to recommend pagan works. Fairy tales and the exploits of epic heroes were particularly regarded as corrupt in content but engrossing in form. Parents, as well as teachers, were frequently exhorted to make biblical narratives as exciting as heroic tales to children.

Of all the narrative techniques recommended for the young, the most importance seems to have been placed on "epic" devices. Indeed, many of the Biblical poems of this period are themselves obviously attempts at epic. At least one of these poems, the *Alethia* of Claudius Marius Victor, a rhetor of Marseilles in the fifth century, was expressly written to train the young.[7] Victor states his teaching intentions in his preface; throughout the poem "epic" devices, which include extravagant descriptions, digressions, and lines taken from Virgil, are added ornamentally, no doubt to engage the young reader in the paraphrase of Genesis which constitutes the main narrative of the poem. That Victor's intention is not only to impress the biblical narrative upon the young but also to assert the supremacy of Old Testament history is indicated throughout, particularly by one charmingly absurd digression aimed at refuting Lucretius' account of the origin of metals. In the *De Rerum Natura* Lucretius had described the origin of metals in a great fire. Victor provides a timely fire of his own, started accidentally by Adam who was hurling a rock at the serpent from outside the gates of Paradise. The rock, thrown at Eve's revengeful suggestion, missed the snake, struck the gates, and began a fire of gigantic proportions, bringing forth molten metal from the earth (*Alethia*, II, 90–112).[8] Victor's knowledge of natural science may have been faulty, but his intentions are clear.

The interest in the narration of fables and fictions (*fictam* is Victor's term) suggested by such poems as Victor's was strongly influential during these centuries. Students in both Greek and Latin schools were taught to rework, embellish, condense, and decorate inherited tales. The handbooks throughout the period are replete with exercises of this kind, frequently emphasizing the need for modern interpretation of older narratives. So pervasive were these exercises that characteristic ways of reworking fables evolved into recognizably different narrative forms. Terms which we use loosely connoted much more specific directives to the student of these centuries. *Paraphrasis,* the elaborate retelling of a tale with appropriate condensations, embellishments, and additions, and *digestus,* the quick summarizing in a manner particularly suitable for legal briefs, are but two of the particular forms children were trained to use.

As was generally true of the teaching of rhetoric at this time, the emphasis in most schoolroom exercises was on form much more than on substance, which was frequently suspect to Christian teachers. Such interest in form extended beyond experiments in narrative to embrace the structure of the image, the line, and the phrase. Again, here, the familiar clash between the natural heritage of the Greek and Latin cultures and the imposed idealization of Hebrew literature was evident. The figures, the tropes, the linguistic flourishes and rhetorical devices which dominated the teaching of this period were those of Greek and Latin literature. They had been most clearly outlined by Quintilian in the *Institutiones Oratoria* and Cicero in *De Inventione*, by far the most influential rhetorical documents in the early Middle Ages. The plainest of the Christian writers did denounce the use of such rhetorical flourishes absolutely, and the best of Christian writers used them with restraint. But the effective use of rhetorical figures was not widely questioned as a standard of literary excellence. Again, of course, the ambivalent attitudes toward the past encouraged teachers to stress empty, formal embellishments over substance. Some Christians, as epitomized by Isidore of Seville in the seventh century,[9] were to claim that all important literary and rhetorical forms had their origin in the Old Testament—an assertion, it must be pointed out, supported by reference not to original texts but to Greek and Latin translations of those texts. A more general attitude, however, was reflected by Augustine, who was content to claim only that all the important forms of elegance were to be satisfactorily illustrated in biblical texts. In Part IV of *De Doctrina Christiana*, for instance, Augustine analyzed several books of the Old and New Testament together with some later Christian writings, comparing them favorably to any work of Latin or Greek literature. Naturally, his standards were those of Latin rhetoric—periodicity, variety, complex use of figures of speech.

Augustine himself neither prescribes nor uses the formal rhetoric of his age excessively. Yet it is easy to see how such essentially fossilized standards of judgment could have only disastrous consequences when used by less capable masters in the classroom. However, there was a yet more pernicious influence associated with the teaching of rhetoric throughout this period. Rhetorical handbooks based typically on the works of Quintilian and Cicero multiplied during these centuries.[10] Often elaborate treatises illustrating various rhetorical devices of style, these books seldom questioned or expanded critical standards. What they did do was further to abstract and formalize the increasingly vapid rules of rhetoric. They preserved the works of classical writers, such as Virgil and Ovid, a half-line at a time. That is, half-lines were extracted from the poetry and used out of context as exempla of rhetorical forms. There is evidence that such piecemeal contact with the great classical writers was all that was given to some students. Certainly, the large number of lines from these books which reappear frequently in the imitative, patchwork poetry of this period testifies to their influence.

In short, since the language of literature was by the third, fourth, and

fifth centuries primarily the language of the past, the teaching of writing
had been reduced essentially to practicing static forms and producing
exercises heavy with absurd stylistic embellishments. This feature of the
early Middle Ages was primarily a result of attempts both to discard and
to preserve the past. Faced with the need to denounce most of the content
of classical poetry or to interpret classical writings in Christian terms,
teachers were forced to pay more attention to stylized patterns and to
treat classical authors almost entirely in terms of their narrative and
poetic embellishments.

Such schoolroom exercises were not without their effects throughout
the literate culture. It is no wonder that children bound to the language
of the past, drenched in an artificial, style-oriented form of rhetoric,
trained to borrow half-lines extensively from classical writers without
reference to their contexts, and taught various ways to embellish, condense, paraphrase, and summarize inherited fables should produce a
sodden mass of highly artificial, highly imitative poetry. Both in its heavy
emphasis on decorative figures of speech and in its adoption of certain
narrative forms, particularly the paraphrase and the digest, the poetry
of this period reveals clearly that the school child was, indeed, the father
of the adult poet.

NOTES

1. Charles S. Baldwin, *Medieval Rhetoric and Poetic* (New York: Macmillan, 1928),
p. 75.

2. Of the many studies dealing with the emergence of Christianity in the Latin world,
particularly in the rhetorical school system, I have found the work of three men most
helpful: Christopher H. Dawson, *Religion and the Rise of Western Culture* (New York:
Sheed and Ward, 1950) and *The Making of Europe* (New York: Macmillan, 1952);
G. Downey, "Education in the Christian Roman Empire: Christian and Pagan Theories
under Constantine and His Successors," *Speculum,* XXXII (1957), 48–61; and M. L. W.
Laistner, *Christianity and Pagan Culture in the Later Roman Empire* (Ithaca, N.Y.:
Cornell University Press, 1951), *The Intellectual Heritage of the Early Middle Ages* (Ithaca,
N.Y.: Cornell University Press, 1957), and "Pagan Schools and Christian Teachers," in
Bernard Bischoff and Suso Brechter, eds., *Liber Floridus: Mittellateinische Studien* (St.
Ottilien: EOS Verlag der Erzabtei, 1949), pp. 47–61.

3. Philo's commentary on the early chapters of Genesis began the long tradition of
allegorical exegesis. Philo himself was a Hellenistic Jew.

4. Although sporadic efforts to merge classical and biblical history were made earlier,
such historical assimilation was systematically developed by Eusebius of Caesarea first in
his *Chronicon,* then more elaborately in his *Ecclesiastical History.*

5. See Laistner, "Pagan Schools and Christian Teachers," for a careful analysis of
Christian attitudes toward pagan studies; Laistner defines four attitudes ranging from a
limited acceptance to a complete rejection of pagan works.

6. Augustine seems to have changed his attitude toward pagan literature, recommending
it hesitantly at first, then rejecting it completely in *De Doctrina Christiana.* In Part IV even

of this later work, however, he still alludes to differences in youthful and mature imaginations.

7. Victor *Alethia,* ed. C. Schenkl, *Corpus Scriptorum Ecclesiasticorum Latinorum,* Vol. XVI (1888).

8. The connection between Victor and Lucretius was first pointed out by J. M. Evans, *Paradise Lost and the Genesis Tradition* (Oxford: Oxford University Press, 1968), pp. 122–23.

9. Isidore of Seville, *Etymologiarum sive Originum,* ed. W. M. Lindsay (2 vols.; Oxford: Oxford University Press, 1911).

10. The best modern collections of these rhetorical handbooks are to be found in Karl von Halm, ed., *Rhetores Latini Minores* (Lipsius, 1863; reprint ed., Dubuque: W. C. Brown, n.d.), and Heinrich Keil, *Grammatici Latini* (Lipsius, 1855–80; reprint ed., Hildesheim: G. Olms, 1961).

4. Children and Literature in Medieval France

Meradith Tilbury McMunn

In France, as elsewhere in Europe in the Middle Ages, it is difficult to distinguish a separate body of literature which was intended primarily for the use of children. Most of the literature which can be shown to have been created especially for medieval children was didactic, although there is some evidence of an oral rhyming-literature composed by children at play. The didactic works are of two main types. Children's primers contained the alphabet, excerpts from Scripture, and edifying catalogues of deadly sins, principal virtues, and the like, but they contained little that could be called entertaining. Besides the primers, a second type of didactic literature specifically designed for children seems to have been the courtesy books. Such works generally consisted of anecdotes with explicit morals and lists of maxims concerning the rules of etiquette. They were intended for boys approximately ten to fifteen years of age, many of whom served as waiters and valets in the homes of wealthy patrons. The advice would be particularly useful to those who aspired to advantageous marriages or positions of social importance. Young girls' courtesy books were similarly instructive, warning them of the folly of being too generous with their affections and the wisdom of obeying parents and guardians. A realistic if somewhat cynical attitude toward them is reflected in the following excerpt from a thirteenth-century fabliau: "Still, she is our child; so we must take care that we marry her and make her an honest woman."[1]

Besides these two types of didactic books, there exists a subgroup of didactic pieces for children—those written for the instruction of medieval children by their own parents, for example the letters from Queen Dhuoda to her son, the *Enseignements* of St. Louis to his children, and the book of the Knight of La Tour Landry for his daughters.[2] These works are significant for the history of children in medieval French literature and culture since they are proof that in France parents from as early as the ninth century were concerned to provide written guidance for their own children.

Moreover, some evidence exists that there was in the Middle Ages a type of poetry created by children at play, similar to the rhymes children invent when jumping rope. Children's rhyming of this type is infrequently preserved in medieval literature, but a rare example has been incorporated in a thirteenth-century fabliau. Children running down the street are depicted chanting: "Gardez le fol, gardez le fol / Qui tient la maçue en son col."[3] These verses have, it is obvious, the rhythm of the *comptine,* and it has been argued that this four-stress rhythm is common to all children's "nursery rhymes."[4] This children's rhyming is, however, necessarily a literature of limited scope, and it is still accurate to say, with the other panelists here today, that there seems to have been no secular literature written or redacted primarily for the entertainment of children. It is probable that the "children's literature" of medieval France was simply the literature of the entire culture.

Medieval literature itself provides evidence concerning the kinds of literature medieval French children enjoyed and their means of access to it. They were a part of the audience who heard the minstrels sing the *chansons-de-geste,* as the twelfth-century author Wace attests.[5] Children, moreover, knew these songs and legends and were able to sing them for themselves like the boy in *Le Garçon et l'aveugle.*[6] Children could also read, as we have heard from previous panelists, and in the twelfth and thirteenth centuries some of their reading matter included the popular vernacular romances. In *Yvain* Chrétien de Troyes narrates a charming scene in which the hero enters a garden where a young girl is reading such a romance to her parents; the young girl in *Li Chevaliers as deus espees* reads a romance to knights and maidens.[7] Evidence of the specific reading preferences of children in their leisure time, though of a later date, is given indirectly by Montaigne, who writes in his essay "On the Education of Children" (c. 1580) that at the age of eight he preferred the fables of the *Metamorphoses* of Ovid to "the Lancelots of the Lake, the

Amadises, the Huons of Bordeaux, and such books of rubbish on which children waste their time."[8] Although Montaigne did not share his contemporaries' taste for the romances he names, his list makes it clear that these popular medieval works were enjoyed for centuries by adults and children alike.

So far, we have been concerned with what is known about medieval literature demonstrably composed especially for children, but since in medieval French vernacular literature much of what we can learn about children's literature must be informed by what we can learn about children in literature, and since a large part of our primary evidence about children, their daily lives and intellectual habits, is found in literature, we must ask, "Does medieval literature accurately reflect medieval childhood?" and "What do medieval child-characters tell us about children in medieval society?" Though Perceval and Aucassin can no more be said to be "typical" children of their period than Oliver Twist or Zazie of theirs, and children in medieval literature were often depicted as idealized "adults in miniature," it is possible nevertheless to discover in medieval literature more than might be expected about the status and lifestyle of medieval children, their fantasies and games, their education and reading habits, and their elders' conceptions of their collective psychology and individual personalities.

The description of children in early French medieval literature indicates very little about their daily lives or intellectual interests. In early epic literature children, like women, are mentioned infrequently. A typical example of such a reference occurs in the *Charroi de Nîmes* when Guillaume d'Orange tells King Louis that he will not take the lands of an infant whose father died in the king's service.[9] Guillaume says, moreover, that he will defend the young Bertram's rights himself, a statement which is heartily applauded by Bertram's retainers, who doubtless had more faith in the strong right arm of a seasoned knight than the valid claims of an infant heir. Nor did all the nobility have Guillaume's scruples. Many of the epics are concerned with the problems caused by the inheritance of fiefs by infant lords and the frequent usurpation of their lands by neighboring barons or adult relatives. The unrest caused by these infant successions was an unwelcome burden to the people, witness the plaintive proverb: "Dolente la terre que enfe governe" ("Unhappy the land that a child governs!").[10]

The lives of heroes are narrated with few details about childhood except those that exemplify precocious prowess, and the exploits themselves are archetypal adult feats—exceptional skill in arms and athletics, the killing of a monster, and the like. Similar idealizations occur in medieval saints' lives, which generally describe the saints as having been supernaturally, or at least ideally, good children and often quick students as well. Since telling the idealized exploits of the hero or the saint was also a means of educating the young by providing them with suitable models to try to imitate, it is probable that heroic legends such as those of Roland, Guillaume, and Alexis were told with an awareness of their potential for instruction as well as entertainment. Nevertheless, the children in these early epics and saints' lives are one-dimensional; the tales focus on their actions, not their thoughts.

In the second half of the twelfth century the child-character in the epics became more prominent. *Enfances,* or the exploits of the young hero, were added to the epic cycles because of the popularity of certain heroes and the demand for more of their adventures. These adventures were usually told chronologically like a biography, beginning with the hero's birth, or even before, and continuing through his education and knighting." Often the adventures of the youth included a separation from his parents or from knightly society, or a struggle to regain an inheritance wrongly taken from him.[12] The similarity of these kinds of adventures to the chivalric quest which developed in the romances is obvious.

The romances of the twelfth and thirteenth centuries offer a wider range of perspectives on medieval childhood than the epic, as well as greater psychological realism. In order to please their public, the authors of the later romances, and some of the later epics influenced by them, enlivened their fictional accounts with details drawn from everyday life. Even idealized representations of children began to include more "naturalistic" particulars which made the child-character a more sympathetic figure, like the little Saracinthe in *L'Estoire del saint graal.* The young Heraclius in *Roman d'Eracle* or Aelis in *Aliscans* exemplify the *senex puer* or "adult in miniature" trope which portrays a child who comports himself as an adult, though clearly distinguished as a child. This trope is, in general, a purely literary conception of childhood. However, there also exists a stage in real childhood when many children precociously assume the attitudes of the adult, playing grownup. It is possible that it is this stage in actual childhood that some medieval authors were representing in this trope.

Philippe Ariès and others claim that medieval people did not perceive psychological differences between children and adults, but this claim is not supported by a close look at medieval literature.[13] Children were represented as more honest than adults, more emotional, and yet more easily pacified. They were capable of much affection, both toward adults and each other. However, their limitations were recognized. They had limited learning abilities and were not able to undertake too much responsibility.[14]

Further evidence about children and their distinctive characteristics can be found in proverbs in manuscripts of the thirteenth and fourteenth centuries. *Enfant* is one of the more numerous entries in Joseph Morawski's index, which lists twenty-one proverbs in which it occurs.[15] Familiar or colloquial words for children, or words denoting kinship, are infrequent: there are no examples of proverbs in Morawski's collection with *gars/garce* ("kid, brat") or *filz* ("son") in them; one with *meschine* ("little girl, maid"); two with *pucelle* ("little girl"); and six with *fille* ("young girl, daughter"). The proverbs reflect a wry awareness of the differences between maturity and childhood, warning the adult against the folly of following the advice of children and cautioning them concerning the effect their mistakes as parents can have on the child's personality.[16]

On the lighter side, children's playfulness is a commonplace, and medieval literature occasionally depicts children realistically at play. Some of their games are copied from adult activities such as playing "knight." Others, such as playing with a ball or rings, seem to be distinctly childish. Even pranks and rhymes are included.[17]

One of the most psychologically realistic portraits of children in medieval literature may be found in the *Roman de Kanor,* a thirteenth-century French prose romance which is the last of the continuations of the *Sept Sages* cycle.[18] Though *Kanor* is fictional in setting and contains much material from Celtic fantasy, the characters themselves are striking in their realism. A typical feature of *Kanor* is the invention of speeches for normally inarticulate characters such as very young children and animals.[19] The author clearly indicates that these are projections of his own imagination, and yet they serve to indicate the psychological state of these infants by representing what they would say "if they could only talk."

The main plot of the romance centers around the quadruplet infant sons of the murdered Emperor of Constantinople, from the moment of their abduction by a lion to the coronation of the eldest as the new emperor. The children are of royal birth, possessed of supernaturally keen senses, and raised in a cave in the forest attended only by a two-hundred-year-old hermit and a young serving girl, but they behave in other respects as we would expect young children to behave. They are curious, impatient, cry when hungry or tired, and have a childishly limited view of the world. In a scene reminiscent of the Perceval story the boys are introduced to courtly society in the form of knights hunting in the wood. The author achieves a psychologically realistic tone by setting the boys' age at seven years so that their naive questions are suitable, though in *Perceval* the teenager's ignorance is farcical.[20] The four boys beg to become knights with horses and dogs, and they have a tantrum when told that they are too young. In an attempt to appease them, the hermit says that they will become knights when it pleases God. "But you *always* say 'Quand Dieu plaira,' " wails the oldest. In their games they imitate adults, riding on sticks for horses, and they have their own system of communication incomprehensible to adults—a "secret code."[21]

From the self-assured youngsters of *Kanor* and other late romances it is a short step to the rascally "varlets" of such fabliau literature as *Le Garçon et l'aveugle*, where children manipulate adults and where the cruel side of childhood with its mischief and insensitivity is portrayed. This literature—the literary side of what might be called the "dissent" of childhood or the "generation gap"—is an aspect of medieval childhood which has been largely ignored. It is the other side of the so-called unity of the worlds of the child and the adult in medieval society suggested by Ariès. One of the most explicit statements of this dissent and an example of the autonomy of children as a group apart from adult society is the defiant speech attributed to participants in the Children's Crusade:

> Long enough have you, knights and warriors, so boastful and so honored, been making your fruitless attempts to rescue the tomb of Christ! God can wait no longer! He is tired of your vain, puny commission! He who calls can insure the victory, and we will show you what children can do![22]

The impudence and the rejection of the authority figure of the knight is here, but here, too, is the impetuosity and the exuberance so universally associated with youth.

These scattered examples of the literature available to French children in the Middle Ages and a brief look at children as depicted in that literature indicate that children were not simply "adults in miniature," but were recognized as distinct individuals in medieval culture. Their literary importance increased as the importance of the individual came into greater prominence in the later twelfth and thirteenth centuries. No nondidactic children's literature developed in the Middle Ages, but it seems reasonable to think that the more realistic representation of child-characters in later medieval literature contributed to the evolution of the modern concept of childhood as a distinct phase of life with its own "children's literature."

NOTES

1. "Toutes voies es ce nos enfes; / Si i devons bien garde prendre / En tant que nous le marions / Et preude femme le faissons," quoted by Ferdinand Fellinger, *Das Kind in der altfranzösischen Literatur* (Göttingen, 1908), p. 236. I am obliged to Professor Keith V. Sinclair for bringing Fellinger's book to my attention.

2. Dhuoda's advice is published under the title *Le Manuel de Dhuoda,* ed. M. E. Bondurand (Paris, 1887); Saint Louis's writings to his daughter and eldest son are collected in *Histoire de France* (Paris, 1840), XX, 26ff. and 302ff.; his instructions to his eldest son are in *Saint Louis, Enseignements à son fils aîné,* ed. Em. A. Van Moë (Paris, 1944); and the counsels of the Knight of La Tour Landry are in *Le Livre du chevalier de la Tour Landry pour l'enseignement de ses filles,* ed. A. de Montaiglon (Paris, 1854).

3. "Watch the fool, watch the fool, / Who holds the club on his shoulder," *Nouveau recueil de fabliaux et contes inédits des poètes français des xiie, xiiie, xive, et xve siècles,* ed. M. Méon (Paris, 1823), II, 183, ll. 319–20.

4. Jacqueline Guéron, "Children's Verse and the Halle-Keyser Theory of Prosody," *Children's Literature,* II (1973), 202, and Constantin Brailoiu, *La Rhythmique enfantine, notions préliminaires* (Paris, 1956).

5. Wace, *Roman de Rou,* ed. H. Andresen (2 vols.; Heilbronn, 1878–79), Vol. I, ll. 1361–67.

6. ". . . car je sai bien de geste canter, / Si vous en deduirai," *Le Garçon et l'aveugle,* ed. Mario Roques (2nd ed. rev.; Paris, 1965), ll. 121–22.

7. Chrétien de Troyes, *Yvain (Le Chevalier au lion),* ed. Wendelin Foerster, rev. T. B. W. Reid (Manchester, 1942), p. 146, ll. 5360–70; *Li Chevaliers as deus espees,* ed. W. Foerster (Halle, 1877), ll. 8951–53.

8. *The Complete Essays of Montaigne,* trans. Donald M. Frame (Stanford, 1957), p. 130 (Bk. I, ch. 26); the text of the original is in *Oeuvres complètes,* ed. Albert Thibaudet and Maurice Rat (Paris, 1962), p. 175.

9. *Le Charroi de Nîmes,* ed. J. L. Perrier (Paris, 1963), p. 12, ll. 365–70.

10. Joseph Morawski, ed., *Proverbes français antérieurs au xve siècle* (Paris, 1925), p. 21, no. 589.

11. *Raoul de Cambrai, Enfances Guillaume,* and *Enfances Renier* are examples of this type, and the *Enfances Alixandre* is an early example of adding an *enfances* section to a romance.

12. There are many examples of epics with these themes; *Galiens li restorés, Enfances Roland,* and *Gui de Warewic* are typical.

13. Philippe Ariès, *Centuries of Childhood,* trans. Robert Baldock (New York, 1962), p. 411; J. H. Plumb, "The Great Change in Children," *Horizon,* XIII (Winter, 1971), 5–13; see also Isabelle Jan, *Essai sur la littérature enfantine* (Paris, 1969), pp. 18–19, for the claim that Jean-Jacques Rousseau invented the modern concept of "childhood."

14. Evidence for these claims is found in examples from Fellinger, *Das Kind,* pp. 97–126 and 183–219. A representative example is also found in Méon, *Nouveau recueil,* II, 396, ll. 62–64: "Por sa juesnese riens ne sot / Li anfes, car d'antor cinq anz / N'est nus anfes saiges ne granz."

15. Joseph Morawski, ed., *Proverbes,* index, pp. 135–46.

16. "De fol et d'enfant garder se doit l'en," Morawski, no. 490; "De petit enfant, petit dueil," no. 538; "Mere piteuse fet fille teigneuse," no. 1223; "De sauvaige pucelle privee putain," no. 554.

17. A scene with boys playing "knight" is found in the *Roman de Kanor,* Paris, B.N., *f.fr.* 22550, fol. 75v^c. A childish prank (with serious consequences) is recounted in *Floovant, chanson-de-geste du xiie siècle,* ed. Sven Andolf (Uppsala, 1941), ll. 72–76. Perhaps the longest catalogue of medieval children's games is given by Jean Froissart, *Espinette amoureuse,* ed. Anthime Fourrier (Paris, 1963), ll. 147–248. Further examples of children playing with balls, rings, and other games are quoted in Fellinger, *Das Kind,* pp. 196–201.

18. I am at present completing a critical edition of the *Roman de Kanor* from the five

existing manuscripts: London, Brit. Mus., MS Harley 4903; Brussels, Bibl. roy., MS 9245; Paris, B.N., *f.fr.* 22550; Paris, B.N., *f.fr.* 93; and Paris, B.N., *f.fr.* 1446.

19. An example of such an infant's "speech" is found in *Kanor,* Paris, B.N., *f.fr.* 22550, fol. 98v^c.

20. See Chrétien de Troyes, *Le Roman de Perceval ou le conte du graal,* ed. William Roach (Geneva, 1959), ll. 69–367. The parallel scenes in *Kanor* are in Paris, B.N., *f.fr.* 22550, fols. 72v^c–76v^b.

21. *Kanor,* Paris, B.N., *f.fr.* 22550, fol. 73r^c.

22. George Zabriskie Gray, *The Children's Crusade* (New York, 1870), p. 47.

5. Children and Literature in Late Medieval England

Bennett A. Brockman

As far as his literary experience was concerned, the child in late medieval England seems to have fared better than his twentieth-century counterpart. The medieval child had access not only to literature written expressly for children (which was invariably didactic) but also, more importantly, to the literature we habitually think of as adult literature: the drama, the romances, the lyrics, the sermons and saints' lives, even Lydgate, Gower, Chaucer, and the *Pearl*-poet, if we can trust the few descriptions of medieval literary audiences which have come down to us. It appears that we can say accurately, although perhaps a bit startlingly, that all the literature of fourteenth- and fifteenth-century England is children's literature. A corollary question, which must be pursued elsewhere, is whether the literature of medieval England is still vital as literature for children.

To consider the literature of late medieval England children's literature we have first to realize, as Mr. and Mrs. McMunn remind us, that the High Middle Ages did not exclude children, even very young children, from occasions during which they could hear romances read, legends recited, or lyrics sung, or witness plays performed. Philippe Ariès must be right in this respect: the medieval child did become an adult at the age of seven, and even earlier, as far as his literary experience was concerned. His general participation in adult activities must certainly have involved him in literary occasions.

The scholarly investigations of Dieter Mehl, Derek Pearsall, and A.

C. Baugh,[1] while not undertaken with this end in mind, enable us to be more specific about this passive participation of the medieval child in his literary world, at least the world of romance. In the fourteenth century the romance audience was typically a wealthy bourgeois household in the city or a provincial aristocratic one (Mehl). Baugh shows that in addition the medieval child could expect to hear romances read or recited in alehouses, in marketplaces, at various popular assemblies or ceremonial occasions, as well as in the baronial hall during meals or at other times. It would probably have been as difficult for the medieval child to evade the romance as to evade the sermon or the cycle plays, which we know were performed in cities, towns, and villages throughout England.

Mr. McMunn has argued that literacy was much more common in the Middle Ages than has been generally assumed. There is evidence in the literature which suggests that children were indeed active participants in the Middle English literary world. They read for themselves, and they read aloud to others. The English redactor of *Yvain* carries over without demur Chrétien's description of a maiden who "red that thai myght here, / A real romance in that place" (line 3088). In *Sir Tristrem,* Isonde is presented as a king's daughter "that gle was lef to here / & romance to rede aright" (l. 1257f.). One of the Harleian lyrics, the "Fair Maid of Ribbesdale," praises a maiden who has "a mury mouht to mele / with lefly rede lippes lele / romaunz forto rede." Conceivably, reading romances privately or aloud was not confined to girls. Sir Eger in *Eger and Grimé* reads a romance to the gathered company; he and presumably real gentlemen like him must have learned to read while children and have exercised their ability privately and publicly.

As far as I have been able to determine, however, we have no record before 1477 of an adult actually encouraging a child to read secular literature. In this year Caxton printed the *Book of Curtesye,* written by one of Lydgate's disciples for "lytyl John," who must have been still a child since the author promises him more advice when he is older. The writer counsels little John to read Gower's *Confessio Amantis,* "so ful of fruyt, sentence, and langage" (l. 329); Hoccleve on the princely virtues (st. 51f); and Lydgate, whose excellence he dares not praise (st. 53–58). He especially urges the virtues of Chaucer, "fader and founder of ornate eloquence / That elumened has alle our bretayne" (st. 48). "His langage," he continues, "was so fayr and pertynente / It semeth vnto mannys heerynge / Not only the worde, / But verely the thynge" (st. 49).

The fifteenth-century writer can indeed vouchsafe for the child what Chaucer, in his "Retractions," was unwilling—at least on record and perhaps with death imminent—to vouchsafe for the adult. Still referring

to Chaucer, he implores, "Redeth, my chylde, redeth his bookes alle, /
Refuseth none." The fifteenth century is the century of the book written
explicitly for children, the courtesy book. But it also asserts clearly what
was only implicit in the earlier works: that Middle English literature is
children's literature.

Late medieval English literature supports the contention of Ariès that
by the fourteenth century children became a subject for sentimental
depiction. But because so much literature of the earlier English Middle
Ages has not survived, one is scarcely able either to defend or to attack
his notions of cultural attitudes toward children prior to the thirteenth
century. On the basis of a work like *Havelok the Dane* (c. 1280), however, one suspects that Ariès is mistaken in his conception of the earlier
age as insensitive to children, especially in his belief that a very high rate
of infant mortality had injured the age to the death of children. Derek
Pearsall echoes the consensus among medievalists when he terms *Havelok* "the genuine expression of popular consciousness." Several episodes
in *Havelok* reflect what can only be considered a genuine affection for
children. Perhaps the most prominent of these scenes reflects also an
evident sensitivity to children's deaths. The narrative has the usurper
Godard confirm his villainy in a most dramatic manner. Forswearing his
oath to the dying King Birkabeyn to protect "hise children yunge"
(l. 368), Godard imprisons Havelok and his two sisters, starves them, and
finally cuts the throats of the two girls. Havelok pleads and bargains for
his own life, but Godard reneges and Havelok escapes only through the
mercy of the fisherman Grim and his wife, whose family Havelok then
becomes part of. The story of the girls' death is repeated twice in the
narrative, and when the day of reckoning comes for Godard, Havelok
sentences him to be flayed alive, drawn over rough ground to a gallows,
and hanged with this inscription over him:

> This is the swike that wende wel
> The king haue reft the lond il del,
> And hise sistres with a knif
> Bothe refte here lif. (ll. 2482–85)

D. S. Brewer has noted that in the fourteenth century probably three-
fourths of all children born died before attaining age five. But while
familiarity with death inevitably bred a casualness toward it which
strikes us as callous, it nevertheless seems clear that, as Brewer puts it,
death "did not seem less horrible, or cause less agony of separation than
it does to us." Whatever the cause of death, or however frequent its
visitations, the sense of bereavement it produced must have been as acute

to them as to us. When death was sentimentalized in medieval works, Brewer continues, "its pain and horror were exaggerated rather than, as with us, minimized."

Another cultural monument of the Middle Ages suggests that medieval people were no less touched by the loss of children to death than we are. Holy Innocents Day was celebrated in the west as early as the fifth century, and the Slaughter of the Innocents remained a popular graphic and dramatic theme throughout the Middle Ages. A fifth-century mosaic, on the arch of the apse of the basilica of S. Maria Maggiore, Rome, shows the Slaughter in the upper register and the entrance of the Innocents as lambs into heaven in the lower register. It is noteworthy that in the eleventh and twelfth centuries the Latin liturgical drama depicted the Slaughter as part of the *Officium Stellae* or as a separate *Ordo Rachelis,* which particularly stresses the lamentations of Israel, personified by the unconsolable Rachel, over the death of her children. The cultural outlook underlying these ecclesiastic artifacts seems not to differ fundamentally from the more detailed elaborations of kindred moments in the literature of the later Middle Ages: in Giotto's intense "Slaughter of the Innocents"; in the scene Chaucer and Dante share, the story of the death of Ugolino and his "sons"; and the mystery plays of the Slaughter of the Innocents and Abraham and Isaac.

One other aspect of Ariès' portrait of the medieval child requires notice: the medieval idea of the child's innocence (see the Penguin translation, pp. 98–124). The post-renaissance world revered the child's innocence as a sexual innocence, and to emphasize the contrast of the modern world, particularly its Victorian heritage, with the medieval, Ariès understandably stresses the former age's acceptance of—even delight in—childish sexuality. But to imply thereby that the Middle Ages did not conceive of childish innocence (p. 104) is at best misleading, as a few examples from Middle English literature will show. We should recall first the lyrics, particularly the lullabies, which associate the Christ child, the Lamb of God, with the human infant, and the mortal child in turn with Christ-like guiltlessness; "Lollai litil child," from ms. Harley 913 (c. 1310) is an example of the latter association, while three poems from John Grimestowe's Commonplace Book of 1372 provide interesting examples of the former. The suggestion of an asexual, theological guiltlessness is made explicit in John Audelay's "Cantalena de puericia" (c. 1425) and is confirmed by the example of *Pearl* and of the little clergeoun of Chaucer's Prioress. To Audelay childish innocence implies specific innocence of the seven deadly sins, a condition the poet believes attainable only in early childhood. Precisely in keeping with medieval educational practice, Chaucer has his Prioress make her little clergeoun seven years old, the age at which the child left the security and restrictions of his mother's knee to enter freely into adult activity. The child victim of the Prioress' tale is thus as old as he can be made and still be regarded as innocent and as young as he can be made and still credibly encounter the adult world. The sentimental point of the tale, the familiar one of the innocent overwhelmed by an alien corruption, is thus established with an arithmetic precision.

Pearl presents a more complex and interesting conception of childhood innocence. Whatever else the poem may mean or its Pearl symbolize, it is clear enough in its presentation of a medieval understanding of the peculiar grace of childhood. In the central stanzas of the poem, Pearl uses the parable of the laborers in the vineyard to show the dreamer that she, though untried in faith, was nevertheless welcomed into the company of heaven, in fact incorporated in the company of the Quen of Cortaysye. She pointedly contrasts the innocent's access to grace with that of the mature sinner:

> The gyltyf may contryssyoun hente
> . . .
> Bot he to gyle that never glent,
> That inoscente is saf and ryghte. (st. 56)

The concluding phrase is repeated thrice as "saf by ryghte." The theology is straightforward. Baptism cleanses the child from inherited sin, and it is not yet capable of sinning on its own:

> Bot innoghe of grace has innocent;
> As sone as thay arn borne, by lyne
> In the water of babtem thay dyssente;
> Then arne thay broght into the vyne. (st. 53)

There can be little doubt that the Middle Ages, at least the late Middle Ages in England, conceived of a childish innocence appropriate to the familiar admonitions of the Evangelists:

> Except ye be converted and become as little children, ye shall
> not enter into the kingdom of heaven. (Matt. 18:31)
> Suffer the little children to come unto me, and forbid them not:
> for of such is the kingdom of heaven. (Mark 10:14)

In fact the *Pearl*-poet in stanzas 60–61 alludes to these verses. We can thus say in sum that, far from not conceiving of childish innocence, the Middle Ages conceived of that innocence in broader, more theological terms than did the nineteenth century; that while it included sexual innocence as part of the child's peculiar guiltlessness, it regarded that component as almost incidental to the child's larger freedom from the other deadly sins; and that, perhaps most importantly, the Middle Ages felt the need to preserve or regain this fuller innocence as urgently as the nineteenth century felt the need to recover or maintain the more restricted innocence it associated with children.

NOTE

1. The following works are cited in the order in which they are referred to in the text. Dieter Mehl, *The Middle English Romances of the Thirteenth and Fourteenth Centuries* (New York: Barnes & Noble, 1969), esp. pp. 1–13. Derek Pearsall, "The Development of Middle English Romance," *Mediaeval Studies,* XXVII (1965), 91–116. A. C. Baugh, "The Middle English Romance: Some Questions of Creation, Presentation, and Preservation," *Speculum,* XLII (1967), 1–31. *Caxton's Book of Curtesye,* ed. F. J. Furnivall (Early English Text Society, extra ser. no. 3, 1868). *The Lay of Havelok the Dane,* ed. K. Sisam (2nd ed.; Oxford, 1915). Philippe Ariès, *Centuries of Childhood* (Paris: Librarie Plon, 1960; English trans. pub. variously by Jonathan Cape, Random House, and Penguin Books). *New Catholic Encyclopedia,* s.v. *Innocents* (an illustration of the fifth-century mosaic). Karl Young, *The Drama of the Medieval Church,* II (Oxford, 1933), 102ff., and *Ordo Rachelis* (University of Wisconsin Studies in Language and Literature, IV, 1919). *Religious Lyrics of the Fourteenth Century,* ed. Carleton Brown (2nd ed., rev. G. V. Smithers; Oxford, 1952), pp. 35–36 and nos. 59, 65, and 75, for the lyrics cited. *The Poems of John Audelay,* ed. Ella Keats Whiting, (Early English Text Society, original ser. no. 184, 1931), poem 41; see also poems 3, 11, and 36. The standard edition of *Pearl* is by E. V. Gordon (Oxford, 1953); several modern English versions are available.

Where Skipping Lambkins Feed

Christopher Smart's Hymns for the Amusement of Children

Linda Feldmeier

Perhaps the greatest barrier to any modern appreciation of the eighteenth-century poet Christopher Smart's *Hymns for the Amusement of Children* lies in understanding how they are at all poems *for* the child. In the first place, the constructions and metaphors often seem much too enigmatic for childish listeners. In Hymn XXII, the personified voice of "Gratitude" addresses the children thus:

> Hear, ye little children, hear me.
> I am God's delightful voice;
> They who sweetly still revere me,
> Still shall make the wisest choice.
>
> Hear me not like Adam trembling
> When I walked in Eden's grove;
> And the host of heav'n assembling
> From the spot the traitor drove.
>
> Hear me rather as the lover
> Of mankind, restor'd and free;
> By the word ye shall recover
> More than that ye lost by Me.[1]

It is difficult to find any clear meaning that would be available to a child in these lines, particularly in the last stanza. It is one thing to tell the child that gratitude is something men owe to God, but quite another to try to impress upon him that gratitude (since "God's delightful voice" is the Word made flesh) is in fact God himself. Smart would have the child understand not only that he must give thanks, but also that he must be grateful for the ability to do so, since man would be incapable of gratitude were it not for Christ's sacrifice. But the paradox of the "fortunate fall" is rather subtle doctrine for a child, and Smart's handling of it does more to obscure than simplify. Not all the hymns are so complex, but many of them are—enough to make us wonder whether Smart was unwilling or merely unable to keep himself within the "little prattler's" range of comprehension.[2]

Another serious obstacle arises when we consider even the simplest poems in the collection, for these hymns are not merely lisping thoughts to be sung to a benevolent Father. In the eighteenth century, "for children" was apparently synonymous with "for the children's moral instruction." And so the full didactic panoply is here in "This pictur'd Hymn-book on a plan, / To make good girls and boys." There are thirty-nine hymns, beginning with one for each of the cardinal virtues, and, when these are exhausted, going on to "Elegance" (" 'Tis in the body, that sweet mien, / Ingenuous Christians all possess, / Grace, easy motions, smiles serene, / Clean hands and seemliness of dress") and "Loveliness," "Generosity," "Honour," "Good-nature to Animals," and the "Long-suffering of God," among others. In "The Conclusion of the Matter," the boys and girls are reminded that, in short, "There's nought like penitence and prayer."

Today, when the once popular eighteenth-century title *Little Goody Two Shoes* has become a term of opprobrium, we are likely to find this unending stream of virtues cloying. But the *Hymns'* apparent flaws are not necessarily evidence of Smart's carelessness or lack of ability. He was an experienced juvenile author, with more than a passing interest in the field. He was John Newbery's son-in-law, and although the relationship between them was not always friendly, he contributed at least one song, a "Morning Hymn," to *The Lilliputian Magazine* and may have had a hand in some of the other Newbery productions.[3] In his last years, he devoted most of his time to writing for children. The *Hymns* were published in 1770, the year before Smart died. They were preceded by two other works for children: a translation of the *Fables* of Phaedrus, published in 1765, and *The Parables of our Lord and Saviour Jesus Christ,* "done into familiar verse, with occasional applications, for the use and improvement of younger minds," published in 1768.

The qualities of Smart's verse that a modern reader finds alien reflect assumptions about the nature of childhood that, in a post-Romantic era, we no longer share. Although an English translation of Rousseau's *Emile* was published in 1763, in 1770 the most influential educational philosopher was still John Locke. When it appeared, Locke's work represented a liberal point of view, since he advised parents to encourage the child to learn, rather than coerce him. Education should be made both useful and appealing; a child might begin to learn to read by playing with blocks inscribed with the letters of the alphabet, and after he has learned his letters, the same principle should apply to his reading matter:

> Some easy pleasant book, suited to [the child's] capacity should be put into his hands, wherein the entertainment that he finds might draw him on, and reward his pains in reading, and yet not such as should fill his head with perfectly useless trumpery, or lay the principles of vice and folly. To this purpose I think Aesop's Fables

the best, which being Stories apt to delight and entertain a child, may yet afford useful reflections to a grown man; and if his memory retain them all his life after, he will not repent to find them there, amongst his manly thoughts and serious business.[4]

This is not altogether a bad aim. Certainly the best children's literature is of the sort that one is not sorry to find "amongst his manly thoughts" —although we have undoubtedly expanded the range of manly thoughts to include much that Locke would have considered useless trumpery. With Locke's theories in mind, we can better understand the rationale behind the too-complex lines in the *Hymns*. They were not necessarily flaws from Smart's point of view: they give the hymns potential for growth. The child's immediate enjoyment of the verse is desirable, but it is not the most important end. He might not understand all of "Gratitude" or "Generosity" when he learned it, but as he grew older, it would be capable of growing with him. The *Hymns* are for children—that is, for the little man, the potential adult.

Modern critics are likely to object that a child's enjoyment is an end in itself and to reject out of hand any children's books that preach too obviously. But taken on its own ground, as a moral work, Smart's *Hymns for the Amusement of Children* has its virtues. It is important to distinguish between didactic literature which tries to make existence meaningful by demonstrating the integrity of a moral universe, and literature which is a perversion of that attempt, which simply turns everything into a "no-no" and preaches for the sake of preaching. Twentieth-century children's literature is not without its own versions of the latter. Jason Epstein describes a modernized adaptation of Beatrix Potter's *Peter Rabbit,* in which the realistic but not very nice detail of the pie Mr. MacGregor made out of Peter's father is suppressed, and over Peter's bed hangs a little plaque inscribed with that fine moral sentiment "Good Bunnies Always Obey."[5] A page from a similarly tasteless fiction from the eighteenth century shows two boys rolling their hoops, accompanied by a frolicking puppy—a happy little scene, to which is appended the following:

Think this to be the wheel of fortune, and thou engaged with labour and industry to keep it turning to thy good liking. Its roundness instructs thee that there is no end to a man's care and toil: that we enter upon life with uncertainty, and must improve every incident with prudence, diligence and anxiety.[6]

This is useless moralizing: the distance between the subject and the application is too great; in fact there is no real connection at all, except the author's own need, like Blake's caterpillar, to choose "the fairest leaves to lay her eggs on."

Two of Smart's hymns provide an instructive contrast:

Hymn XXXIII
For Saturday

Now's the time for mirth and play,
Saturday's an holiday;
Praise to heav'n unceasing yield,
I've found a lark's nest in the field.

A lark's nest, then your play-mate begs
You'd spare herself and speckled eggs;
Soon she shall ascend and sing
Your praises to th'eternal King.

The anonymous author of the wheel of fortune analogy denies the child's playfulness; Smart delights in it. When he tells the child not to hurt the lark or her eggs, and then pictures the lark singing for the child to God, it is not for the sake of forbidding. It is not merely that kind acts are nicer than naughty ones. The child is asked to choose a world informed by Charity, where a thoughtless cruelty is barren, but even a small act of kindness is alive and generates its own eternal song of gratitude and love. Religion is not a gloomy affair; among all the other virtues there is even a place for "Mirth":

Hymn XXV
Mirth

If you are merry sing away,
    And touch the organs sweet;
This is the Lord's triumphant day,
Ye children in the gall'ries gay,
    Shout from each goodly seat.

It shall be May to-morrow's morn,
    Afield then let us run,
And deck us in the blooming thorn,
Soon as the cock begins to warn,
    And long before the sun.

I give the praise to Christ alone,
    My pinks already shew;
And my streak'd roses fully blown,
The sweetness of the Lord make known,
    And to his glory grow.

> Ye little prattlers that repair
>   For cowslips in the mead,
> Of those exulting colts beware,
> But blythe security is there,
>   Where skipping lambkins feed.
>
> With white and crimson laughs the sky,
>   With birds the hedge-rows ring;
> To give the praise to God most high,
> And all the sulky fiends defy,
>   Is a most joyful thing.

Again, there is a note of restraint, but it is not gratuitous. Smart's vivid sense of the pleasure of a pre-dawn escape to the fields, away from society, is as strong as his moral fervor. If the child is cautioned against the untamed exultation of the colts, it is because Smart saw a more glorious world in the lamb's pasture. And whether or not we find it an enviable goal, it is true that "blythe security" is the product of a moral universe, and not a natural one.

It would be misleading to select only the more appealing hymns for comment. Others are less happily realized. In striving for memorable rhythms Smart often achieved no better than doggerel rhyme, as in "Pray Remember the Poor":

> I just came by the prison-door,
>   I gave a penny to the poor:
> Papa did this good act approve,
>   And poor Mamma cried out for love.

There are bright, original moments in these hymns, but there are also too many moments when Smart depends upon a stock epithet of pat advice: the children are cautioned to "shun the wily lures of sin" and to beware the tendencies of their "dang'rous giddy youth." Smart never descends to turning a child's joy into anxiety, but he never misses an opportunity to make the telling moral point, and this gives a certain relentless quality to the work as a whole. All the virtues are catalogued, with fine enough lines of distinction drawn so that we have not only "Temperance" but "Moderation," not only "Truth" but "Honesty." The child who took all this seriously would be a prig. Even worse, the imposition of a set of standards too difficult for any human child to attain results not in the child's peace and blithe security, but in guilt and frustration. Smart's own life presents the best exemplum of the vices of too much virtue. He was confined to an asylum for a number of years, obsessed with his inability to attain spiritual perfection. Inspired by the biblical injunction to "pray unceasingly" he would fall to his knees in the middle of the street, and insist that others pray with him. By the time he came to write the *Hymns,* however, little of this fanaticism remained. They are gently, if somewhat overwhelmingly, didactic.

While as a model for children's poetry the *Hymns* can be faulted both in content and technique, they are still valuable because they show the passion and concern with which children's books can be written, and as such provide a welcome antidote to children's literature that is cute and condescending. In assessing the place of the *Hymns* within the Smart canon, Arthur Sherbo finds that "although Smart dedicated his *Hymns* to a child and wrote them for children, they are more than mere hack work, tossed off with speed and indifference. . . . Into these poems, some of them of a bare simplicity and naiveté that have few equals in literature of merit anywhere, Smart brought together for a last time some of the major themes of his poetry."[7] Perhaps he would not sacrifice the mystical paradoxes of a poem like "Gratitude" for more readily comprehensible doctrine because he wished to communicate the fullness of what was essential to him. This is not an easy goal, and perhaps can never be fully realized. But a contemporary children's author would do well to follow Smart in offering his readers not what he conceives might hold their attention, but what he can communicate to them of that which he finds vital. *Hymns for the Amusement of Children* remains an example, if not of the best that can be achieved, still, of the highest that can be attempted.

NOTES

1. All quotations from the *Hymns* are taken from a facsimile of the third edition (1775) published by Basil Blackwell for the Luttrell Society in 1947.

2. Other critics have commented on the occasional complexity of the *Hymns.* Arthur Sherbo, in *Christopher Smart: Scholar of the University* (East Lansing, Michigan State University Press, 1967), p. 261, notes wryly that "the first stanza of 'Generosity' probably gave some difficulty. . . . And the whole of 'Learning' . . . must have caused little brows to knot in perplexity." Edmund Blunden, in his introduction to the Luttrell Society's edition of the *Hymns,* remarks that Smart "sometimes gives his young audience conceptions beyond their years" (p. xiii).

3. See Roland B. Botting, "Christopher Smart and *The Lilliputian Magazine,*" *Journal of English Literary History,* IX (1942), 286–87.

4. John Locke, *Some Thoughts Concerning Education,* ed. F. W. Garforth (1963; reprint ed., Woodbury, N.Y.: Barron's, 1964), p. 189.

5. Jason Epstein, "Good Bunnies Always Obey: Books for American Children," *Commentary* (Feb. 1963), reprinted in *Only Connect,* ed. Sheila Egoff, G. T. Stubbs, and L. F. Ashley (Toronto: Oxford University Press, 1969), pp. 70–90.

6. Andrew W. Tuer, *Pages and Pictures from Forgotten Children's Books* (1898; reprint ed., Detroit: Singing Tree Press, 1969), p. 15.

7. Sherbo, p. 260.

Romanian Folklore and Ion Creangă's
Recollections of Childhood

R. L. Taylor

Ion Creangă occupies a place in Romanian letters analogous to that of Hans Christian Andersen in Danish or the Grimm brothers in German literature. He is the main figure to give literary expression to the rich stores of Romanian folk and fairy tales. For nearly a century his work has been popular with children throughout Europe, and his tales have often been reprinted in colorful illustrated editions. Yet equal in popularity to his stories have been his *Recollections from Childhood,* of which one can form a rough idea by imagining *Tom Sawyer* and *Huckleberry Finn* written in the form of Clemens' own diary or autobiography. The folk tales and his own "recollections" are closely related, suggesting an intimate and mutual influence between "art" and "life." Unlike many children's authors, Creangă has retained the interest of adults and has achieved great critical acclaim.

Creangă was born in 1837 in the little village of Humuleşti, on the eastern slope of the Carpathian mountains, just at the edge of the Moldovan plain which stretches eastward toward Bessarabia. The village has changed little since the nineteenth century: ducks and pigs still dominate the streets. The house where he grew up has undergone the curious transformation into itself which occurs when a home becomes a museum, preserving childhood intact as if sealed in plastic—an odd monument to a man fascinated by the fluidity of imagination and the hard, almost cruel, way in which children learn to accept life and death.

Creangă trained for the priesthood, was ordained, and practiced in Iaşi, the capital of Moldova. However his blunt temperament and sardonic outlook did not blend well with the piety he was expected to exhibit. Certain habits of his, including shooting the crows which settled on the roof of his church, were displeasing to ecclesiastic authority, and he was relieved of his duties. In the meantime, various companions turned his attention toward writing. In the 1880's Iaşi was the cultural center of Romania, which was then undergoing a wave of nationalistic enthusiasm, characterized largely by a discovery of roots. A prominent feature of this movement was the uncovering of Latin elements which had been submerged by Slavic authority in the church and by Turkish and Austro-Hungarian political power. Most of the leading literary figures participated in this revival—Caragiale in the theatre; Eminescu in lyric poetry; Alaxandri in the discovery of the traditional ballad.

The influence of the articulate circles of Iaşi, in particular the "Junimea" literary society, whose journal, *Convorbiri Literare,* published most of his work, directed Creangă back to the village of his youth for inspiration and sources. Although he draws heavily on traditional folk sources, his style is highly self-conscious. By the latter half of the nineteenth century, the search for folk material had spread from Germany and England throughout Europe and had recently become fashionable in Romania. Mihai Eminescu had studied in Germany, where he certainly became familiar with the work of Grimm, Brentano, and others. Vasile Alexandri, like Walter Scott in Scotland a century before, travelled around the Romanian countryside collecting ballads, many of which he "improved" by sentimentalizing them and by setting them into a more "polished" form.

In the treatment of his folk material Creangă differs markedly from his contemporaries and immediate predecessors. His writing preserves and at times exaggerates the village attitudes and oral character of his material. He remains at all times the village storyteller, a role which his education and literary friendships seemed only to crystallize. His exploitation of folk language can be analyzed on many levels, the first of which is dialect.

For the Romanian reader, Creangă's tales are somewhat like the Uncle Wiggley or Br'er Rabbit stories for the American reader. The dialect is so pronounced that the average native speaker finds himself in a linguistic world which may be hauntingly familiar, but in which many times he is forced to guess at the precise meaning of particular expressions. Iorgu Iordan has exhaustively analyzed the phonetic, lexical, morphological, and syntactic peculiarities of Creangă's dialect. There has been much learned debate over the vertical, horizontal, and temporal range of his dialect elements—whether they are specific just for Humuleşti, for Moldova, for Northern Romania in general, whether they are regionalisms, slang, archaic forms, specific to particular social classes, and so forth. Although many of these arguments are of interest mainly to the specialist, one aspect of the dialect problem remains important for any serious reader.

Village storytellers often employ dialect as symptom. In a traditional society, the language a person uses immediately identifies him according to various parameters—education, social class, proximity to the dialect region, and the like. The narrator can rely on his listeners' familiarity with a large body of such conventions. Understanding the dialogue and sometimes the story itself may be dependent on recognizing the boundary of a dialect range. For example, if a character begins using language inappropriate to his status he is immediately rendered ludicrous; in other cases, a particular verb form may identify a person as coming from another village which has a specific reputation or relationship to the narrator's village. For such reasons it is desirable to recognize changes in dialect which denote variations in tone or relationship between the characters.

Of greater significance, however, than Creangă's use of the variant speech patterns normally classified as dialectal is his ability to capture the normal speech of the average Romanian, who, in the nineteenth century, happened also to be a peasant. Three generations of Romanian scholars have sought to explain how his dialogue manages to sound as convincing as it does. It is very difficult for a person writing in English in the twentieth century to devise a language which similarly strikes a majority of readers as sounding just like speech. One difficulty is that British and American speech relies heavily on slang, which rarely lasts more than a decade. Although Creangă's language is highly colloquial, it is more durable than slang.

Several factors contribute to this durability. For one thing, his characters tend to punctuate almost every event with a proverb, which provides a mode of classifying and thereby "understanding" the event. Even in "formal" tales of magic and fantasy, these proverbs tend to be earthy, skeptical and sardonic: "Wherever there are lakes there are always enough frogs; You have to cool down in the same shirt that you get hot in; You cannot stop wind, water, or men's voices." In most cases such proverbs act to summarize a narrative sequence, but sometimes proverbial construction will be part of the narrative line itself. In his autobiography, describing the point when his interest shifted from killing flies to chasing girls, Creangă concludes, "and then the mill began to grind other corn," an expression admirably suited for describing any change in interest or fortune. Sometimes the narrative line will be carried forward by snatches of verse or song with proverbial content:

> Youthful rider, ancient horse
> Can't agree upon their course.

Somewhat similar in form to the proverbs are certain fixed constructions, often fragments of verse or song, which differ from the proverbs in operating as vestigial magic spells. These tend to be active or causative, whereas proverbs tend to reveal acceptance (often caustic or bitter) of things as they are. These expressions may be highly idiomatic or metaphorical, perhaps because they retain the magic character of hidden knowledge:

Fă-mă, mamă, cu noroc,
Și macar m-aruncă-n foc.

(Make me, mother, full of luck
And I will throw the crane into the fire.)

That is, "I can do things myself, without anyone's assistance."

Another frequently used form consists of interrogation with argumentative or diminutive intent. When opponents begin using the same tactics, the result can be a highly charged but absurd conversation which goes nowhere:

Where are you from?
I am from my village.
Well, where is your village?
That one over on the other side of the hill.
Which village on the other side of the hill are you talking about?
I am talking about my village.

Another such conversation takes place between St. Peter and an applicant at Heaven's gate:

Who is there?
I.
Who is I?

The humor in this conversation lies not only in the applicant's presumptuousness but in St. Peter's use of the pronoun *I* as a proper name instead of employing the more conventional pattern, "who are you?" The function of these responses is to provide nonanswers in the form of answers, an appropriate reaction to questions which function primarily as provocations. Creangă's work is filled with such conversational cul-de-sacs.

Another way in which Creangă exploits formulaic patterns is by the use of repetition, of which there are many differing instances:

Și merge Ivan și merge și merge
(And Ivan went, and went, and went)

Nu mă duc Mama Nu mă duc
(I'm not going, Mama, I'm not going)

Și eu fuga și ea fuga și eu fuga și ea fuga
(and I ran and she ran and I ran and she ran).

such repetition has the effect of heightening the tone, whether it be humorous or serious. Other oral forms which Creangă employs are interjections and pure sound elements such as stutters, morphological features including diminutives, colloquial, and idiomatic syntactic constructions, and various types of figured speech—inversion, metaphor, ellipsis, and so on.

In addition to the formulaic nature of his dialogue, Creangă's characters, plots, and themes tend to be entirely traditional. His characters may be divided into two broad categories. The first, figures with stock roles, are of three types: parental or authority roles, including the vulnerable single mother with children, the evil step or surrogate parents, the henpecked husband (in particular by a second wife), and the obtrusive mother-in-law; sibling conflict, including good and bad daughters and the good or competent youngest son working his way out from under evil or incompetent older brothers; and religious figures, including the devil (under many euphemisms), the good priest (a happy normal family man), the deranged monk (abnormal, a bit of anti-Catholicism), and St. Peter (usually a bit bewildered). The second category, figures representing stock attributes, includes the lazy man or woman, the malevolent man or woman, the greedy man or woman (usually old and unhappy), the disobedient woman or child, the trickster, the wise fool (often an archetype of saint who leaves fate to God), and various archetypal animals (wolf, bear, sheep, pig, wild bird). The distinction between role and attribute is complementary rather than absolute. It is assumed that a particular role will promote certain characteristics. Thus all mothers-in-law are considered nosy, all second wives or step-mothers are cranky, and so on. Much of the formulaic treatment of character lies in accepting the rigidity of such assumptions, and the creativity allowed the storyteller consists of embellishing the relationships which everyone takes for granted.

Creangă's tales, except for a few didactic pieces, are usually divided into *povești,* which are noble or fantastic tales presenting positive models of behavior such as kings' sons, "true" heroes, or good people disguised in rags, and *povestiri,* which are comic in tone and grotesque in form, and whose characters are aberrant to the point of being disfigured—the man who was too lazy to eat, or the stupid man who tried to carry sunshine into his house in a bucket. The themes and events for these tales are drawn from the universal store of the European folk tale, including initiation rituals (the quest, the trial); cycles of fate or judgment (transformations, reversals of initial status, triumph of "justice"); devices for wish fulfillment (incantation and magic, revenge, accident or the pot of gold); and models of behavior or archetypes of social control (ridicule of lazy or disobedient characters, natural wisdom or goodness of animals).

Creangă's creativity does not lie in challenging oral, folk, and formulaic conventions of language, character, or theme but in embracing
and embellishing them in a manner analogous to the work of Chaucer
or Mozart. The following example illustrates his procedure at the verbal
level. The conventional Romanian formula for beginning a fairy tale is
a fost odata (there once was), equivalent to the English "once upon a
time." In Creangă's tales, however, one can come across such openings
as, "A fost odata, cînd a fost, că, dacă n-ar fi fost, nu s-ar povesti." In
English this could be rendered: "Once upon a time there was a time
which, if that time had never been, there wouldn't be a tale." One can
find this curiously exuberant playing with the formulae at almost every
level where one can find the formulae themselves. The effect is that,
although the sacrosanctity of the formulae appears to be called into
question, no clear alternatives to the formulae emerge. Many of his fairy
tales appear in fact to be parodies of fairy tales, yet, by persistently
leading back into the form, the parodies wind up serving the same social
or psychological functions as the original tales.

In one story, *Ivan and His Sack,* parody at the level of theme appears
to extend to the level of parody of the genre itself. The tale, which is a
burlesque on the "trials of Hercules" theme, opens with a discharged
soldier staggering drunkenly down the street. His singing and erratic
behavior frighten St. Peter, who is walking just ahead of him in the
company of the Lord, who assures him that they have nothing to fear
from a man as long as he is singing. The soldier accosts the pair of
travelers, addressing them in rudely familiar language. From here the
story proceeds through a bizarre series of adventures as the soldier
contends with death and the devil. The tone is extravagant, resembling
the tall tale, yet the victims of satire are numerous and explicit. When
Ivan approaches the Golden Gate he inquires of St. Peter:

Is there liquor in heaven?
None at all.
Are there fiddlers in heaven?
None at all.
Are there women in heaven?

The Romanian response to that question is a sardonically ambiguous
intensifier *(Ba),* which could be applied either to an affirmative or negative answer. "What poverty there is in heaven!" Ivan comments, and goes
down to hell in search of something more interesting. When his questions
are answered in the affirmative he rushes eagerly into hell exclaiming,
"haraşo, haraşo! Aici e de mine" (Wonderful, wonderful, here's the place

for me). There are pointed political implications in the use of slavic
vocabulary in this context. Somewhat later Ivan finds himself guarding
the Golden Gate when Death comes by to get fresh orders from the Lord,
an ironic twist on the conventional chain of command, which puts Death
under Satan. In a tone of bureaucratic officiousness, Ivan informs Death
that he has no business with the Lord.

As the objects of satire vary throughout this story, the point of view
seems also to change. Thus the comments about women in hell echo the
traditional Christian attitude, the observations about the poverty of
heaven appeal to the rationalist, the political comments have a chauvinis-
tic center, and Ivan's contemptuous dismissal of death answers a deep
human need. Yet, although the tone throughout the piece is sardonic
gusto, orthodox values always seem to sort themselves out and survive
the parody. In spite of all Ivan's earthly inclinations, as long as the Lord
is with him, he is invulnerable to Satan and to death.

The furthest Creangă moves from the use of folk and oral formulae
is in the *Recollections from Childhood,* an autobiography tracing his
development from his earliest memories, throughout his childhood, to
the point where he finally leaves his village. Superficially, this work falls
into the popular *Bildungsroman* format, which in one sense is as opposed
as possible to formulaic writing and the fairy tale. The "romantic"
assumption of the novel of education is that the hero is unique and that
the purpose of the novel is to trace the irreproducible set of circumstances which contributed to his singular character or talents.

Structurally, however, the influence of the *Bildungsroman* is less important than the forms of the fairy tales Creangă had been publishing for
the previous seven years. First of all, the author of the *Recollections*
constantly stresses his ordinariness, emphasizing that what happened to
him has happened likewise to everyone in similar circumstances. Furthermore, just as James Joyce organized each of the chapters of *Portrait
of the Artist* around a dominant epiphany, Creangă broke up the narrative line of *Recollections,* made each of the four chapters structurally
self-contained, and based each one on the form of a separate fairy tale.

The first chapter is modeled on the cycle of the prodigal son. There
is a conflict between the children, who engage in such pranks as catching
flies by slamming them between the pages of the *Book of Hours,* and the
priests and schoolmasters, who provide religious instruction with the aid
of "Saint Nicholas," a leather whip. A beating was called "consolation
from the Saint." Eventually an argument develops between the father
and the mother over the value of the child's getting an education. Although the mother supports the boy, the father sees no sense to such

foolishness. Finally the boy is sent off to live with an unpleasant foster family. He enacts vengeance on them (albeit accidentally) by rolling a huge stone down the hillside, destroying the house and killing the goat. He then runs away, goes through a series of endurance tests, and returns (in triumph) to sing in the choir on Easter morning. Although his triumph is marred by the fact that he returns with a case of the mange, nonetheless the archetype is preserved intact. The chapter is characterized by a curious amalgamation of tones. The humorous episodes, jokes, and pranks are often revealed to have serious implications, such as carrying out justice, while events of great moment tend to have some ludicrous aspects.

In the second chapter the roles of his parents are reversed. The mother becomes the authoritative figure while the father becomes indulgent and understanding. The chapter's theme is the magical transformation, which is taken to symbolize the "incomprehensible" process of maturation. In the opening pages the mother is portrayed as having witch-like powers. She knows many herbs and teas for curing illness and sadness, and she can control the weather. In a poetic bit of witchery she tells the boy to go out and smile at the sun in order to drive away the clouds. The sun obediently comes out from the clouds because "he knew with whom he was dealing. I was my mother's son." Language itself becomes associated with her arcane knowledge since she helps him with his reading and teaches him many stories.

The bulk of the chapter is then taken up by a string of pranks undertaken by the incorrigible youth. His mother finally "cures" him of his foolishness by stealing his clothes while he is in swimming, thus "exposing" him to the laughter of some girls who are washing clothes nearby. In one of Creangă's fairy tales almost the identical trick is used to gain control over the devil.

The third chapter moves out of a mythic and archetypal realm into the "real" world of the village, which is complemented by and contrasted with its immediately adjacent precincts—the famed monasteries, old ruined castles, nearby villages with strange customs, and the like. In theme and technique this chapter moves from the universal to the particular. The stylistic emphasis is on description rather than incident. Education continues to be a major subject, but now the reader sees the content rather than merely the effect of the education; there continue to be practical jokes, but now they are played on peers rather than on parents or authority figures. In this chapter the transition away from childhood is registered by a style which emphasizes the particular more than the formulaic patterns of the fairy tales and the earlier chapters.

The fourth chapter is little more than a narrative epilogue describing Creangă's final journey to Iaşi, which is a definitive break, both with the village and with its outlook. Perhaps the major difference lies in the sense of time, which changes from circular or recurrent village time into linear, irredeemable modern time.

The closing chapters of this book are as far as Creangă moves from the oral formulae of the village storyteller. For the most part he was happy to remain within the constraints of these formulae, yet throughout his writing his treatment of them was consistently innovative. Marianne Moore called for a poetry which provides the reader with imaginary gardens with real toads in them. Creangă gives his reader a fairy tale world filled with archetypal peasants who talk and think just like human beings.

BIBLIOGRAPHICAL NOTE

A brief survey of the publication of Creangă's work would seem helpful. His earliest publications consist of short didactic poems for use in primary education. These appeared in a series of primary school texts bearing such titles as *New Methods for Reading and Writing for Use in the First Grades* (a phonetic approach), 1868. An article on "Jesuitism in Romania" appeared in 1872. Didactic tales for children began appearing in 1874. The first of his better-known tales appeared in 1875 in *Convorbiri Literare,* which ran the original versions of almost all his tales. The first section of *Recollections from Childhood* appeared in January 1881 in Iaşi *(Convorbiri Literare)* and two weeks later in *Timpul* in Bucureşti. The other three parts of this work appeared in both journals incrementally throughout the same year. After its publication in these journals, Creangă made many changes in the text. His collected works were first published in 1890 and his complete works in 1900. Since then his complete or collected works have been republished 68 times, excluding translations. Individual tales have been published many times, often with lavish illustrations. A definitive two-volume edition of the complete works (with full scholarly apparatus) has been made by Iorgu Iordan and Elisabeta Brancuş (Bucureşti: Editura Minerva, 1970).

Creangă's works have been popular as the base for dramatic pieces for children and puppet shows. Iordan and Brancuş list 23 entries under this category, perhaps the most interesting of which is a "tableau" devised by the avant-garde poet Saşa Pana in 1958.

(In 1970, a complete list of separate translations of Creangă's works contained 140 entries. He has been translated into almost every major European language, including French, German, Italian, Spanish, Portugese, Russian, Ukranian, Hungarian, Polish, and Serbo-Croatian as well as Chinese, Hindustani, and Vietnamese. His complete works were published in French in 1965 (Bucureşti: Editura Meridiane). Translations into English include two translations of the

Recollections from Childhood, one by Lucy Byng (London and Toronto: J. M. Bent, 1930), the other by A. L. Lloyd (London: Lawrence & Wishart, 1956); and a collection of the folk tales (incomplete) translated by Mabel Nandriş, issued in London by Routledge and Kegan Paul in 1952 and in New York by Roy in 1953 (this translation has a few holes—for example, in deference to the ladies, references to the presence of women in hell have been scrupulously omitted). Translations of individual stories into English include "The Story of a Sluggard," tr. Leila Hamilton, *The Ring of Bells* (Devon, 1909), pp. 23–24; "The Mother in Law," tr. Cynthia Jopson, *Slavonic Review,* VII (1930), 524–30. None of the English translations can be considered adequate substitutes for the original. They tend to turn Creangă's sardonic wit into something bland and saccharine. For example, in the first few lines of the *Recollections,* he refers to himself as a "dragaliţa-Doamne," which means literally "beloved Lord." In practice, when this kind of expression is applied to children or to persons of lower status, its implication is almost invariably sarcastic—something like "He's too lazy to get out of bed." The term in context leads into the conflict between his parents over the value of his wasting time and money on an education. Byng (p. 13) renders it "little dear." Until a translation is available which captures the stylistic coloring, Creangă's work cannot be appreciated by an English-speaking audience.

Scholarship and criticism on Creangă has been voluminous. The Iordan and Brancus bibliography lists 920 books, articles, and notes on him, or somewhat more than two books or articles for every page that he wrote. Perhaps the best study of his style is by G. I. Tohăneanu, *Stilul Artistic al Lui Ion Creangă* (Bucureşti: Editura Stiintifica, 1969). This excellent book contains chapters on the nature of oral language, narrative art, the art of dialogue, and handling of description. Several of this paper's observations on the transformation of oral formulae into a literary style have been drawn from this book. Among the rest of the embarrassment of riches characterizing Creangă criticism mention should be made of Iorgu Iordan's excellent description of the phonetic characteristics of Creangă's peasant dialect; G. Calinescu's study of variants and sources (1938); Eugene Todoran's two articles on the basis of Creangă's humor; and Lazar Saineanu's article comparing Romanian folk tales with classical legends. Creangă has been very popular in France. The best study of his work outside Romania is Jean Boutière's *La Vie et l'oeuvre de Ion Creangă* (Paris, 1930). No criticism, original or in translation, is available in English.

An Epic in Arcadia

The Pastoral World of The Wind in the Willows

Geraldine D. Poss

Throughout Kenneth Grahame's two collections of short stories, *The Golden Age* and *Dream Days,* his narrator writes fondly of the romantic characters that he, his brothers, and his sisters read about during their childhood. The children liked to choose roles and act out the Arthurian romances, and on the particular day described below, Harold, the youngest boy, seized the occasion of his oldest brother's absence to be Sir Lancelot. Charlotte insisted on being Tristram, and the narrator, who was more inclined that day to dream than to act, accepted a subordinate role without protest:

> "I don't care," I said: "I'll be anything. I'll be Sir Kay. Come on!"
> Then once more in this country's story the mail-clad knights paced through the greenwood shaw, questing adventure, redressing wrong; and bandits, five to one, broke and fled discomfited to their caves. Once again were damsels rescued, dragons disembowelled, and giants, in every corner of the orchard, deprived of their already superfluous number of heads. . . . The varying fortune of the day swung doubtful—now on this side, now on that; till at last Lancelot, grim and great, thrusting through the press, unhorsed Sir Tristram (an easy task), and bestrode her, threatening doom; while the Cornish knight, forgetting hard-won fame of old, cried piteously, "You're hurting me, I tell you! and you're tearing my frock!"[1]

The nostalgia, mock-heroism, and affection expressed in this passage are typical of Grahame's attitude toward romance. He equates the innocence of the children with its ideal world and, to the extent that both are irretrievable, the equation is valid. But he is also aware that the worlds of Homer and Malory are fallen; heroes need villains in order to demonstrate their valor. And he knows that it is only through the uncritical eyes of childhood that the heroic world can truly seem Utopian. For Grahame, the innocent, green world of Arcadia is by far the more appealing, and from time to time, quite casually, in the short stories, he allows us a glimpse of it as it was perceived by the uncomprehending child. Though the Arcadian vision remains intermittent and basically undeveloped in the stories, we can find in them the elements—both positive and negative—that would eventually lead Grahame to fashion the sweet epic in Arcadia that exists in *The Wind in the Willows.*

"The Roman Road," another story in *The Golden Age,* outlines the Arcadian alternative at its most poignant and melancholy. The narrator opens by relating how on a day "when things were very black within" (p. 156) he took a walk along a road which he felt might truly, as the proverb promised, lead to Rome. He meets an artist who, by some coincidence, claims to spend half his year there, and the little boy begins asking questions about the city. As the conversation develops, it becomes evident that the place they are discussing is a creation of fantasy only, and that its inhabitants are those people who have for some reason had to leave the world of poor, working mortals:

> "Well, there's Lancelot," I went on. "The book says he died,
> but it never seemed to read right, somehow. He just went away,
> like Arthur. And Crusoe, when he got tired of wearing clothes
> and being respectable. And all the nice men in the stories who
> don't marry the Princess, 'cos only one man ever gets married in a
> book, you know. They'll be there!"
> "And the men who never come off," he said, "who try like the
> rest, but get knocked out, or somehow miss,—or break down or
> get bowled over in the *mêlée,*—and get no Princess, nor even a
> second-class kingdom,—some of them'll be there, I hope?" (pp.
> 165–66)

The world which they envision is one which simply ignores death, women, and pressure to achieve. Rejecting the idea of his death, the little boy includes Lancelot, but it is clearly with the others, the gentle folk who never made it as heroes, that the adult narrator has the greatest affinity. And perhaps such types struck a respondent chord in that hero-worshiping little boy too, who so easily bypassed Arthur and Gawain to slip into the subsidiary role of Sir Kay. If we hear a wistful note here, about not getting the princess and fighting the dragons, we sense relief too, for there is something foolish and even vaguely repellent to the writer in all that activity, and he can imagine a much more satisfactory world, without the "alarums and excursions." His "reluctant dragon," a sensible spokesman for pacifism, elsewhere explains to the earnest and perplexed St. George why he will not participate in a contest:

> "Believe me, St. George," [he says]. "There's nobody in the world
> I'd sooner oblige than you and this young gentleman here. But the
> whole thing's nonsense, and conventionality, and popular
> thick-headedness. There's absolutely nothing to fight about from

beginning to end. And anyhow I'm not going to, so that settles it!"[2]

What the dragon seeks, and what finally moves him to agree to fight and succumb on the third charge, is a chance to socialize with the villagers, narrow-minded though they may be, and to find a sympathetic audience for his poetry.

If only one man can win the princess, it seems implicit in the little boy's statement that he did not expect—nor perhaps want—to be that man. The narrator, and by inference Grahame, reveals his ambivalence about women throughout his essays, in the distaste he evinces for the typical female behavior of his older sister Selina and for the tendencies he occasionally notes in his younger sister Charlotte to follow in her footsteps—even though the little girl was still smart enough in *The Golden Age* to want to be Tristram rather than Iseult. In "The Finding of the Princess," another essay in that volume, Grahame approaches the issue with his characteristic charm and indirectness, reflecting upon the subject with perhaps as much light as he was willing to give it.

By way of contrast with its title, and to establish conditions existing in his own family circle at the time of the incident, the story opens with a discussion of toothbrushes. The narrator muses on the reasons why his sisters received them before he and his brothers: "why, we boys could never rightly understand, except that it was part and parcel of a system of studied favouritism on behalf of creatures both physically inferior and (as shown by a fondness for tale-bearing) of weaker mental fibre" (p. 51). With this observation as a prelude, the story then moves to the child's romance. He is walking alone through a wood which leads to a garden. All his literary experience tells him that it is in such places that princesses are found, and notwithstanding his disdain for his sisters, he approaches hopefully:

> Conditions declared her presence patently as trumpets; without this centre such surrounding could not exist. . . . There, if anywhere, she should be enshrined. Instinct, and some knowledge of the habits of princesses, triumphed; for (indeed) there She was! In no tranced repose, however, but laughingly, struggling to disengage her hand from the grasp of a grown-up man who occupied the marble bench with her. (pp. 56–57)

The man asks amiably where he "sprang from"; he replies that he "came up stream" in search of the princess, and then adds: " 'But she's wide awake, so I suppose somebody kissed her.' This very natural deduction moved the grown-up man to laughter; but the Princess, turning red and jumping up, declared that it was time for lunch" (p. 58). Indulging his own whimsy, the young man dubs him "water baby," and invites him to stay for the meal. Thus, the little boy is able to sustain his fantasy through the afternoon. When he finally leaves the couple, at their gentle suggestion, the man gives him two half-crowns, "for the other water babies," and the princess gives him a kiss. The story ends as the child drifts into a pleasant sleep, filled with dreams of this kiss. But the narrator notes that at the time he was actually more affected by the man's generosity, which he described (no pun, I think, intended) as a "crowning mark of friendship" (p. 60). This is understandable: a gift not for oneself but for one's friends is a gesture of regard and affection much easier to accept gracefully than an inevitably embarrassing kiss. But the judgment also suggests that the magic the child had tried so hard to attach to his real princess ultimately failed him. She was not as satisfying as the dream into which he finally incorporated her. Throughout the essay the reader can sense this contrast between the romance the little boy is trying to cast and the good-natured yet necessarily limited flesh-and-blood characters who are being called up on to fill the roles, careless of their place in history and the eyes of the chronicler upon them. From the very start the scene was wrong; the princess was awake, and maybe just a bit too awkward and embarrassed herself. How much more beautiful it would have been had she been asleep.

Heroism, heterosexual love, and death—all are approached gingerly, with occasional humor and gentle irony, in the stories of the 1890's. But a decade later, in *The Wind in the Willows,* Grahame finally develops a golden age of his own imagining rather than Malory's, and the ambivalence is, in his own way, resolved.[3] The ideal world that blossoms in his novel is like the world at the end of the Roman Road. It is an unpressured world of good-natured fellows who eschew nonsensical fighting. And as for the princess, no one need worry about competing for her, or living with her once she has awakened, for she is simply not there. What remains is an Arcadian world bounded by a lovely river, a Wild Wood that really threatens no evil, and a Wide World that one need never bother about at all. Through his book Grahame weaves the gentler trappings of epic, dividing it into a classical twelve chapters, but omitting from the work all aspects of the heroic life that might cause strife and pain and eventually death.

The book opens, in the epic manner, with a statement of theme: it is to be about the "spirit of divine discontent and longing," a spirit so strong in spring that it reaches to the "dark and lowly little house" of

the domestic Mole, luring him out in search of some gentle adventure.[4]
Later this same spirit draws him back home, if only for a visit, and this
we recognize as the epic pattern in little: the journey out and the journey
back. As in picture books, it is diminutive and relatively safe, because
it is a journey within an innocent pastoral milieu. At his most heroic, the
childlike Mole must make his necessary passage to the Wild Wood, and
the Rat must strap on his guns to follow him, but this too quickly leads
to warmth and comfort and piles of buttered toast. The Rat is there to
protect the Mole, the Badger to protect them both, and the ubiquitous
Friend and Helper ultimately to protect them all.

With his creation of the Friend and Helper, Grahame has neatly seized
control of the gods, scaling another epic problem down to comfortable
size. In "The Olympians," prefaced to *The Golden Age*, he had characterized adults by their power to affect lives with their foolishness and
petulance, to blame children for the wrong offenses, and to ignore those
pleasures that beckoned so obviously to the young. The Homeric gods
stood in a similar relation to men, exacting vengeance, playing favorites,
and generating continual concern about sacrifice, devotion, and protocol.
Such Olympians, whether as adults or gods, have been eliminated from
The Wind in the Willows. The animals in Grahame's ideal world are
truly innocent, and so they are spared the anguish that questioning,
knowledge, and the inevitable desire to influence their fate would produce. What they have, instead, is the benign, all but unsexed figure of
Pan, who sits at the center of the book, but demands no recognition and
no offerings. And unlike the Olympian gods, who were always leaving
awesome and intimidating signs of their presence—whether by dazzling
men with their beauty, or by metamorphosing into birds at the ends of
their earthly visits—Pan bestows the gift of forgetfulness, asking no
thanks for his benevolence. Dimly, in the seventh chapter, the Rat can
hear this song: *"Lest the awe should dwell—And turn your frolic to fret
—You shall look on my power at the helping hour—But then you shall
forget"* (p. 132). And as he and the Mole move closer, the Rat says
finally: "This time, at last, it is the real, the unmistakable thing, simple
—passionate—perfect" (p. 132). But he cannot repeat it and shortly falls
asleep, as the song fades into the gentle reed talk produced by the wind
in the willows.

If gods and religion are at the center of the strife that plagues the
Homeric world, women are the traditional, if unwitting, agents. Odysseus lays the blame for the Trojan War squarely on Helen's shoulders,
and, contemplating the fate of Agamemnon, he declares: "Alas! . . .
All-seeing Zeus has indeed proved himself a relentless foe to the House

of Atreus, and from the beginning he has worked his will through women's crooked ways. It was for Helen's sake that so many of us met our deaths, and it was Clytaemnestra who hatched the plot against her absent lord."[5] Even Penelope and a reformed and penitent Helen cannot adequately redress the balance. So Grahame, who could never find a lady to match the sleeping princess of romance, and who was evidently unhappy in his own marriage,[6] wisely disposed of these instruments of the gods as one more safeguard against unhappiness. Occasionally, in his descriptive passages, his prose will carry him past the limits of his chaste, bachelor's paradise, and he will celebrate the sexual aspect of the natural cycles: "June at last was here. One member of the company was still awaited; the shepherd-boy for the nymphs to woo, the knight for whom the ladies waited at the window, the prince that was to kiss the sleeping summer back to life and love" (p. 42). But the passion he alludes to metaphorically is utterly missing (or, as for the Rat, forgotten) in his animal world.

Laurence Lerner describes the two ways in which Arcadias can traditionally accommodate sex. The first is to offer fulfillment of desire; the second to eliminate desire all together.[7] But if, in the latter case, the characters must make a conscious effort to conquer or deny desire that they actually feel, then they are experiencing the rigors of asceticism and moving toward heroism again. The most natural path to a happy, asexual world is the path back to childhood, and Lerner translates a passage from Virgil's *Eclogues* which recalls this innocent state:

> When you were small I saw you (I was then your guide) with
> your mother, picking the dewy apples in our orchard. I had just
> entered the year after my eleventh year; already I could touch the
> delicate branches from the ground. I saw you and, ah, was lost:
> this wicked treachery of love caught me.[8]

The world that Virgil regards with such sophisticated nostalgia is like the world of Grahame's child-men, who, despite their enjoyment of the manly and epic pleasures of hearth and home and a story well told, will never enter the year after their eleventh year. They may be threatened by the social upstarts from the Wild Wood,[9] but they will never have their Arcadia destroyed by the passion or treachery of love.

Yet even without the help of gods and women, the comic Toad manages to create a hell for himself. The most active character in this pastoral paradise, and the only actual wanderer, Toad is also the most shallow of the lot. Perhaps this is not completely ironic, for it reflects the sin-

gleminded intensity of purpose that the hero—or at any rate the man of
action—needs in order to complete his task. And if Toad's only task is
to heed that spirit of divine discontent and longing presumably wherever
it takes him, Grahame nevertheless indicates that it should not be taking
him where it is. His pursuit of activity and novelty for its own sake is
not ennobling and heroic as Toad fancies, but rather a mischanneling of
a natural instinct. The other animals may travel less, but they seem to
be experiencing much more. Grahame has obvious affection for Toad
(Green suggests that he represents the submerged bohemian in Grahame
himself),[10] yet he is still demonstrating in Toad the problems of an
unexamined life devoted to acquisition and external adventure in a world
that is retreating further and further from nature.

Green writes that "most of Toad's adventures bear a certain ludicrous
resemblance to Ulysses' exploits in the *Odyssey;* and the resemblance
becomes detailed and explicit in the last chapter, which parodies the
hero's return and the slaying of the suitors."[11] In general, however, *The
Wind in the Willows* parallels epic in a way that is more reverential than
parody is. Grahame is simply being eclectic about what he can include
in his own ideal world. If Toad's adventures mimic those of Odysseus,
the joke is almost always on Toad. He incorporates the hero's idiosyncra-
cies, but he is all style, without the center of strength and intelligence
of Odysseus, and without the hero's true capacity for anguish.

First and most obviously, Toad shares Odysseus' delight in singing his
own praises. After he seizes the same motor car for the second time, he
composes a small paean of praise to his resourcefulness:

> The motor-car went Poop-poop-poop,
>   As it raced along the road.
> Who was it steered it into a pond?
> Ingenious Mr. Toad! (p. 196)

Seconds later he realizes he is being pursued and shifts: "O my! . . . What
an *ass* I am" (p. 197). While Odysseus taunts Polyphemus with the fact
that it was he, "Odysseus, Sacker of Cities,"[12] who had blinded him, and
never thinks to blame himself for the seven years on Calypso's island that
the boast costs him, we are nevertheless aware of his compensating
qualities. Without such arrogance, he would not be a sacker of cities, and
had he not planned his escape from the Cyclops' cave, he and his men
would have died. Had Toad, on the other hand, shown a little restraint,
he might simply have spared himself and his friends a lot of trouble.

Toad's second seizure of the car followed what might have been a
twenty-year jail term, rounded off by a magistrate of medieval speech

patterns and Olympian irrationality from nineteen ("fifteen years for the cheek" [p. 114]). It would have been an epic term, had he served it, the same length of time Odysseus spent away from home before Athene secured Zeus' permission to free him from Calypso. Toad's escape is likewise arranged through the efforts of a woman, the gaoler's daughter, who, like Athene (and perhaps Nausicaa?), appeals to her father for mercy and plans on her own to let him slip out, disguising his aristocratic toad's body in the clothing of a washerwoman, as Odysseus was disguised and withered, upon his return to Ithaca, to look like an old warrior. The gaoler's daughter is goddess-like both in her control and in her affectionate tolerance of Toad's boasting.[13] She is clearly a different order of being from Toad. The only other point at which the distinction between human and animal seems as pronounced is when the barge woman discovers Toad's identity and cries: "Well, I never! A horrid, nasty, crawly Toad! And in my nice clean barge, too!" (p. 183). It is a wonder that the two women have any place in *The Wind in the Willows,* but they remain part of the wide world, which is full of all sorts of perils and which is kept forever separate from the enchanted circle on the river bank.

Throughout *The Odyssey,* Odysseus longs for the pleasures of home, for his wife, and for the son he left in infancy. The longing tinges all his voyages with urgency and sadness, and the ambivalence lends depth to the character and the story. But for Toad there is never ambivalence; his exaggerated swings from joy to remorse seem due to an inability to accommodate two contrary states of feeling simultaneously. He loves his friends, but once he has left them, and until he gets into trouble, he forgets them completely. And neither is he nostalgic for his home. Instead, what seems to stir him is pride of ownership. His description to the gaoler's daughter—"Toad Hall . . . is an eligible self-contained gentleman's residence, very unique; dating in part from the fourteenth century, but replete with every modern convenience" (p. 138)—is, as the lady says, more in the nature of a classified advertisement than an affectionate remembrance, and she replies perceptively: "Tell me something *real* about it" (p. 138). Even the excitement of travel that he relates to the Mole and the Rat seems false on his lips. He speaks of "the open road, the dusty highway. . . . Here to-day, up and off to somewhere else to-morrow! Travel, change, interest, excitement! The whole world before you, and a horizon that's always changing" (p. 28), and the statement may faithfully record Grahame's own enthusiasm for travel. But one wonders how Toad could know, for not only does he never stay out of trouble long enough to enjoy any of his trips, but when he is momentarily free, he is preoccupied with himself exclusively. When he finally plans the pre-, during-, and after-dinner speeches that his friends never let him deliver (perhaps in ironic imitation of Odysseus' long and deeply appreciated tale to the pleasure-loving Phaeacians), we anticipate nothing that will touch or excite us. It will be all ever-expanding self-congratulation.

As dramatic change does not necessarily imply growth or excitement in *The Wind in the Willows,* permanence does not imply boredom or stagnation. Enjoyment of the life on the river bank merely involves Thoreau's ability to hear a different drummer, one who is quieter, requiring greater patience and sensitivity from the listener. That pattern of pastoralism, the Mole, is not dead to the calls around him. "We others," Grahame writes (pp. 80–81),

> who have long lost the more subtle of the physical senses, have
> not even proper terms to express an animal's intercommunications
> with his surroundings, living or otherwise, and have only the word
> "smell," for instance, to include the whole range of delicate thrills
> which murmur in the nose of the animal night and day,
> summoning, warning, inciting, repelling. It was one of these
> mysterious fairy calls from out of the void that suddenly reached
> Mole in the darkness making him tingle through and through. . . .
> He stopped dead in his tracks, his nose searching hither and
> thither in its efforts to recapture the fine filament, the telegraphic
> current, that had so strongly moved him. A moment, and he had
> caught it again; and with it this time came recollection in fullest
> flood.
>   Home!

Athene produced a mist which so obscured the shores of Ithaca that Odysseus did not know he had finally returned. No one could have so befuddled the faithful Mole, who was not to be diverted, and desensitized, by journeys: "For others the asperities, the stubborn endurance, or the clash of actual conflict, that went with Nature in the rough; he must be wise, must keep to the pleasant places in which his lines were laid and which held adventure enough, in their way, to last for a lifetime" (p. 76).

That the Mole recognizes other modes of existence and makes this conscious decision to limit himself is in keeping with pastoral tradition. Reflecting on the genre, Patrick Cullen observes:

> Arcadian pastoral can and does satirize the artifices and
> corruptions of the nonpastoral world . . . but there is, implicitly or
> explicitly, a counterpoising awareness of the limitations of pastoral

values and with that a greater sense of the multivalence of experience, a sense of the potential legitimacy of urban and heroic modes.[14]

This "potential legitimacy" is not realized in the Toad, who is satirized for his recklessness (" 'Smashes, or machines?' asked the Rat. 'O, well, after all, it's the same thing—with Toad' " [p. 63]). In the chapter entitled "Wayfarers All," however, Grahame does suggest what these other modes of existence might be. Disturbed at the autumn departure of his friends who are following the longing to go south, the Rat must face the call of adventure himself, and while the migration of the birds may be all instinct, the case of the Sea Rat cannot be so clearly explained. Grahame allows his River Rat to be enchanted by the words and the way of life of the other animal, without suggesting where instinct ends and conscious will begins. Is the River Rat tied to the river, as the birds are seasonally to the north and south? Or does the Rat's allegiance to the river spring from habit that can be changed? When the chapter is over and the Rat's seizure past, our relief for him is mingled with a sense of the validity of other styles of life, even though for the Rat and the Mole, Grahame has reaffirmed the value of pastoral, with "adventure enough, in [its] way, to last for a lifetime" (p. 76).

It is often stated that, with the possible exception of "The Reluctant Dragon," the essays and short stories that Grahame wrote in the 1890's are not children's literature. Deciding on which shelf to place *The Wind in the Willows* is more difficult. There do not seem to be many children today who share Alistair Grahame's prodigious verbal faculties (he was once called "a baby who had swallowed a dictionary"[15]), and most of the encouragement about introducing the novel to children may be found in books that are as idealistic and nostalgic as Grahame's work itself. The reasons for the difficulties children have with the book may go beyond the occasional near-archaic words and complex metaphors. Perhaps it is the sophisticated intelligence that informs *The Wind in the Willows* that is hardest for the child to appreciate. It is the same spirit, the longing for a golden age, that infused his short stories, and although the obtrusive elegance of the narrative voice has receded, the ironies remain. Part of the pleasure of reading an Arcadia lies in the perception both of its limited but highly artful simplicity and of its ever-budding but never fully blossoming allegory. To a great extent such sophisticated perception exists for adults in all children's literature. The writer selects and guides his naive reader, manipulating facts, breaking harsh truths gently, attempting, however unconsciously, to instill an appreciation of those values that he holds most dear. But the ideal reader remains, or should remain, the child, who will take it all quite seriously, and innocently allow the writer silently to pull the strings. The ideal reader of *The Wind in the Willows*, however, knows as much as the writer. He not only understands "how jolly it was to be the only idle dog among all these busy citizens" (p. 3) and comprehends the metaphor of "Nature's Grand Hotel" (p. 154), but more important, knows, with Virgil, how it feels to be no longer too young to reach the branches, and has some sense of the "spirit of divine discontent and longing" from which the work springs.

NOTES

1. "Alarums and Excursions," *The Golden Age* (New York and London: John Lane, 1902), pp. 38–39. Subsequent page references are to this edition and will appear in the text.

2. "The Reluctant Dragon," *Dream Days* (Garden City, N.Y.: Garden City Pub. Co., 1898), p. 220.

3. Peter Green writes of the period preceding the composition of *The Wind in the Willows:* "[Grahame] progressively stifled his conscious urge towards personal anarchy and artistic individualism; he came to terms with his successful career in the City; and close on top of this he made an emotionally disastrous marriage. The inevitable result was that —as in the cases of Lear and Carroll—his imaginative, creative impulses were driven down deep into his subconscious mind. His son Alistair provided the focal point for their transmutation and eventual release. . . . Repressed, unhappy, driven in on himself, badly bruised by contact with adult passion, Grahame turned . . . to the world of symbol and myth. In so doing he released the full strength of his genius" (*Kenneth Grahame: A Study of His Life, Work and Times* [London: John Murray, 1959], p. 265).

4. *The Wind in the Willows*, illus. Ernest Shepherd, intro. Frances Clarke Sayers (New York: Scribners, 1908, 1959), p. 1. Subsequent references are to this edition and will appear in the text.

5. *The Odyssey*, trans. E. V. Rieu (Baltimore: Penguin, 1946), p. 183.

6. See Green, pp. 196–238, and note 3 above.

7. *The Uses of Nostalgia: Studies in Pastoral Poetry* (New York: Schoecken, 1972), pp. 86–87.

8. Lerner, p. 86. The passage is from *Eclogue* VIII, ll. 38–42.

9. Green writes: "The Wild Wooders, stoats, weasels, and the rest, are clearly identified in Grahame's mind with the stunted, malevolent proletariat of contemporary upper-middle-class caricature" (p. 246).

10. Green believes that "Toad . . . is a sublimation of all [Grahame's] unrecognized desires, and is harried by all the forces which Grahame himself found particularly terrifying" (p. 251).

11. Green, p. 260.

12. *The Odyssey*, p. 153.

13. Athene responds to one of Odysseus' cautious lies with admiration and affection: "The bright-eyed goddess smiled at Odysseus' tale and caressed him with her hand. . . . 'What a cunning knave it would take,' she said, 'to beat you at your tricks! Even a god would be hard put to it.' " (*The Odyssey*, pp. 209–10).

14. *Spenser, Marvell and the Renaissance Pastoral* (Cambridge: Harvard University Press, 1970), p. 3.

15. Quoted in Green, p. 237.

Kipling and Fantasy

Peter Havholm

Boris Ford voiced the opinion of many when he wrote: "Except for children, there seems little to be said on behalf of [Kipling's] imagination; but of course, though children probably do enjoy *Puck of Pook's Hill* and the *Jungle Books,* Kipling rather hoped that adults would like them too."[1] I object both to this view of Kipling's prose fiction and to another, less harsh judgment found on the crowded critical battlefield that spreads around this most evaluated of writers. The other view is that Kipling did not really come into his own until he developed what is commonly referred to as his "late manner" after 1900.[2] There is a third view which embraces all of Kipling and dismisses his negative critics as the victims of political prejudice,[3] but measured rejection on the one hand and equally measured selection of the mature work on the other mark the bounds of worthwhile Kipling criticism.

Indeed, these views are trying to get at the same thing in Kipling, but they share an error of interpretation that has so far not been pointed out. Both Ford and those who boost the later work as mature take a superficial view of stories "children probably do enjoy." Ford assumes that grown-ups ought not to enjoy such stories. Those who take the other side seem to agree with him because they look for a maturity they do not find in early Kipling. On one side, simplicity of substance is rejected because it is not complex; on the other, simplicity is virtually ignored on the ground that it disappears later on.

Through an examination of a few of Kipling's works, I wish to show that while there is reason to believe he could not achieve the particular kind of complexity we associate with tragedy, he did achieve brilliantly a kind of simplicity we associate with some stories "children probably do enjoy." "Complex" and "simple" are appropriate (though all too value-tinged) words because the kind of story at which Kipling fails and the kind at which he succeeds require our assent to different views of human possibility. The view I call complex assumes that the great challenges in life are within us. More simple is the view that human beings are either good or bad, and that consequently great challenges come always from outside the self. Thus, measured on the single scale of human possibility, the simple assumption is that we can do only what evil outside us and a limiting Providence will allow. The complex view is that we can do what we will. The simple view is that we are what we are made. The complex view is that we are what we make ourselves.

91

This pronouncement should not be taken very broadly; I am concerned only with what Kipling could and could not do well. I have no wish to argue either that children cannot enjoy the kind of complexity Kipling could not create or that such complexity is always absent from stories commonly considered "for children."

My argument runs as follows. In *The Light that Failed,* there is evidence Kipling was trying to write a species of tragedy. He fails because he cannot adopt the complex view of human possibility. But in certain of the Mowgli stories in the *Jungle Books,* we find Kipling succeeding brilliantly at an effect quite as soul-shaking in its way as is successful tragedy. J. R. R. Tolkien has called this effect "The Consolation of the Happy Ending" in his discussion of fairy stories.[4] Once Kipling adopts the convention of fantasy, a kind of heroism that has nothing to do with blameable human error is available to him, and he uses the gift of joy, Tolkien's *eucatastrophe,* again and again in his later work. I shall show in detail how it operates in "They," a story very much in Kipling's "late manner."

Kipling could accomplish one thing superbly despite his inability to accomplish another, and it is not very fruitful to look in his work for the complex. But it is futile to damn him for succeeding in stories "children probably do enjoy." Adults have always been able to enjoy such stories, and will not, I hope, lose the capability. If we understand one of the things Kipling can do in the proper light, evaluation of his work will become both more temperate and more accurate.

I am not the first to be disappointed by *The Light that Failed.*[5] Edmund Gosse summed up contemporary critical response in 1891: "I confess that it is *The Light that Failed* that has wakened me to the fact that there are limits to this dazzling new talent, the *eclat* of which had almost lifted us off our critical feet."[6] Max Beerbohm, reviewing a dramatic version in 1903, suggested scathingly that because there is so much effeminate man-worship in the story "Rudyard Kipling" might well be a woman's pseudonym.[7] With the assistance of Charles Carrington's authorized biography, Mark Kinkead-Weekes concluded in 1964: "Kipling cannot finally see beyond his own private agonies and violences; this means that he is less and less able to achieve any real focus at all."[8]

Though the novel is still in print, it might be well to give a brief summary here. We meet Dick Heldar and his nemesis, Maisie, as children in a grim foster home. There occur puppy love and a nasty powder burn on Dick's forehead. We next meet Dick as a rough, knockabout vagabond artist whose chosen subject is men at war. In the Sudan (he is following Kitchener's expedition to Khartoum), he is taken up by Torpenhow, a war-correspondent, and begins to send his sketches to Torpenhow's paper. Dick's work is a great hit at home, though it is thought too violently and dirtily "realistic" by some. The first wonderful flush of success causes him to use callously as a model one Binat, an alcoholic ex-painter in Port Said, to mistreat violently a rapacious publisher in London, and to paint for gold a much-prettified picture called "His Last Shot." His journalist friends attempt to set him straight, but he remains desperately cynical about his public. In the meantime, however, he has met Maisie again and again fallen in love with her. But Maisie is determined to achieve popular success with her own pallid paintings and cares nought for Dick except as a sort of footman-teacher. After a good deal of painfully unrequited love, Dick begins to go blind as a result of the old powder burn overlaid by a sword cut in the Sudan. He suffers a last, terrible double disappointment when Maisie rejects him even though he is blind and Bessie (an ex-prostitute, whom he has prevented from vamping Torpenhow) ruins the masterpiece finished just before his blindness becomes complete. Finally, Dick goes to the Sudan, where all his journalist friends have gone to cover another military campaign, and makes his way to the front just in time to die in Torpenhow's arms, shot through the head.

One could dismiss all this as mere autobiographical rambling or as a pathetic story of the most obvious kind were it not for a very important aspect of the novel only partly apparent in my summary. This aspect is pointed to by critical comments about how unlikeable Dick is (readers who feel they are meant to pity Dick have difficulty in doing so unreservedly because he is so obnoxious in the middle chapters)[9] and by Lionel Trilling's remark: "If [as a boy] one ever fell in love with the cult of art, it was not because one had been proselytized by some intelligent Frenchman, but because one had absorbed Kipling's credal utterances about the virtues of craft and had read *The Light that Failed* literally to pieces."[10]

I think Kipling meant the credal utterances and Dick's arrogance to indicate that Dick's prolonged suffering is the result of his own error. Indeed, Dick sees his blindness as a punishment visited upon him by a "very just Providence." Soon after he has been told he will be blind within the year, he prays, "Allah Almighty! . . . Help me through the time of waiting, and I won't whine when my punishment comes" (p. 197). Later, when he has finished the *Melancolia*, his masterpiece, he says "Just God! what could I not do ten years hence, if I can do this now!" (p. 209).

The reason God is just, taking this line of interpretation, is that Dick has thought the very hard life he has led means he is *owed* success. That he is quite wrong to make such demands on Providence, to say nothing of his Public, is clear from Torpenhow's remark just after Dick has re-met Maisie, fallen in love with her again, and realized "there's everything in . . . [her] face but love" (p. 82): "It's no business of mine, of course, but it's comforting to think that somewhere under the stars there's saving up for you a tremendous thrashing. Whether it'll come from heaven or earth, I don't know, but it's bound to come and break you up a little. You want hammering" (pp. 85–86). We are meant to see Maisie, the blindness indirectly caused by her, and even the destruction of the *Melancolia* as a "tremendous thrashing" administered in return for Dick's arrogance in making demands on Fate and his Public.

The novel was meant to proceed in a manner not entirely unlike Thomas Hardy's *Mayor of Casterbridge*. In such a story, the protagonist suffers because of his own error and then, through defiant action in the teeth of that error's train of vicious consequences, redeems himself in our eyes. Such a story differs from the ordinary, pathetic, have-a-nice-cry-dearie tear-jerker in that the protagonist is sufficiently noble in character both to be responsible for his own suffering and to be able to achieve redemption through his own effort. Fate may operate malevolently, but we never lose our sense that Fate has been given its cue by the victim's own mistakes.

J. M. S. Tompkins, in the best full-length appreciation of Kipling, seems to agree with this estimate of what *The Light that Failed* was meant to be:

> There is, however, one design . . . which holds the book together
> . . . by a genuine though unmatured life that runs throughout all
> its parts. This is the question of degradation, the possible
> degradations of art, of love, and of life. It is from these that Dick
> is to be saved, by Torpenhow, by Maisie, and finally even by
> Bessie's spite in destroying the *Melancolia,* so that he cannot
> traffic in it to buy an inglorious physical comfort. . . . [In the
> book's last chapters, Dick] has "paid for everything" and is free of
> self-pity. He is back among the sounds and smells of the East . . .
> and in Dick's last words—"Put me, I pray, in the forefront of the
> battle,"—Kipling's excited Muse, under the cover of quotation,
> reached for the proud amplitude of Jacobean speech. The allusion
> is to Uriah, and the unspoken words are "that I may be smitten,
> and die." (*Art,* pp. 15–16)

I think the pattern is there in embryo. Dick wastes his art on "His Last Shot," his love on Maisie, and nearly his life on Bessie and the imagined

profits from the *Melancolia*. Kipling means Dick to save himself from
all of this by the realization that such waste is unworthy and by the
consequent journey back to the Sudan. Providence keeps after him until
he realizes what he *must* do, and turns to that rather than what he *will* do.

But the novel as Kipling finally wrote it refuses to allow Dick really
to be to blame for what happens to him. Moreover, Kipling childishly
makes sure that everyone who hurts Dick is thoroughly punished for
what he has done. Neither of these lapses is consistent with the apparent
"design" of the novel. Together, they ruin it.

We cannot blame Dick because the train of misfortune that overwhelms
him is too clearly linked to the independent malevolence of Maisie and
Bessie and God. Despite Kipling's excuses for Maisie, she ends up a
thoroughly selfish tease. Yes, she tells Dick several times that his romantic
hopes are baseless. Yes, "His Last Shot" proves that success can make
even the best of artists do trivial, Maisie-like things. And yes, Dick himself
reminds us that he has shown Maisie a ruined canvas as his best work.
But all this falls into the background at her exit from the novel:

> There she sat in the almost dismantled drawing-room and thought
> of Dick in his blindness, useless till the end of life, and of herself
> in her own eyes. Behind the sorrow, the shame, and the
> humiliation, lay fear of the cold wrath of the red-haired girl when
> Maisie should return. Maisie had never feared her companion
> before. Not until she found herself saying, "Well, he never asked
> me," did she realize her scorn of herself.
> And that is the end of Maisie. (p. 254)

Few heroines have received quite so vehement a dismissal.

It would have been consistent with her insensitivity to have had Maisie
quite unaware of her fault in the matter. But Kipling cannot let her go
unpunished. It would have been equally appropriate to have Bessie, the
agent of a "just Providence," remain unaware of the ruined *Melancolia*'s
value. But Kipling must have her aware of how much money she has lost
—"she knew the value of money" (p. 287)—and then heap further
contempt upon her: "Now through a slip of the tongue, and a little
feminine desire to give a little, not too much, pain, she had lost the
money, the blessed idleness and the pretty things, the companionship,
and the chance of looking outwardly as respectable as a real lady"
(p. 293). These punishments indicate that Kipling really does not believe
Dick's suffering is fair. Since Kipling cannot believe it, he cannot convince his reader, and we are left with what seems like chapter after
chapter of excessive pity for Dick.

The final departure for the Sudan is motivated not by "a very just

Providence" but by "a very just Providence *who delights in causing pain*" (pp. 290–91, italics mine). Such a Providence must take Its place alongside Maisie and Bessie as the real cause of Dick's misfortunes, leaving Dick a hounded, bathetic victim.

In his short stories at about this time in his career, Kipling created a number of very successful victims: Learoyd in "On Greenhow Hill," Holden in "Without Benefit of Clergy," Georgina in "Georgie Porgie," and Punch in "Baa Baa, Black Sheep." They are "successful" because the stories in which they suffer are designed only to make us pity their innocent pain at the hands of outside forces—and we do, we do. But when Kipling tries to make Mulvaney a tragic hero in "The Courting of Dinah Shadd" (in which are evoked the images of Mulvaney as Hamlet and as Prometheus), he again comes a cropper.[11] Mulvaney's "error" in the story is twenty minutes' drunken flirtation with another woman once he has become engaged to Dinah Shadd. The result, perhaps assisted by an alcoholic curse from the other woman's mother, is the loss of his only child, a life of alcoholism, and no promotion. The punishment so overwhelms the youthful indescretion that we must see the notions of human responsibility in this story and in *The Light that Failed* as similar.

Kipling's notion for the novel was to give his protagonist a heroic glory through suffering brought on by his own pride. That Kipling cannot bring off redemption through suffering results not only from his own real suffering at the hands of Florence Garrard, Harper Brothers, and the British critics in 1890, but also from his inability to imagine a good man committing a blameable wrong. Instead, in Kipling's cosmos, if a good man doesn't watch out he will be struck down by a Providence who "delights in causing pain." Clearly, such an attitude cannot produce the kind of tragedy I have called "complex," for such a work depends upon the possibility of terrible error in the best of men.

Dick Heldar's story ends with a whimper. But in a thoroughly different vein, Kipling's fiction finds in many readers a response nearly as strong as that he seems to have wished for *The Light that Failed.* We first find this achievement in the non-didactic Mowgli stories in the *Jungle Books.*[12]

I specify non-didactic because critics have a tendency to treat all the Mowgli stories as if they were fables like "How Fear Came" and "The King's Ankus."[13] But if "Red Dog," for instance, were fable rather than adventure, someone would surely have demanded by now that children not be allowed to read it. For the story opposes Mowgli and the Pack against the Hun-like Red Dog of Dekkan, who are anathematized not just because they kill needlessly but also because they produce larger litters than the wolves. Mowgli "despised and hated them because they did not smell like the Free People, because they did not live in caves, and, above all, because they had hair between their toes while he and his friends were clean-footed" (p. 225). Following the fabular line, Mowgli's leading the dholes through the bee-cliffs is the atrocity made "necessary" by the threat to the civilized tribe. The story would then end with genocide: "But of all the Pack of two hundred fighting dholes, whose boast was that all Jungles were their Jungle, and that no living thing could stand before them, not one returned to the Dekkan to carry that word" (p. 256).

What actually happens is that Kipling finds in fantasy the absolute evil that makes blameable human error as the prerequisite to glory quite unnecessary. In the "real" world, where Kipling places Dick Heldar and Terence Mulvaney, we know absolute evil is hard to find—and we are unwilling to find it in Maisie, Bessie, and the carefully low-class Sheehy women of "Dinah Shadd." But the world of fantasy is a different matter.

G. K. Chesterton points out in "The Ethics of Elfland"[14] that the "philosophic manner of fairy tales" assumes all connections between discrete physical events to be magic. Thus, in the context of fantasy, Cinderella's midnight transformation is no more improbable than the appearance of an apple on a tree. Chesterton uses the example to proclaim the apple as much a miracle as the disappearing ball gown, but it can be turned the other way. Once magic begins to operate openly, the consequences of overstaying the fairy godmother's time limit are as natural as the fairy godmother herself: we accept the laws of magic in precisely the same way we accept the laws of nature once we realize an author is operating within the fantasist's convention.

This goes far enough to produce rather abrupt moral imperatives. Some frogs may turn into princes, but there are certain trolls and a witch or two who are better off eliminated. The creation of animals who are evil by definition is merely a special form of the fantasist's miraculous laws. From the wolf who is out to get Little Red Riding Hood to the dholes who threaten the Pack is a short step indeed. By definition, by law, by magic, the troll or the witch or the slavering wolf or the dhole is inherently evil.

Once such a simplification is accepted, all Mowgli's heroism and invention in "Red Dog" at the expense of the dholes achieve a wonderfully straightforward glory of the kind unavailable to Dick Heldar.

A good argument could be made that fantasy is almost by definition wish-fulfillment. At least it must be a major temptation for the artist who takes on the freedom to organize the world to fit his notions of how it ought to be. Such a possibility brings to mind Edmund Wilson's suggestion in "The Kipling that Nobody Read":

> This increasing addiction of Kipling to animals, insects and machines is evidently to be explained by his need to find characters which will yield themselves unresistingly to being presented as parts of a system. In the *Jungle Books,* the animal characters are each one all of a piece, though in their ensemble they still provide a variety, and they are dominated by a "Law of the Jungle," which lays down their duties and rights. The animals have organized the Jungle, and the Jungle is presided over by Mowgli in his function as forest ranger, so that it falls into its subsidiary place in the larger organisation of the Empire. (pp. 50–51)

What happens, however, is that the notions Wilson extracts from the stories (notions that were certainly Kipling's) fall into place as sections of the background for Mowgli's adventures. In "Red Dog," Mowgli's final triumph in no way depends upon Kipling's organization of the jungle in the sense Wilson means.[15] Instead, Mowgli's stature ultimately depends upon the same love and innocent courage that motivate most of the behavior in the *Jungle Books.*

Victorious over the dholes, running to help cut off their retreat, Mowgli falls to his knees beside the dying Akela: " 'Said I not it would be my last fight?' Akela panted. 'It is good hunting. And thou, Little Brother?' " Mowgli replies: " 'I live, having killed many,' " and the wolf goes on, " 'Even so. I die, and I would—I would die by thee, Little Brother' " (p. 254). Akela tells Mowgli to return to his own people, but the boy refuses to go until "Mowgli drives Mowgli."

> "There is no more to say," said Akela. "Little Brother, canst thou raise me to my feet? I also was a leader of the Free People."
> Very carefully and gently Mowgli lifted the bodies aside, and raised Akela to his feet, both arms around him, and the Lone Wolf drew a long breath, and began the Death Song that a leader of the Pack should sing when he dies. It gathered strength as he went on, lifting and lifting, and ringing far across the river, till it came to the last "Good hunting!" and Akela shook himself clear of Mowgli for an instant, and, leaping into the air, fell backward dead upon his last and most terrible kill. (pp. 255–56).

In his last words Dick Heldar reaches through "the proud amplitude of Jacobean speech" for a noble death. The notion of a "good death" in the sense that it meets standards of decorum arising from a life of battle is pretty much lost to us now except in Western movies (which have abundant fantasy conventions of their own to depend upon). And Dick's last words, ending a life whose keynote is pathetic innocence, seem silly rather than noble. But in the admittedly brutal, necessarily simple Jungle, the Lone Wolf finds such a death. Even more significantly, he is as innocently strong as Dick is innocently weak.

In the "real world," we adults have difficulty considering noble a person incapable of doing something blameably wrong. But what about a wolf? Or a boy? To understand the very strong emotional force of Akela's "I die, and I would—I would die by thee, Little Brother," we must turn to what J. R. R. Tolkien has called the "Consolation of the Happy Ending" or the *eucatastrophe* of fairy tales ("On Fairy-Stories," pp. 68–69).

Tolkien explains the affective power of the *eucatastrophe* as analogous to "The Christian joy, the *Gloria*" (p. 72), which is the ultimate and true consolation. But I prefer to stop at the place where he describes the feeling:

> The consolation of fairy-stories, the joy of the happy ending: or more correctly of the good catastrophe, the sudden joyous "turn" . . . . : this joy, which is one of the things which fairy-stories can produce supremely well, is not essentially "escapist," nor "fugitive." In its fairy-tale—or otherworld—setting, it is a sudden and miraculous grace: never to be counted on to recur. It does not deny the existence of *dyscatastrophe,* of sorrow and failure; the possibility of these is necessary to the joy of deliverance; it denies (in the face of much evidence, if you will) universal final defeat and in so far is *evangelium,* giving a fleeting glimpse of Joy, Joy beyond the walls of the world, poignant as grief.
>
> It is the mark of a good fairy-story, of the higher or more complete kind, that however wild its events, however fantastic or terrible the adventures, it can give to child or man who hears it, when the "turn" comes, a catch of the breath, a beat and lifting of the heart, near to (or indeed accompanied by) tears, as keen as that given by any form of literary art, and having a peculiar quality. (pp. 68–69)

This passage describes accurately the feeling we have when Akela asks to die by Mowgli.

It is Akela's good death by Mowgli's side that is the climax of "Red Dog," not Mowgli's defeat of the dholes. And "heroism" is the wrong word for Mowgli's stature when Akela asks to die by him. In fact,

Mowgli has risked nothing. There is the possibility of his doing so when he has committed himself to the fight, but Kaa's plan for leading the dholes through the bee-cliffs effectively solves the problem. Mowgli makes a jump from those cliffs he tells us is not so terrible as others he has made before, and Kaa waits for him in the river. When Mowgli fights the dholes, he has his four wolf brothers ranged round him for protection.

There is no indication in the story that Mowgli has "earned" Akela's tribute except by being the same good person he was when, barely able to stand, he was first found by Mother and Father Wolf. The triumph of innocent goodness is no triumph in the "real world" where, as we all know, innocence is often a liability. But in a fantasy designed to make it not a liability but a glory, it is a wonderful possibility the side of our minds Tolkien associates with Christian *Gloria* can accept happily.

In the last of the Mowgli stories, "The Spring Running," Mowgli discovers (somewhat belatedly at seventeen, the "realistic" critic might comment) that, in what the animals call "The Time of the New Talk" in the Spring, the jungle holds no pleasure for him. A series of events leads him to decide to return to people, and he wishes to tell all the jungle at Council Rock of his decision. But because it is Spring, no one comes except his four wolf brothers, Kaa, old Baloo, and finally Bagheera.

Mowgli's last adventure is no adventure at all, but ends with a boy sobbing, "with his head on the blind bear's side and his arms around his neck, while Baloo tried feebly to lick his feet" (p. 292). As he walks to the village of men, he hears the song of the Three behind him, ending: "Jungle-Favor go with thee!"

"Jungle-Favor" is the love of the Three, the love Mowgli has earned as a child "earns" love—by being innocently good-hearted. What Mowgli goes to is not suffering; what he leaves he does not leave by his own choice. But in going, he receives another tribute like the one Akela gave him. It is a dream of loving fealty, with all the emphasis on love. The term "Master of the Jungle" becomes an endearment when Baloo uses it. Indeed, Mowgli is proved no master (though again, that is not his fault) by the appearance only of his brothers and the Three at his last and most urgent call.

Precisely the same limitations can be found in Mowgli's character as in Dick Heldar's. But in Mowgli, they are not flaws because he aspires no higher than innocence. Dick is no boy; Maisie, Bessie, and the Head of the Central Syndicate are no animals, and we cannot accept the paces Kipling puts them through. But in the Jungle of Kipling's fantasy, animals and a boy succeed or fail depending upon their strength against enemies and Fate.

"A fleeting glimpse of Joy, Joy beyond the walls of the world, poignant as grief," describes our response to the wonders Kipling aims at in a number of stories written after the *Jungle Books*. Repeating the pattern of "Red Dog," Kipling's masterpiece *Kim* ends with a tribute to its boy hero from his mentor, the Lama. Kim has "deserved" the Lama's care from the beginning as Mowgli "deserved" that of the Three: by being the "Little Friend of all the World." Chance and Providence intervene in Kipling nearly as often as they do in Hardy, but in Kipling's later stories, their intervention is likely to be benign. That the gift of joy is occasionally preceded by a good deal of suffering makes it no less a type of the *eucatastrophe*. In "An Habitation Enforced," "The House Surgeon," "In the Same Boat," "Friendly Brook," and " 'My Son's Wife,' " those who do good help, are helped by, or are rewarded by remarkable coincidence or the frankly otherworldly. Christ appears in "The Gardener" to help relieve the protagonist of her burden of guilt. "Uncovenanted Mercies," a kind of apotheosis in this vein, pulls a reversal by finding a happy ending through the "intervention" of human love in Hell.[16]

One of the very best of Kipling's stories in the "late manner" is "They," published in 1904.[17] It is the story of a man who discovers a house prepared by its owner to be a refuge for dead children not quite ready to leave this world. The climax of the story is the narrator's realization—at his own dead daughter's remembered touch—that this is what the house is and why he is in it.

I first read the story when I was about twelve, but I did not understand it until much later. On first reading, I was awe-struck by the bravura descriptions of the Sussex countryside, the beautiful house, and its owner, but I did not know what it was the story's narrator "knew" at its end—despite a very real sense that there was much there teasing me on to realize something not stated outright. I should have had no problem with the explicit idea of a dead child wishing to say goodby to her father, but Kipling's elliptic style, always hinting and never relaxing into straightforward statement, left me baffled. Because of the way the story is told, I think few children today could do any better.

Out for a drive, the narrator comes on the house by mistake and nearly drives onto its lawn before he is stopped by a clipped yew "horseman's green spear laid at my breast." The pointing spear becomes significant only at the story's climax when we realize that the narrator's discovery of this house is no accident.

Once the narrator has met the house's owner, a beautiful blind woman, the hints proliferate. In her second speech, she says, "You—you haven't seen any one, have you—perhaps?" We know he has seen two children, but the hesitation in her speech might be over "seen" because she is blind.

This supposition seems confirmed a little later by "Oh, lucky you!
. . . I hear them, of course, but that's all. You've seen them and heard
them?" But the confirmation is made ambivalent again by her odd introduction of the narrator to her butler, Madden: "Is that you, Madden?
I want you to show this gentleman the way to the cross-roads. He has
lost his way but—he has seen them."

This is one line of clues, the line which leads to our knowledge (and
the narrator's) of what is going on in the house. In this line is Madden's
questioning of the narrator about *whether* he has seen the children rather
than which children or where. Later is the business of "Jenny's turn to
walk in de wood nex' week along" when Jenny's child is dying and the
wood is the one surrounding the house. Finally, on the narrator's last
visit to the house, there is the animal fear of the tenant farmer when he
is forced to enter the house at night.

The other line of clues begins with the lady's question: "You're fond
of children?" and the narrator's description of his response: "I gave her
one or two reasons why I did not altogether hate them." Why such
reticence? Why not "I told her I had two of my own," or something
similar? Perhaps it is because there is something more to tell than that.
What that something might be is hinted when she comments, "And they
tell me that one never sees a dead person's face in a dream. Is that true?"
(why does she ask him as if he might know?), and the narrator replies:

"I believe it is—now I come to think of it."
"But how is it with yourself—yourself?" The blind eyes turned
toward me.
"I have never seen the faces of my dead in any dream," I
answered.

"My dead" and "How is it with yourself—yourself" imply a bond already made, an understanding between the two that the reader has
somehow missed. Perhaps it occurred in the "one or two reasons why
I did not altogether hate them."

The two lines of clues come together at the story's climax:

The little brushing kiss fell in the centre of my palm—*as a gift
on which the fingers were, once, expected to close:* as the all faithful
half-reproachful signal of a waiting child not used to neglect even
when grown-ups were busiest—*a fragment of the mute code
devised very long ago.*
Then I knew. And it was as though I had known from the first
day when I looked across the lawn at the high window.

The words I have italicized above are as impersonal (note "of *a* waiting child") as all the other clues in the story, yet they culminate the two lines of hints such that, if we have followed the story carefully, we have the same rush of discovery as its narrator at the line: "Then I knew." What he knows, what we "know" at this lovely moment is "The Consolation of the Happy Ending" as Tolkien describes it: poignant as grief.

Though there must be some ten-year-olds somewhere for whom tragedy at the level of *The Mayor of Casterbridge* is moving, I suspect many of them are more intrigued by the kind of glory Mowgli finds. That adults can respond with equal fervor to this kind of glory is apparent in critical response to stories like "They" and "The Gardener" among Kipling's later work. In these stories, Kipling finds new and frequently quite complex ways of producing the *eucatastrophic* effect, but he does not abandon it. And only the way in which a story like "They" is presented makes it relatively unavailable to children. There is nothing complex about its matter.

The joy of such stories is always given, whatever the struggles that precede it. Indeed, as Tolkien hints, it derives some of its power as a literary device from its other worldly connections. Mowgli's innocence and good heart are given him. The narrator in "They" is given the joy of knowing: the yew horseman's spear at his chest singles him out for it at the story's beginning. On the other hand, the affirmation of tragedy assumes our knowledge that the ultimate hazard is within rather than without, and the greatest glory our ability to transcend our very human limitations unaided and against the most tremendous odds.

One thing we mean by the word "child" is "a being growing into complexity." Such a definition avoids substantively the flat assumption that a child is simple. But it suggests that there are some complexities about which a child is still learning. And since tragedy in the classic sense is something we spend our adult lives learning about, it is no great criticism to say that a child cannot appreciate it in the way an adult can.

We could criticize Kipling for never achieving the tragedy he falls so far short of in *The Light that Failed.* Or we could proclaim the complexity of manner in "They" as complexity of matter. But in either case, we imply that, because the *eucatastrophe* is not so complex as the end of tragedy, it must be rejected. I can imagine the Olympian heights from which such an argument might be made, but I prefer to remain on a level from which I can respond—along with the children—to the glimpses of joy Kipling gives us in his best work.

NOTES

1. In "A Case for Kipling?" reprinted from *The Importance of Scrutiny,* ed. Eric Bentley, in E. L. Gilbert, ed., *Kipling and the Critics* (New York: New York University Press, 1965), p. 62.

2. The View is most clear in Edmund Wilson's "The Kipling that Nobody Read," reprinted from *The Wound and the Bow* in Andrew Rutherford, ed., *Kipling's Mind and Art: Selected Critical Essays* (Stanford: Stanford University Press, 1964), pp. 17–69. See particularly pp. 63 and 69. J. M. S. Tompkins, though she has a perceptive appreciation for all of Kipling, suggests the same view in *The Art of Rudyard Kipling* (2nd ed.; London: Methuen, 1965), pp. ix-x, 115–18. The assumption underlies C. A. Bodelsen's *Aspects of Kipling's Art* (Manchester: Manchester University Press, 1964).

3. See Roger Lancelyn Green's "Introduction" to his *Kipling: The Critical Heritage* (New York: Barnes and Noble, 1971), pp. 1–33, particularly pp. 1–2.

4. "On Fairy-Stories," in *Tree and Leaf* (Boston: Houghton, 1965), pp. 3–84.

5. My text is that in Vol. IX of the "Outward Bound" edition of *The Writings in Prose and Verse of Rudyard Kipling* (New York: Scribner's, 1897–1937).

6. "Rudyard Kipling" in Green's *Critical Heritage,* p. 116, reprinted from *Century Magazine,* XLII (1891), 901–10.

7. Max Beerbohm, "Kipling's Entire," in *Around Theatres* (New York: Knopf, 1930), pp. 314–18.

8. In "Vision in Kipling's Novels," *Mind and Art,* p. 210. Carrington discusses the close relationship of life to art in *The Life of Rudyard Kipling* (New York: Doubleday, 1955), pp. 130–33, and in "Some Conjectures about *The Light that Failed,*" *Kipling Journal,* XXV, no. 125 (1958), 9–14.

9. See Gosse, p. 116, and J. M. Barrie, "Mr. Kipling's Stories," in *Critical Heritage,* p. 85.

10. In "Kipling," reprinted from *The Liberal Imagination* in *Kipling and the Critics,* p. 91.

11. "Georgie Porgie" and "Baa Baa, Black Sheep" were first published in 1888 and first collected in *Life's Handicap* (1890) and *Wee Willie Winkie* (1888), respectively. "On Greenhow Hill," "Without Benefit of Clergy," and "The Courting of Dinah Shadd" were all first published in 1890 and first collected in *Life's Handicap.*

12. Collected in Vol. VII of the "Outward Bound" edition, to which my page numbers refer.

13. The first is a story of animal original sin which places Fear in control of the jungle. The second is a cautionary tale about the consequences of human greed.

14. In *Orthodoxy* (New York: Dodd, Mead, 1908), pp. 81–118.

15. Wilson depends too much on the notion that "In the Rukh," in which Mowgli becomes a forest ranger, is the climax of Mowgli's story. In fact, it preceded "Mowgli's Brothers" in composition and was the product of a different line of inspiration. See Roger Lancelyn Green, "Two Notes on *The Jungle Book,*" *KJ,* XXV, no. 128 (1958), 12–15, and C. E. Carrington, "Casual Notes on the Mowgli Stories," *KJ,* XXVI, no. 129 (1959), 23–24.

16. *Kim* was published in 1900. "An Habitation Enforced" (1905) and "The House Surgeon" (1909) were collected in *Actions and Reactions.* "In the Same Boat" (1911), "Friendly Brook" (1914), and " 'My Son's Wife' " (1917) were collected in *A Diversity of Creatures.* "The Gardener" (1926) was collected in *Debits and Credits* and "Uncovenanted Mercies" (1932) in *Limits and Renewals.*

17. Collected in *Traffics and Discoveries,* Vol. XXIV of the "Outward Bound" edition, pp. 132–56. I have not given page references because the story is so short.

Laura Ingalls Wilder's Orange Notebooks and the Art of the Little House Books

Rosa Ann Moore

"The road pushes against the grassy land and breaks off short. And that's the end of it," said Laura.

"It can't be," Mary objected. "The road goes all the way to Silver Lake."

"I know it does," Laura answered.

"Well, then I don't think you ought to say things like that," Mary told her gently. "We should always be careful to say exactly what we mean."

"I was saying what I meant," Laura protested. But she could not explain. There were so many ways of seeing things and so many ways of saying them.[1]

The easy flow of her language and the enormous recall of details of her life deceive the reader into imagining that Laura Ingalls Wilder must have found writing her autobiographical novels for children a matter of no more than sitting down to record exactly what she meant, in order from the earliest memories until her marriage. That she worked "over her material painstakingly, revising and polishing it and verifying dates," Elizabeth Rider Montgomery tells us.[2] But how hard she worked to choose between the "many ways of seeing things and . . . many ways of saying them" becomes clearer when one examines the evidence of her work itself.

The possibilities of what the well-known orange notebooks from the Springfield Grocer Company might tell us did not seem urgent until the posthumous publication of three of them in 1971, under the title *The First Four Years*. Roger Lea MacBride, in his "Introduction," warns the reader that because Mrs. Wilder "lost interest in revising and completing it for publication" after Almanzo's death, "there is a difference from the earlier books in the way the story is told."[3] Any child notices the difference, and may accept it, through his great faith in Mrs. Wilder. But the adult is struck by its relative flatness, the lack-lustre quality of its language, the very different character of Laura from the one he has learned to know and love, the disheartening series of misfortunes. One is also struck by many episodes' being told again, less well it seems than the first time. The impulse to discover the character of the dissimilarities leads one to compare familiar portions of *The First Four Years* with the same events as they are related in *These Happy Golden Years*,[4] published during her lifetime. The latter novel is drawn in part from events also related in *The First Four Years*, and revised by Mrs. Wilder in a manner that presumably satisfied her exacting standards of language, form, and mood. Some key to Mrs. Wilder's approach to her art may surface from a systematic examination of these differences.

The "Prologue" of *The First Four Years* corresponds to the middle portion of Chapter 23, "Barnum Walks," in *These Happy Golden Years*. In two brief pages, the "Prologue" describes a horse-drawn buggy out under the stars, bearing "the driver and the white-clothed form in the seat beside him." At length "a sweet contralto voice rose softly on the air" and sang "in the starlight," "for it was June . . . and lovers were abroad in the still, sweet evenings." In *These Happy Golden Years*, the same scene occurs directly after the closing session of Mr. Clewett's singing school. But the event is transformed. The distance established by anonymous characters and the mere outlines of human forms in the "Prologue" is broken down when the driver and his companion become Almanzo and Laura, and when the close observation of detail and the injection of dialogue fill in the picture so the the reader shares the experience. "Barnum no longer reared and plunged. He started quickly, with a little jump, into a smooth trot. The air was chilled with the breath of coming winter. . . . There was no sound but the soft clip-clop of Barnum's feet as he walked along the grassy prairie road."[5] Almanzo asks Laura to sing the starlight song, which she does, and then, where "lovers were abroad," we have dramatized for us the scene in which these particular lovers discuss with a vestige of Restoration detachment whether or not Laura would like an engagement ring.

The reader of *The First Four Years* knows that Chapter One, "The First Year," gives an account of another event he has read of before— the preparation for the wedding in Chapter 31 of *These Happy Golden Years*. But the major surprise is in characterization, especially that of Laura. In "The First Year," she sees Almanzo's buggy coming in time to pick up her hat and gloves and be ready when he arrives. Their conversation during the ride has to do with the need to marry soon, partly to avoid allowing Almanzo's sister an opportunity to stage-manage the wedding, partly to get it out of the way before the harvest will require Almanzo's full attention. Laura's demurrer jars a bit: she doesn't want to marry a farmer, and for the very practical reason that

a farm is such a hard place for a woman. There are so many chores for her to do. . . . Besides a farmer never has any money.

PERFORATED AND PERMANENTLY BOUND

Name *The Hard Winter* Grade_____

School *No 1*_____

Changed to The Long Winter

Cover of Wilder's notebook labeled "The Hard Winter, No. 1, Changed to The *Long* Winter."

He can never make any because the people in towns tell him what
they will pay for what he has to sell and then they charge him
what they please for what he has to buy. It is not fair. (p. 4)

At last, Laura agrees "to try it for three years. She liked the horses and
enjoyed the freedom. . . . Two quarter sections of this land, each with
160 acres of rich black soil, would be theirs. . . . It would be much more
fun living on the land than on the town street" (pp. 6–7). Almanzo
promises in return that, if farming has proven unsuccessful at the end
of three years, he will "quit and do anything" she wants him to (p. 5).
The last source of debate is Laura's reluctance to marry as early as
Almanzo would like because she will not yet have been paid for her last
month of teaching, and will not have the money to buy new clothes. Yet
the arguments for early marriage are persuasive "because of the help it
would be to have a home and housekeeper in the rush of fall work coming
on" (p. 8).

This Laura, practical, cautious, doubtful almost to the point of appearing ready to decide not to marry at all—one might say "modern"—is not
the Laura of Chapter 31 in *These Happy Golden Years*, which covers the
same ground. When Almanzo comes to fetch her for the ride she runs
out to meet him with her familiar disregard for propriety: the bonnet is
a concession to Ma's years of urging; gloves would be uncharacteristic,
and they are not mentioned. The young couple's discussion of the date
of the marriage is limited to the need for haste in order to avoid both
the interference of Eliza and the expense of an affair which neither of
them can afford. No debate takes place about the risky economics of
farming, nor do they bargain about what to do should it fail. Instead of
the three-year proviso, Laura only asks that Almanzo not require her to
promise to obey him. The revised Laura still is strong and independent
but not penurious, and her love bears the marks of courage, optimism,
and endurance, as well as genuine devotion.

The "Prologue" moves straight along to the wedding, and dispatches
all in two pages—the preparation, the quick performance of the marriage, and the return "to the old home for a noon dinner, and in the midst
of good wishes and cheerful good-bys, once more into the buggy and
away for the new home on the other side of town. The first year was
begun" (p. 10).

The same events in *These Happy Golden Years*, Chapter 33, are
related, contrastingly, in a leisurely detail which imparts both form and
feeling to the novel, as well as to the entire series of books about Laura.
Her family is present and approving, helping to make Laura ready for

Almanzo's arrival. While the pair waits for the Reverend Brown in his sitting room, Laura observes details of its furnishings: its "crocheted rag rug" on the floor, and a "picture of a woman clinging to a white cross planted on a rock, with lightning streaking the sky above her and huge waves dashing high around her" (p. 280). The rug and the picture function in several ways. Most simply, they create a concreteness of presence that, like the revised scene in the buggy, brings the lives of these characters into the life of the reader. They also create, in the midst of rapidly changing and emotionally whirling events, the singular clarity with which one sometimes perceives those irrelevant details that endow a moment in one's life with its uniqueness, that make it a "spot of time" which becomes immutable and permanent, if only in memory. Finally, the careful tracing of the picture is perhaps Mrs. Wilder's way of giving us all the accounting that she wishes us to have of the wearisome train of death, fire, disillusionment with friends, and failure of effort in *The First Four Years.*

"So they were married." An ending and a beginning. At home, though Ma has set the table with linen and silver, nothing tastes right. There is the enormous sense of change, of girlhood being over, of the past meeting the future. Pa helps Laura into the buggy for the last time, Carrie brings Laura her "old slat sunbonnet," and Prince and Lady, who presided over the beginnings of the romance, bring the couple home. Home is described in loving detail, and the first supper together.

> Laura's heart was full of happiness. She knew she need never be homesick for the old home. It was so near that she could go to it whenever she wished, while she and Almanzo made the new home in their own little house.
> All this was theirs; their own horses, their own cow, their own claim. The many leaves of their little trees rustled softly in the gentle breeze. (p. 289)

The consciousness of possession is softened by expunging the tone of avarice and calculation, even of reasonable practicality, and by allowing the sense of things as symbols of continuity with the past and of support in facing the future to dominate the moment. The little girl has come to womanhood, the story of Laura is finished, the cycle in which adults stand between their children and the difficult realities of survival is about to begin again, with the point of view of the protagonist shifted from the protected center, where children often stand, to the dangerous circumference, the place for adults, unbuffered against the brutalities of nature and of people. This shift may, in fact, have thrown up very recalcitrant obstacles to the satisfactory revision and publication of *The First Four Years* as an entity.

Collation of passages describing events common to both *The First Four Years* and *These Happy Golden Years* reveals at least five distinctions between them. Most prominent is the poetic and philosophic dimension which characterizes the latter. Regularly, those portions which we have examined are specified in *Golden Years* with considerable detail, named characters, conversation. In short, they are dramatized. In that book, too, information which may have been judged to be unpleasant, inappropriate, or lacking in appeal to children is omitted. Portrayal of character is altered in the interest of consistency or vividness, except in cases where omission because of unpleasantness, inappropriateness, or lack of appeal takes precedence. Finally, the sense of form controls much more firmly than in the notebooks the relation of parts to each other and to the whole —whole book, whole series—with consequences for point of view as well.

Do the other notebooks, one wonders, bear the same relationship to their corresponding published versions? The two manuscripts in the Detroit Public Library indicate that they do. And in addition to the five large categories of revision mentioned above, they show Mrs. Wilder's marginal notes interspersed among paragraphs of narrative. For example, in "These Happy Golden Years" (MS.), she has Pa sing three full verses of "Love's Old Sweet Song." She adds a brief paragraph of narrative, then appends this: "Note (I don't know if all this song should be used. I love it all but perhaps it is too much. It seems to me to fit right here. The last song Laura hears Pa and the fiddle sing)."[6] The published novel omits the narrative paragraph and includes the whole song. It culminates an evening of the family's reviewing its past through its most loved songs, and closes the chapter, perfectly preparing for the story of Laura and Almanzo's marriage in the next:

> So to the end when life's dim shadows fall,
> Love will be found the sweetest song of all.

Indeed, it did fit right there.

Another insight into authorial uncertainty occurs in "The Hard Winter" (MS.). At the bottom of page 198 the following paragraph is crossed out: "And the lonely little town, with its little lonely houses, each surrounded by piles of drifted snow, cowered, hushed and quiet on the desolate prairie, in the fury of the storm." The next page of the manuscript, also numbered 198, contains only a rewrite: "And the little, lonely houses, in the lonely, little town cowered on the frozen prairie in the fury of the storm." Beneath it is this sign of the Laura who sometimes shocked Mary: "(I have read the darned thing until I don't know which is best" [sic]. Neither version is very different from the other nor so inadequate that it fails to convey a relatively forceful idea of the setting. Collation with the finally published story shows that "the darned thing" fermented until she hit upon still a third version which confirms our initial observations. We have it at last from Laura's point of view, one of the most consistent of Mrs. Wilder's revisions. Laura's consciousness of the struggle of solitary men against malevolent nature with cosmic force not only gathers intensity, but sets up poetic and philosophic overtones as well:

> Huddled close together and shivering under the covers they
> listened to it. Laura thought of the lost and lonely houses each
> one alone and blind and cowering in the fury of the storm. There
> were houses in town, but not even a light from one of them could
> reach another. And the town was all alone on the frozen, endless
> prairie, where snow drifted and winds howled and the whirling
> blizzard put out the stars and the sun.[7]

From here onward, the five large groups of revision can be documented repeatedly on almost every page of the manuscripts. The published account of Almanzo and Cap's trek through the snow for wheat (*The Long Winter,* pp. 268–74) is a glittering story of courage, wit, endurance, faith. The notebook hardly prepares us for it:

> "Believe I'll warm up too," Cap called and ran beside his sled.
> When they were tired and warm, they rode on the sleds again,
> while the horses trotted briskly.
> The sun was directly overhead and it was noon when Almanzo
> saw a wisp of smoke rising from a hollow in the prairie.
> "There is some kind of a house ahead there," he shouted to
> Cap.
> "Looks as though that smoke came out of a snowbank," Cap
> shouted back. ("The Hard Winter," MS., p. 224)

The mystery of what transforms Mrs. Wilder's memory of facts and events into fiction is at work here. Paragraphs two and three of the quoted passage are spun out—not merely lengthened, but dramatized, with Almanzo and Cap's everlasting struggle against cold, the horses' falling through the snow's crust, their uncertain destination, the impulse to turn back. She does not tell us "it was noon." Instead, "The small, cold sun seemed to hang motionless but it was climbing. The shadows narrowed, the waves of snow and the prairie's curves seemed to flatten. The white wilderness leveled out, bleak and empty" (pp. 271–72). With

half the day gone, there is still an unknown distance to travel before the
boys will find wheat and feel they have earned the right to turn back. So
one feels the pressure of time, also. One does not merely know what
happened, one experiences it.

Though many passages undergo the metamorphosis of drama and
detail, not all of Mrs. Wilder's revisions were effected by additions to the
manuscripts. At times, she omitted material that, for whatever reason,
did not serve her purposes. Sometimes she left out a song and retained
only its title in her finished work. Occasionally, the omission was more
significant, both in length and in effect. Chapter 10, "Pa Goes to Volga,"
in *The Long Winter,* is one of those instances in which the retention of
Laura's point of view cuts out some of the story. Laura and Carrie see
Pa off one morning on a railroad handcar with some other men to meet
the train at Volga and help dig the track clear of snow on their way. On
the third day Pa returns home on the work train, bringing along Mr.
Edwards, an old friend who has figured in the Ingalls' life before. He is
fondly remembered by the children, for whom he swam a flooded creek
one winter, bringing Christmas presents. The wildest story he has to tell
relates his encounter with a tax collector, for whose business he has so
little regard that he fabricated a wife and five children to deduct. Mr.
Edwards is kindhearted, independent, impatient of any government even
so modestly centralized as a county, and drawn toward the free far West.
The Long Winter draws a wholesome curtain across what happened at
Volga; "The Hard Winter" presents a scene that only Pa, not Laura,
would have been able to relate:

> After supper the men all gathered around the stove in the hotel
> bar-room. Some talked and told stories. A couple played checkers.
> The two strangers from the handcar and two men who had come
> on the train started a game of cards.
> Mr Edwards left Pa and sauntered over to watch the game.
> "Sit in?" one of the players invited.
> "I'll watch awhile and see how it goes. It ain't played like seven
> up, is it?" Mr Edwards answered.
> "Not exactly. This is poker," the man replied as he winked at
> another of the players.
> The game went on a few minutes longer, then again the player
> invited, "better sit in now. You will soon learn the game." "I sure
> will. It looks easy and you fellers can show me how," Mr
> Edwards said as he drew a chair up to the table.
> Pa didn't like to have Mr Edwards play with those men. He felt
> sure they were regular gamblers, but he knew Mr Edwards hadn't
> much money to lose.

They were still playing when Pa went up the stairs to bed after telling the hotel keeper to put Mr Edwards in his room.

Some time in the night, Pa was wakened by Mr Edwards coming into the room and saw him carefully lock the door, then prop a chair against it.

"What is the idea Edwards?" he asked.

"Just this here," Mr Edwards answered as he began to pull money out of his pockets, $5. bills and $10. bills and twentys [sic] and fifties and a couple of hundred dollar bills.

Pa sat up in bed and helped Mr Edwards count. In all there was eighteen hundred dollars.

"What in the world Edwards! Have you robbed the bank?" Pa demanded.

"I just let that crowd of bums show me how to play poker," Mr Edwards explained.

"And you told them you didn't know how!" Pa accused him.

"I said it wasn't like seven up. And is it?" Mr Edwards enquired. "I can learn a card game mighty fast and I can play sixty five different games tolerably well."

Pa roared with laughter. "So that's it!" he said. "Beat them at their own game of handling the cards! How many card tricks can you do?"

Mr Edwards said he couldn't remember but he knew enough to do him.

"You won't need to shovel snow tomorrow, not with this much money," Pa chortled.

"But I aim to," Mr Edwards told him. "I'll be safer out in a snow bank than I will in town with this on me," and he stuffed the money back in his pockets. Then taking off his shoes and pants and shirt, but keeping on his underthings as Pa had, he lay down in the bed and soon they both were asleep. ("The Hard Winter," MS., pp. 88–91)

On the way back to De Smet, Mr. Edwards becomes so impatient with the work train's progress that he plays the Fast Sooner Hound: he bets Gerald Fuller, another passenger, five dollars that he can leave the train and catch up with the engine on foot. He wins ("The Hard Winter," MS., pp. 92–93). Once in De Smet, Mr. Edwards insists upon stopping in a saloon en route to the Ingalls' house, and orders whiskey. He toasts Pa Ingalls, who is drinking water:

> "Here's to you as good as you are
> And here's to me as bad as I am
> But as good as you are and as bad as I am
> I'm as good as you are as bad as I am."
>   ("The Hard Winter," MS., p. 94)

At home, over a dinner of mashed potatoes, creamed turnips, and apple pie, Pa recounts the adventures of the last two days.

> They all listened breathlessly but Mr. Edwards looked embarrassed.
> "I know you don't hold with playing cards Mam," he said to Ma. But it wasn't rightly their money, so I took it from them. I didn't know whose money it was so I just kept it. I hope you don't think hard of me Mam." ("The Hard Winter," MS., p. 96)

After dinner and Mr. Edwards' departure, the family discovers that he has secretly tucked a twenty dollar bill under the handkerchief in blind Mary's lap. " 'That Edwards can palm a card or scatter his bank roll so neatly that no one ever sees him,' Pa said" ("The Hard Winter," MS., p. 97).

And so to Mr. Edwards' exemplary traits must be added card shark, hustler, gambler, liar, and toper. Pa's response to him indicates no disapproval, however, but gratitude for his generosity and admiration for and enjoyment of his salty skills. All of this is deleted from the published version. Only the conversation about his tax evasion remains (*The Long Winter*, pp. 112–13), and his surreptitious gift is acknowledged by Ma's "He has a heart of gold" (p. 114). Pa's extended comment is reduced to "That Edwards" Mr. Edwards represents a change, a contact with the unencumbered outside world, an old friend moving on, a moment of enjoyment for the little family facing a winter to be worse than what has gone before, and in all of those good ways he survives in the final work. Yet the humanity of Pa's ability to enjoy the earthy dubiety of Mr. Edward's morality, flourishing in the unrestrained milieu of the westward movement, and that derring-do itself, are washed away, perhaps out of a nice respect for what children probably should be protected from for a while longer.

This is but one example of changes in the representation of character. There are others, like those we have already seen in Laura. Frequently when Laura and Mary appear together, a change takes from one and gives to the other. Readers think of Mary as being the good, patient, literal child, and of Laura as the reckless, restless, metaphoric one. The image is made carefully consistent. But they were not always thus.

> "Let's go in Mary," she said. "I don't like the weather."
> "It *is* cold," Mary answered. "I can feel the sun on my face, but the air feels savage someway. Can you see the cloud?"
> "There is no cloud," Laura assured her. ("The Hard Winter," MS., p. 236)

In the published text, the dialogue is rearranged. Laura speaks:

> "But I don't like the weather. The air feels savage, somehow."
> "The air is only air," Mary replied. "You mean it is cold."
> "I don't either mean it's cold. I mean it's savage!" Laura
> snapped. (*The Long Winter,* pp. 286–87)

The imagination that poor Mary accidentally shows is re-assigned, both to contribute to and to conform to the image of Laura as the one whose untrammeled mind runs to personification and peevishness, while Mary continues literal and legislative.

Ma, who comes in for her share of revision, seems to suffer most from it. Her treatment is similar to Pa's, though more pronounced than his. Often her responses are so altered that she appears almost suspiciously pious and refined, when one suspects that a good deal of gusto, zest for life, and a large degree of tolerance were more likely tools for survival in her kind of life. In the notebook, *These Happy Golden Years,* when Uncle Tom comes to visit and proposes rolling out a blanket on the floor for the night, she is permitted to say, "Shucks! . . . I guess Charles and I can sleep on a straw tick for once" (p. 104). The expletive is informal, indicative of relaxed speech, possibly of relaxed manners—and absent from the published book (p. 110). For a mother watchful of her daughters' adverbs, it is out of character. When Laura complains to her parents of some of her teaching problems, Ma replies: "Be as wise as a serpent and harmless as a dove" ("These Happy Golden Years," MS., p. 46). Published, Ma gives good sensible advice from her own teaching experience to deal with the problem student:

> "That's right, Laura, listen to your Ma," said Pa. " 'Wise as a
> serpent and gentle as a dove.' "
> "Charles!" said Ma. Pa took up his fiddle and began saucily
> playing to her, "Can she make a cherry pie, Billy boy . . . ?"
> (*These Happy Golden Years,* pp. 54–55)

It seems impossible to read the "Charles!" without a chiding tone in the mind's ear. When Ma is no longer permitted to cite the axiom herself, neither is she allowed a sense of humor to respond when her husband does.

Another change even less favorable to Ma has to do with Indians. Pa returns to the homestead after a visit to town, where he happened to encounter an old Indian who warned of the coming of an extraordinarily severe winter. In manuscript there is nothing condescending about the description of the Indian. Ma, building a fire while Pa describes to her the Indian's recital, makes no comment about the Indian and indicates only that she does not wish to move from the claim shanty into town ("The Hard Winter," MS., pp. 49, 52). Today's reader finds that a highly normal reaction and wonders why the scene is revised to this:

> "But what's the need to hurry so?" Ma asked.
> "I feel like hurrying," Pa said. "I'm like the muskrat, something tells me to get you and the girls inside thick walls. I've been feeling this way for some time, and now that Indian . . ."
> He stopped.
> "What Indian?" Ma asked him. She looked as if she were smelling the smell of an Indian whenever she said the word. Ma despised Indians. She was afraid of them, too. (*The Long Winter*, p. 64)

While this attitude was undoubtedly widespread among settlers, it is curious that it should be attributed to Ma after reflection if it should not have been in the original portrayal. The last sentence perhaps offers faint exoneration, however, for most children, whether consciously or not, can appreciate the idea of fear as a pardonable basis for dislike.

It almost appears that anything at all rough and ready about Pa, who is both a strong and gentle man by any account, is polished away, while Ma's heartiness is assigned to him and she is left nothing much except priggishness. Certainly one cannot think her portrayal is deliberately intended to give this impression, and while one does at times tire of her gentle reprimands, one also realizes that this negative idea of her is magnified by witnessing the change from what she is in the notebooks to what she becomes in the published novels.

One must ask, particularly in the easy retrospect afforded by our present day position of intense consciousness and sense of national guilt with regard to minorities, broadened acceptance of conduct with less regard for "good taste," and increased permissiveness towards what our children may read and know, whether the motive underlying Mrs. Wilder's revisions of character was oriented toward a sufficiently durable aesthetic principle. Whatever the answer to the question, one must nevertheless admit that she executed these revisions with the greatest care and consistency.

The same control over form is apparent in the revisions. Besides the observations already made, including that in note 4, there are numerous instances of the combination or redistribution of published chapters so that they begin or end in places different from those in the notebooks. More importantly, events are re-arranged to produce a greater sense of completion in a given event, or to create more anxiety in connection with it. For example, during the weeks of Laura's teaching at the Brewster school, Almanzo brings her home in his sleigh each Friday after school and takes her back on Sunday evening. Life at the Brewsters' is so unpleasant that the respite at home is a godsend, yet Laura fears that Almanzo will infer from her accepting his kindness a more favorable regard for him than he should. So she resolves to tell him exactly why she rides with him. In the manuscript, she makes her little speech *on the way home* at the end of the second week. "I am going with you because I want to get home," she says ("These Happy Golden Years," MS., p. 52), but little is made of it. He takes her back on Sunday and comes the following Friday as usual, after a scene in the town with Cap Garland helping to ready him for what turns out to be a dangerously cold drive. The narrative proceeds through the weeks. Mrs. Brewster, a pitiful woman who looks like a fugitive from *Giants in the Earth,* threatens her husband with a knife in the night, disappears unaccountably from the house, and so events proceed until the ordeal is over and Laura goes home permanently.

The published version offers a more sophisticated treatment. Not until after Laura's fourth week at school has gone by, and she is returning to the Brewsters' *after* her fourth weekend at home, does she make herself clear to Almanzo—realizing all the while that he may choose now not to rescue her as usual the following Friday. With that doubt in her mind at Brewsters', rather than at home—after all, her father could take her to teach if necessary—she must go through a whole unhappy week, culminating in Mrs. Brewster's poor, mad knife scene, and an unpromising Friday at twenty degrees below zero. These fairly simple rearrangements of events make what Almanzo does seem more important, and the uncertainty of his deeds more interesting. By rigidly restricting this portion of the tale to Laura's point of view, the sense of the need for escape is more intense and we do not know any more than she that he and Cap Garland have planned anything until he drives up at school for her with bells jingling.

Examples of effective restructuring can be multiplied. These kinds of revision give an impression similar to that left by some of Robert Frost's poetry in which the rhyme strikes us as both so commonplace and so perfect that we are tempted to think we have been speaking poetry all our lives. The essential materials of Mrs. Wilder's original drafts are fully recognizable, yet modified often in slight ways, so that some grace beyond the reach of art seems to shape them into the important work that they are. Her control is natural and so instinctively right that

negative criticisms, such as may be made about the characterization of
Ma, are absorbed and balanced out in the portrayal of a hardy and loving
family that did more than survive: they carried a cultural tradition into
a new world of experience, where it gave them strength to endure and
create. They became a touchstone both of literature and of life for
American children.

Virginia Kirkus, the editor at Harper's who "discovered" Laura Ingalls Wilder in 1931, wrote in the special Wilder issue of *The Horn Book
Magazine* that her response to the manuscript of *Little House in the Big
Woods* "was an emphatic 'Yes,' " for reasons that "lay in the manuscript
itself."[8] In a recent letter, she recalled that "the Wilder manuscripts
. . . required singularly little editing. . . . I felt that the writing had a
distinctive folk flavor; was honestly conceived on the basis of her own
childhood experiences."[9] Ursula Nordstrom, later Mrs. Wilder's editor,
put the matter even more strongly: "None of the manuscripts ever
needed any editing. Not any. They were read and then copy-edited and
sent to the printer."[10]

The editing had already been done, for what appears in the notebooks
to be unretouched autobiography becomes in the finished work both less
literal and more true and beautiful. One wonders whether Mrs. Wilder,
in *The First Four Years,* was indeed experimenting with another way of
saying what she had seen, with the intention of eventually publishing the
book, whole. Her habitual use of her material suggests she probably was
not. But even if she was, it is difficult to imagine that her sight could be
clearer or her voice surer than in the preceding books for which she is
justly revered and loved.

NOTES

1. Laura Ingalls Wilder, *By the Shores of Silver Lake,* (New York: Harper and Row,
1953), p. 58.

2. *The Story behind Modern Books* (New York: Dodd, Mead, 1949), p. 180.

3. Laura Ingalls Wilder, *The First Four Years* (New York: Harper and Row, 1971),
p. xiv. Subsequent reference to this volume will be indicated by page number only, inserted
parenthetically in the text.

4. In his "Introduction" to *The First Four Years,* Roger Lea MacBride writes, "My own
guess is that she wrote this one in the late 1940's" (p. xiv). That would presumably place
its writing after *These Happy Golden Years,* which was copyrighted in 1943. The books
themselves, however, cause one to wonder whether *The First Four Years,* in notebook, may
not have preceded the final draft of *These Happy Golden Years.* There are three reasons:
One, it is odd to think that Mrs. Wilder, after having published the story of her courtship
and marriage, would go back over any of the same ground in a subsequent book. Such
reviewing and overlapping of events occurs in none of the other books in the series. Second,
for her to have borrowed from another manuscript the material to round off *Golden Years*

is entirely possible, as the contents of the other two available notebooks do not coincide precisely with their published counterparts. For example, the notebook entitled *The Hard Winter*, on which *The Long Winter* (1940) was based, tells in Chapter 11 the story of Ben Woodworth's birthday party at the rail depot. Perhaps to intensify the cheerlessness of the winter, that happy episode is omitted and published later as Chapter 20 in *Little Town on the Prairie* (1941). Finally, the relationship of events in *The First Four Years* to the expanded telling of them in *Golden Years* is consistent with the observations which one can make about other manuscripts in relation to their final versions, as my discussion will show.

When I pursued this question with Mr. MacBride, however, he responded that he didn't "think that 'The First Four Years' (which in manuscript was titled 'The First Three Years and a Year of Grace') was written before 'These Happy Golden Years.' I am 90% certain that Rose told me that her mother had drafted the book after writing 'Golden Years', but laid it aside as perhaps being a bit painful" (letter, September 30, 1974).

In any case, one can only be grateful to Mr. MacBride and Harper and Row for publishing *The First Four Years* and opening these insights into the work of a very great American writer for children.

5. Laura Ingalls Wilder, *These Happy Golden Years* (New York: Harper and Row, 1971), p. 213. Subsequent reference to this volume will be indicated parenthetically in the text.

6. Laura Ingalls Wilder, "These Happy Golden Years" (MS.) microfilm. This one and a microfilm of *The Hard Winter*, retitled *The Long Winter*, both belonging to the Gifts and Rare Books Division of the Detroit Public Library, are the only two which, insofar as I can discover, are available for study. Others, housed in the Laura Ingalls Wilder Home in Mansfield, Missouri, and in the Pomona Public Library, Pomona, California, are for display purposes only. According to Roger Lea MacBride, "The decision to make those in Mansfield available [to qualified scholars] has not yet been made" (Roger Lea MacBride in a letter to Rosa Ann Moore, October 5, 1972). I am grateful to Mr. MacBride and the estate of Mrs. Wilder for permission to quote from the Detroit manuscripts in this paper.

7. Laura Ingalls Wilder, *The Long Winter* (New York: Harper and Row, 1967), p. 224. Subsequent reference to this volume will be indicated parenthetically in the text.

8. Virginia Kirkus, "The Discovery of Laura Ingalls Wilder," *The Horn Book Magazine,* reprinted from the Laura Ingalls Wilder Issue (December, 1953), p. 428.

9. Virginia Kirkus Glick in a letter to Rosa Ann Moore, September 27, 1974.

10. "Re-Issuing the Wilder Books," *Top of the News,* reprint by American Library Association (April 1967), unpaged.

Harriet the Spy

*Milestone, Masterpiece?**

Virginia L. Wolf

Ten years after the publication of Louise Fitzhugh's *Harriet the Spy,*
there remains considerable uneasiness about the novel's status as literature. Ms. Fitzhugh, who was also the author of a sequel, *The Long Secret*
(Harper, 1965), and the co-author with Sandra Scoppettone of *Suzuki
Beane* (Doubleday, 1961) and *Bang, Bang, You're Dead* (Harper, 1969),
died on November 19, 1974. On the publication of HARRIET, she was
called "one of the brightest talents of 1964"[1] Several short reviews
praised the novel for its vigor and originality.[2] On the other hand, in the
most extensive review which the book received, Ruth Hill Viguers objected strongly to its "disagreeable people and situations" and questioned
its "realism" and its suitability for children.[3]

Today, now that many books are even more overt and harsh in their
criticism of contemporary society, such objections are less common.[4] To
my knowledge, critics have only briefly and rarely mentioned the novel
in recent years. The only prize it has ever received is the Sequoyah
Award in 1967, given by the children of Oklahoma. It has been a peren-
nial bestseller for both Harper and Dell. It would seem that the novel
survives principally because children are devoted to it. *The Arbuthnot
Anthology* does recognize the novel as a milestone of children's literature,
praising it as "contemporaneous" and implying that it is a forerunner of
those more recent novels valuable for their immediate social relevance.[5]
However, since no book ever survives for very long on the basis of its
contemporaneousness, such praise is at best a dubious honor.

The novel can be read as social criticism. It is, on one level, an
illuminating portrait of contemporary, urban, American life. Harriet's
parents are so caught up in their own lives that they do not get to know
their own daughter until she is eleven years old. The Robinsons sit in
stony silence when alone together and come alive only when they have
a chance to display their latest acquisition to a visitor. The Dei Santi
family's preoccupation with their store prevents their understanding of
one of their sons. The rich divorcee Agatha Plummer retreats to her bed
in order to get attention. Harrison Withers lives alone in two rooms with
his bird cages and his twenty some cats, trying to outwit the Health
Department. The image which arises is one of a fast-paced, materialistic,

*A version of a paper presented at the MMLA forum on Children's Literature, St. Louis,
Missouri, November 2, 1974.

complex society in which individuals are isolated in their own private worlds.

This isolation results in a failure of communication and consequently in a scarcity of meaningful human relationships. It results in a misunderstanding of unique individuals such as Harrison Withers and Harriet while it encourages conformity. Harriet's world is full of people who have no real understanding of their own special interests or abilities. This is especially evident of her classmates. Pinky Whitehead is a nonentity. Marion Hawthorne and Rachel Hennessey merely ape their mothers. In Harriet's words, "THEY ARE JUST BATS. HALF OF THEM DON'T EVEN HAVE A PROFESSION."[6] Living by means of pretense, the people of Harriet's world are afraid to hear or to seek the truth.

To read the novel as social criticism, however, is to see it in only one dimension. To read it as simply a socially relevant message is to ignore its structure. In its form, the novel is reminiscent of many contemporary adult novels which are constructed on the premise that reality is inevitably a matter of individual perception.[7] In such novels, our experience of the fictive world is structured by the point of view from which the novel is told. Perceiving, thinking, and feeling as one character does, we learn more about him or her than we do about the world which he or she describes. In other words, limiting us to Harriet's point of view, *Harriet the Spy* is fundamentally a thorough characterization of Harriet.[8] The enveloping point of view is, for the most part, third person, telling us what Harriet feels and thinks but emphasizing what she does, sees, and hears. The notebook entries, which are in the first person, record her actual language and reveal the content and thinking process of her mind. Each point of view enriches the other. The notebook entries reveal the limitations of Harriet's mind as a vehicle for understanding her world, and that which we see over her shoulder, as it were, fleshes out our understanding of the nature and sources of these limitations, allowing us to perceive both her and her world more fully than she does.

The previous description of contemporary society is not Harriet's. We obtain it by synthesizing bits and pieces of what we see by means of Harriet. Furthermore, this portrait of her world allows us insight into Harriet which she only gradually and then only intuitively possesses. We are allowed to see the extent to which this world has shaped and inhibited her. Harriet, too, is virtually isolated from intimacy with other people. This explains her need for window-peeping and writing in her notebooks. Given her environment, these activities are her only opportunities for self-discovery and growth. Imaginatively and ingeniously, she attempts to break out of her isolation, as a spy.

Harriet is, of course, unconscious of this way in which her environ-

ment has influenced her. As her notebook entries reveal, she understands
herself on a much more superficial level. Ole Golly, her nurse, has given
her faith in herself and an enthusiasm for knowing life and for finding
her own way:

> OLE GOLLY SAYS THERE IS AS MANY WAYS TO LIVE
> AS THERE ARE PEOPLE ON THE EARTH AND I
> SHOULDN'T GO ROUND WITH BLINDERS BUT SHOULD
> SEE EVERY WAY I CAN. THEN I'LL KNOW WHAT WAY
> I WANT TO LIVE AND NOT JUST LIVE LIKE MY
> FAMILY. (p. 32)

With naive self-confidence and extraordinary energy, Harriet attempts
to follow this advice. Finding her sources of information limited, she sets
up her spy route. So often puzzled by what she observes, she communi-
cates her opinions and questions to a notebook, frequently with a nota-
tion such as "THINK ABOUT THAT" (p. 141). Her notebook entries
reveal, on the one hand, that she is engaged in self-discovery, learning
what she likes and dislikes in the process of honestly stating her responses to what she sees. On the other hand, they are a record of mind
unfettered by sympathy and almost totally self-absorbed. Seen through
Harriet, the world is no more than a spy-route, no more than a place and
an opportunity for amusement and knowledge. Furthermore, in this role,
Harriet is no more than a spy. She is an observer rather than a partici-
pant. While she is exposed to many different life styles, her experience
is only vicarious. She can learn to be honest with herself, but she cannot
learn to share. She can learn to evaluate but only to a lesser degree to
empathize.

The key to the limitations of Harriet's quest for knowledge occurs very
early in the novel with Ole Golly's quotation of a passage from Dostoievsky:

> Love all God's creation, the whole and every grain of sand in it.
> Love every leaf, every ray of God's light. Love the animals, love
> the plants, love everything. If you love everything, you will
> perceive the divine mystery in things. Once you perceive it, you
> will begin to comprehend it better every day. And you will come
> at last to love the whole world with an all-embracing love.
> (pp. 22, 24).

Harriet translates this in terms of her own egocentric experience of the
world: " 'I want to know everything, everything,' screeched Harriet
suddenly, lying back and bouncing up and down on the bed. 'Everything
in the world, everything, everything' " (p. 24).

The novel portrays the process whereby Harriet begins to learn to love. Her experience with life for eleven years has been almost totally self-centered; it has been a process of imbibing rather than of giving. It is not until she loses Ole Golly, her notebook, and finally her friends that she is forced to give a little. Isolated and misunderstood, she is directly confronted with her need for people and by the demand to conform. At first, she meets this demand head on, refusing to give an inch. She forces her parents to find a way of understanding her, and she finally relents only after Ole Golly's letter arrives. By the end of the novel, we must feel that Harriet has moved closer to the human community and that she has done so by accepting that "OLE GOLLY IS RIGHT. SOMETIMES YOU HAVE TO LIE" (p. 297).

Many adults have been horrified by this piece of advice, yet quite simply and straight-forwardly it states a fact of existence with which all children must come to terms. Negative criticism, especially from a child, usually evokes hostility, and children therefore learn to repress their disagreement and dislike. Unfortunately, in the process of doing so, many, out of fear or guilt, lose touch with these feelings. Having done so, their critical abilities and their trust in their own perceptions are, to varying degrees, lost. They learn to conform, to accept the other person's perception. They become the boring and bored Marion Hawthornes and Robinsons of this world. The beauty of Ole Golly's advice is that it does not question Harriet's truth. It allows her to retain her own individual identity.

Harriet's ability to empathize is still not fully developed at the end of the novel. She is still to some extent locked in her own world. But she has grown. She has learned how to be an onion; she has written a story about Harrison Withers; and in the closing scene of the novel, she is able to imagine what it is like to be Sport and Janie. "She made herself walk in Sport's shoes, feeling the holes in his socks rub against his ankles. She pretended she had an itchy nose when Janie put one abstracted hand up to scratch. She felt what it would feel like to have freckles and yellow hair like Janie, then funny ears and skinny shoulders like Sport" (p. 297).

The novel gives us the experience of Harriet's inner growth. Ultimately, then, it is psychological realism. Realizing this, we should be able to understand why the charge that the novel lacks realism is false or, better, irrelevant.[9] The novel does not attempt to portray reality fully or journalistically. It is rooted in Harriet's experience, and that is a limited experience. If, then, characters seem like caricatures or types, this is justified. We can only experience them when and as Harriet does. The merits of this limited point of view result from the distortion it causes.

In addition to characterizing Harriet, this structural device is the source of the novel's criticism of contemporary urban American society. I do not mean to imply that Harriet is merely Ms. Fitzhugh's mouthpiece. As we have seen, Harriet is often incapable of understanding those whom she observes. Her judgments are simply her emotional reactions to particular individuals. It is not what Harriet says which is the source of our understanding. It is Harriet's quest, her attempt to observe as many ways of life as she can for the sake of finding her own way. Experiencing life with Harriet, we are repeatedly engaged in evaluating a vast range of people in terms of Harriet's likes and dislikes. This process sets up a pattern for us with Harriet as *our* standard of measurement. The sharp contrast between Harriet and her world implicitly criticizes the sterility and conformity which she encounters. Harriet's personality illustrates that happiness and creativity are the results of the freedom to be and to find oneself. Having had such freedom, Harriet is an individual.

To be sure, the novel does not exalt the American ideal of individuality as some kind of panacea. We are aware of the distorted perspective. Harriet is insensitive. Her invasion of others' privacy demonstrates the danger of extreme individualism as does the pain her friends feel on reading what she has written of them in her notebook. We feel the limits of this ideal most fully in Harriet's suffering after she loses Ole Golly, her friends, and her notebook. Her need for love and understanding is overwhelming, and her isolation is deadening. For the first time, she becomes bored with her own mind.

At this point, Harriet is helpless. She cannot see that she has done anything wrong and responds to her friends' abuse with a total lack of understanding: "I HAVE A FEELING THAT EVERYONE IN THIS SCHOOL IS INSANE" (p. 192). Her descriptions of her friends in her notebook are, from her point of view, merely the truth, written down for her own use and not for the sake of hurting them. Understanding Harriet, we can share her conviction that her friends are wrong. But we can also see vividly that the simple truth is not enough, that Harriet is trapped by her inability to understand other people's feelings. Without love, there is no way out of this situation. Someone has to give.

It becomes clear that *Harriet the Spy* is at its deepest level a celebration and an exploration of the nature and the development of love. Ole Golly's quotation from Dostoievsky is central to our understanding. In its portrait of Harriet, the novel allows us to see that self-love is rooted in self-discovery; love of others, in self-love; and knowledge of others, in love. Harriet's quest for self-discovery is the first stage. This is transcended and the second stage begun when she fully comprehends her need for understanding from others. Next comes her discovery that she can maintain her own sense of the truth (her integrity) without being insensitive to others. This allows her to give, and having given, she moves on to the final stage, a growing awareness of others. By the end of the novel, Harriet has learned "THAT SOME PEOPLE ARE ONE WAY AND SOME PEOPLE ARE ANOTHER AND THAT'S THAT" (p. 277). Less articulate than Dostoievsky, this is nevertheless Harriet's restatement of the heart of Ole Golly's quotation: "if you love everything, you will perceive the divine mystery in things" (p. 24).

We have not exhausted the novel's implications. These are rich and multiple. But this discussion suggests that the novel is more than the overt, simplistic social criticism of so many of the recent realistic novels for children. *Harriet the Spy* is not a message book. It is first and foremost an experience. On the primary level, we are immersed in Harriet and, by means of her, her world. The fusion of Harriet and her world is the source of the novel's richness. This structural device sets up a pattern of comparison and contrast which, on the symbolic level, achieves theme. In T. S. Eliot's words, we are given an "objective correlative," in Ezra Pound's, a "vortex." We are confronted with vivid, unforgettable images: that of a child looking into a series of rooms and those of a series of rooms in which people play out their private dramas, virtually unaware of the rest of the world. With the spy route superimposed on the spy, we get a dialectic radiating throughout the novel with one image reflecting, qualifying or opposing another.

Obviously, I believe that *Harriet the Spy* will survive. Harriet and her adventures are memorable. Like all good literature, the novel transcends the particular, evoking the inner spirit of a character and her world to explore eternal questions about love and happiness and truth. Significantly, the novel is not a fantasy like so many children's masterpieces. Perhaps this is revelatory of the mid-twentieth century. In any case, it is fortuitous for children's literature. Louise Fitzhugh has proven that contemporary, realistic fiction of psychological and philosophical depth is a viable possibility for children. *Harriet the Spy* is a milestone and a masterpiece of children's literature—perhaps *the* masterpiece of the mid-twentieth century.

NOTES

1. Margaret F. O'Connell, "The Pick of the Racks," *The New York Times Book Review,* November 1967, p. 54.

2. For example, see *The Bulletin of the Center for Children's Books,* XVIII (1964), 53–54; *Library Journal,* LXXXIX (1964), 64; and *The New York Times Book Review,* February 25, 1968, p. 18.

3. "On Spies and Applesauce and Such," *The Hornbook,* XLI (1965), 74–75.

4. Nevertheless, in my part of the country (the midwest), such objections have been and continue to be the basis for censorship of the novel. It has been periodically removed from the shelves of school libraries, as recently as the spring of 1974, because adults have complained that children are imitating or might imitate Harriet's window-peeping.

5. May Hill Arbuthnot, Dorothy Broderick, Shelton L. Root, Jr., Mark Taylor, and Evelyn L. Wenzel, eds. (3rd ed.; Glenview, Illinois: Scott, Foresman, 1971), p. 1078.

6. (New York: Dell, 1964), p. 278; hereafter, references to this work will be cited parenthetically.

7. For example, Nabokov's *Pnin* or Barth's *The Floating Opera;* both highly complex novels play with distortions arising out of a single point of view.

8. See my article, "The Root and Measure of Realism," *Wilson Library Bulletin,* XLIV (1969), 409–15, for a more detailed study of Harriet's personality.

9. Sheila Egoff attempts to deal with this charge in "Precepts and Pleasures: Changing Emphasis in the Writing and Criticism of Children's Literature" in *Only Connect: Readings on Children's Literature,* ed. Sheila Egoff, G. T. Stubbs, and L. F. A. Ashley (Toronto: Oxford University Press, 1969), pp. 439–40; basically I agree with Ms. Egoff's opinion that the novel's realism is that of inner reality, but I do not agree that the author's approach "is best described as 'naturalistic' rather than 'realistic' " (p. 439).

Contemporary Children's Literature in India

Kamal Sheoran

India is a country of many contradictions. Contemporary children's literature is one of them. It is the unpalatable truth that in a country where thousands of children are doomed to illiteracy, the urgent need is to provide textbooks and other basic needs for rudimentary education. At this point, to speak of children's literature as a specialized field is far-fetched and fanciful. This fact is accompanied by an unusual phenomenon. India has the greatest living oral narrative tradition in the world. It fulfils and feeds the needs of every young and growing child in that he gets his complete "story" quota orally. Thus if children's literature exists at all as a separate entity on the accepted scale of written literature, it exists in spite of rather than because of prevailing conditions. And in this context children's literature in India remains perhaps the greatest paradox of all.

Because of its nature, children's literature in India cannot be put into a neat compact section, nicely labeled, sealed, and stamped. The subject remains as vast and varied as the subcontinent itself—and as old. It becomes difficult to corral it under one heading. Applying any single code or criterion of judgment is equally impossible. The only way such an elastic and sprawling literature can be dealt with is to divide it into levels, taking each level individually and on its own merit.

On one level we have the traditional children's literature, which, for the most part, is oral narrative. It is a living literature that spills into various forms of the spoken and written word. On the other hand is the "modern," printed children's literature dealing with present-day styles and subjects. It is a more didactic form, less creative and still slow in development, irrespective of language.

On another level there is the language. Literature for children in English forms a separate section and remains quite different both in form and content from its counterparts, Hindi and the regional languages. English, which is the medium of instruction in almost every major city in India, caters to the more affluent section of society. Children's literature in English displays marked "Western" characteristics in style, subject, and treatment. Hindi and other regional languages are more insular, more "relevant" in content. The regional languages have access even to remote corners of the country and, although different from each other in treatment, nevertheless draw their themes from traditional folklore.

127

Indian folklore is rich and imaginative and remains the most interesting source for children's literature. Included here are the Panchatantra, written in Sanskrit in 200 B.C., the Jatakas, the Puranas, the Ramayana and the Mahabharata epics, as well as a large number of ancient Indian Sanskrit classics. Like the Norwegian collection of folklore, the *Norske Folkeeventyr,* Indian mythology is not specifically for children but it is most popular with children.

The Panchatantra tales in the oral narrative form are believed to have found their way into traditional folklore of almost every country in the world. Animal fables from this source are predominant and remain as always society's traditional vehicle of social and moral instruction. Tales of animal wisdom, cunning, and foolishness, in which conventional animal characteristics are ignored, are peculiar to India. Thus it is not at all unusual to find a clever quail, an intelligent crow, a smart jackal, or a stupid tiger; the owl is regarded as an ill omen, but not the raven; the peacock, far from being vain, is said to weep because he has such ugly feet, and the snake is not considered dangerous and vile but a protector of the innocent. These fables are retold in many languages and are universal to the country's multilingual literature.

Indian folklore, much of which has yet to be printed, remains a curious mixture of tradition and pure fantasy. Stories of ogres, ghosts, restless spirits, and other such representatives of the underworld as Yama the God of Death, and holy sages, "rishis," and "munis" who could curse a whole kingdom to ashes or bring alive the dead with a mantra, are chronicles of timeless concepts that assume authentic dimensions not only with children but also with adults to this day.

Fantasy, as represented in myth, legend, and epic forms, is stimulating and unusual enough to keep even the twentieth-century child wonder-struck for hours. Story concepts are imaginative and are best put across to a receptive audience in oral narrative, which allows full scope to the storyteller's interpretations, according to the mood and expectations of the audience.

Fear and excitement go hand in hand. Modern storytelling tendencies which shun situations that create unwanted tensions tend to be insipid because they not only lack the pace of the folklore but also fail to keep up with the imagination of the child, for whom nothing is impossible, nothing implausible, and nothing so strange that it cannot be enjoyed. This is particularly noticeable in the children's story hour programs on All India Radio which broadcast songs, ballads, and riddles for children.

Although oral narrative is still a tradition in every home in India, story forms are changing. The old grandmother, wizened with age but full of stories, is an institution still found in most houses where the joint family system exists. Stories of gods and goddesses engaged in a battle of good and evil, the love of the brother Lakshman for Ram, the wicked step-mother Kaikeyi, the pranks of Krishna when he was a child, are stories which have not gone stale with repetition. In many cases the tone of the story remains amoral and free of inhibitive tendencies—which most adapted versions exclude. The settings of most myths and epics are, however, woven into the fabric of the story and the content perforce remains unchanged. Thus polygamy is the rule rather than the exception where kings were concerned, and wicked *asuras* (demons) who carry off girls to their dens are as much a part of traditional lore as children born out of wedlock. Oral rendering of such lore is common to every regional language and dialect. In the English language, imaginative and inspired translations are found in such collections as *Tales from Indian Classics,* the *Panchatantra Tales* in a series of hardbound volumes brought out by the Children's Book Trust, and *Jataka Tales* published by Echo.

Historical narrative symbolizes brave and courageous deeds of well-known Indian historical figures. Every child is familiar with Rani of Jhansi, Chatrapathi Shivaji, and Prithviraj even before he reads about them in storybooks widely available both in English or Hindi or studies them in classrooms.

Folk tales, as distinct from folklore, in themselves form a separate class. These folk tales are realistic rather than imaginative and are cha-racterized by pungent humor, satire, sharp objectivity, and common sense. Stories about Birbal and his wit and of the clever-minded Tenali Raman are gems of great verve and sparkling humor. Most folk tales carry the individual stamp of the region they hail from. Thus folk tales of the south are influenced to a greater degree by mythology than those of the northern regions. And if we split hairs even in states at such close quarters as Punjab and Himachal Pradesh, the folk tales are sufficiently different in content to inspire a series of collections by Sterling Paper-backs titled *Folk Tales of Kashmir, Folk Tales of Haryana,* and so on, covering almost all the regional states of India. However, it must be admitted that in the retelling and adaption by modern authors, much of the natural spontaneity and humor so evident in the dialect is lost.

In dealing with *written* literature for children one is faced with a peculiar problem. No other country has such a variety of recognized individual languages in current use as India, and the fact that there is no common language for the five hundred million people affects the entire literature of the country. The fourteen regional languages are on a par and equal in development and sophistication to any spoken lan-

guage in any part of the world. They vie as much with each other as with
Hindi, the national language, and English, the language in vogue. Bearing this in mind, one can appreciate how difficult and awesome is the task
of compiling any kind of reliable data for the purpose of a critical study.
Therefore, in dealing with children's literature in the regional languages,
I have touched upon only those languages which record a long history
of association with *written* literature for children.

Children's books in Malayalam began as early as the eighteenth century. The first recognized children's author in Malayalam was Kunchan
Nambiyar, a poet and humorist. His *Sree Krishna Lila* remains unusu-
ally fresh and simple. It was during the latter half of the nineteenth
century, however, that the subject was taken up in earnest. Kerala
Varma, as chairman of the Text Book Committee, brought out many
biographies and essays for children. An exciting literary venture, the
Mahacharitra Sangam, published in 1895, was a collection of biographies of 107 great men of the world. But much of the literature during
this period remains pedantic. The publication, some decades later, of
supplementary reading resulted in an ambitious series of fairy and folk
tales and classics, both of the East and West. A total of 225 titles were
published, but the illustration and production remained crude and
shabby.

It is only as recently as 1950, when a unique cooperative publishing
concern was established in Kottayam, that well-produced children's
books in Malayalam were first displayed. Altogether about a thousand
titles of published literature for children are available. Oral narrative
remains the most popular vehicle of children literature. Although this
state boasts the highest percentage of literacy in India and contains as
many as 10,000 primary schools, 1,200 high schools, and a student
population of 12 *lakhs* (1,200,000), the scope and depth of creative
writing for children is still not up to the standard one might expect.

If books for children in Malayalam have been few and far between,
children's magazines in that language have made spectacular progress.
They are coming out on an average of one a year. Currently, there are
no less than twelve different magazines printed in large quantities.
Chanda-ama is the Malayalam version of an English original published
in Madras. *Thaliru* is a fortnightly brought out by the state government
from Trivandram. Most of the other magazines are "projections" of
well-known journals and newspapers—like *Balarama,* brought out by
the *Manorama* group of journals—and are extremely popular with children.

Children's literature in Marathi dates only from the beginning of this century, although in development and stature it is highly regarded today, and some of the oldest monthly magazines for children belong to the Marathi language. Typical of popular children's literature, *Anand* and *Shalapatrak* have completed over seventy-five years of existence and stood the test of changing times and styles. P. K. Atne is a name associated in Marathi literature with the beginning of a new movement. He was the first well-known author to produce textbooks for children in a simple and interesting style. With the establishment of children's literature as a separate field, many young writers set out to explore the medium, producing a spate of fresh and original writings which may not stand up to a critical literary analysis but which, nonetheless, were exceedingly popular with children. A number of child heroes were created about this time (the mid-thirties) and retained their color and popularity till the late forties. Serious attention was also given to the illustration and format of books.

Soon after independence various prizes were instituted at central and state levels to encourage children's literature. The Mouji Prakashan and Popular Book Depot are two publishing houses that have brought out books exemplary both in form and content. A curious phenomenon must be highlighted here. The children's theatre movement has taken strong roots in Maharashtra. Many adult playwrights have produced excellent plays for children, a medium for which children of this region have a well-developed taste. Vijay Tendulkar and C. T. Kanolkar, for example, have produced thoughtfully conceived plays and poetry. The fact that children enjoy them attests not only to the child's heightened awareness of a sophisticated subject but to the exploration of newer horizons for the child on the part of the writers. Novelettes, poetry, and plays are media especially well developed in this part of India. Recently the husband-wife team of Leela and Bha Sa Bhagwat have brought out a well-conceived book of nursery rhymes as well as a series of adventure stories in which a new child hero has emerged. Sumati Payagoakar is at present a well-known writer and has been writing for children over the last fifteen years.

A new and encouraging step has been taken by Shri Kumtha, a bookseller and publisher. A book week is held once a year at which only children's books are made available. The event is becoming increasingly popular and may well be the beginning of a new trend.

Children's literature in Bengali has ancient roots both orally and in the written form. Translations of Indian classics and mythology appear as early as the beginning of the eighteenth century. Middle Eastern literature—the tales of Arabia and Persia—has been imported and adapted to such an extent that a Bengali child considers it part of his heritage. With the advent of the Christian missionaries a new impetus was given to the production of religious tracts and textbooks for children.

Children's literature in this language took on disciplined lines with the publication of a children's magazine by two brilliant writers, Ishwarchandra Vidyasagar and Aukhoy Kumar Dutta, who can be said to be the architects of children's literautre in Bengal. These established writers also wrote a number of small books for children. These books, albeit written in an archaic style, are still sought after today by parents and teachers alike.

A period of prolific creativity in poetry followed, and fresh, lively renderings of the rules and laws of arithemetic in humorous verse appeared for the first time. Needless to say they are popular with children to this day.

Bengali children's literature is marked by the keen interest taken in it by every famed man of letters. This interest has given it a status and style enjoyed by none of the other regional literatures for children. The association of such names as Tagore, Shastri, and Keshav Chand Sen with juvenile literature has raised it to dizzying heights and a fascinating number of splendid books can be found. Although the production of books in terms of illustration, typography, and design is not of high standard, the extraordinarily well-written texts often lead the reader to overlook the physical appearance of the books.

At the beginning of the twentieth century, Upendra Kishore Roy brought out the highly reputed monthly children's magazine *Sandesh,* which appears to be a most popular magazine even today. Apart from *Sandesh,* numerous children's magazines appeared in print and a few have survived. A multitude of gifted writers like D. R. M. Majumdar and Yogindranath produced a rich and diverse literature for the young. Their plots are striking in that they touch upon sickness, hunger, work, and loyalty in a way that is appreciated by children of all ages.

Contemporary children's literature in Bengali is extremely progressive. Well-known names today are Satyajit Ray, Lila Majumdar, Kishore Bharati, Sukhatara, and Ananda. A startling trend in current literary efforts is "specializiation" on the part of the writers. This is unusual in India, where children's literature is marked by spasmodic and irregular standards of published material. In Bengali children's literature, writers achieve recognition in a particular field. Thus, H. Kumar Roy and S. M. Mukerji are known for their adventure stories. Y. N. Gupta and S. Banerji specialize in historical narrative. Humor and light-hearted stories concern Jagannath Pandit. Similarly, short modern stories reflecting current modes have a large following of established writers. Specialists in subjects like myth and fairy tales like Sita Devi and Shanta Devi do not attempt biography, which is the domain of N. K. Chatterji and D. N. Bhattacharya. Limericks and humorous verse as distinct from "moral" verse is dealt with by other authors. Sukumar Dey is established in the field of animal stories, just as J. Roy and Amarnath are in the sphere of science fiction, of which there is a fine representation.

Many contemporary Bengali writers concern themselves with increasing the range of a child's vision. Merely telling a story is not enough. An interest is taken in the mental development and character of the child. This has been the touchstone of all children's literature in Bengal. Recently, however, a handful of nonconformists have rebelled against such a "puritan dogma." They have used plots and language which underscore the urgency of present-day situations. Realism is their key word. These young writers have not hesitated to touch upon such forbidden subjects as sex and love, parental conflicts, and teenage rebellion and principles—for the older age group. This neo-literature has come under heavy criticism, but it continues to grow. It must be remembered that Bengal, the pace setter as far as art and literature are concerned, takes up many experimental programs with enthusiasm. Children's literature at present, in Bengal, is a fully developed field as far as purely literary merits go. Production and technical standards do not measure up, however, with the result that to a non-Bengali the books are unattractive and of poor quality.

Hindi, the national language of the country, is still to come into its own. It faces stiff competition from the regional languages on the one hand and English on the other. Children's literature in Hindi dates back a hundred years. Curiously, the birth of modern Hindi literature and children's literature in Hindi took place at the same time; the first children's magazine, *Bal Bodhini,* began in 1874. Moreover, more than in any other language in India, it is the poet rather than the prose writer who has contributed to the development of children's writing. Bharatendu Harish Chander was not only the first writer of note to cement the shaky foundations of modern Hindi literature but was also, in a sense, the pioneer of children's literature in Hindi. Until about sixty years ago, Maithli Sharan Gupta and Ram Naresh Tripathi were towering figures in children's literature because of their simple, catchy rhymes and imaginative poems. In 1942, Sohan Lal Dwivedi wrote verse for children on patriotic themes and won immediate recognition.

But it was only in 1947 that many established adult writers turned their attention to writing for children. In short, children's writing has been taken seriously, as an endeavor worth undertaking, only in the last twenty-seven years. Nevertheless, writers and publishers, having once made up their minds, made big strides. A large number of books were brought out, a prominent series being a hundred titles on folk tales of the world. Traditional Sanskrit classics as well as a number of stories from ancient Indian mythology were translated. The translation of the "World's Classics" established a new trend: the old school of thought, which selected material written only for children, gave way to selecting such literature which when adapted could be enjoyed by children. A "See India" series culminated in a well-conceived program of "See the World."

Children's literature in Hindi has developed along very disciplined lines. A series on great scientists of the world, for example, would be followed by great philosophers of the world, great revolutionaries, and so on, with the result that a comprehensive literature earmarked for children can be found on almost all subjects of note.

Currently the National Book Trust, National Publishing House, Children's Book Trust, Atma Ram and Sons, Rajpal and Sons, and Arya Book Depot are well-known publishing houses for children's literature in Hindi. As elsewhere, the layout and production of books remain mediocre. Currently, Hindi is also the only language which boasts of two doctorates in children's literature, granted to Dr. Hari Krishan Devasari and Dr. Mast Ram Kapoor in recognition of their work in this sphere.

The two most popular magazines for children, *Parag* and *Nandan,* take the distinction of having the largest circulation figures in all the regional languages and English—over 130,000 each. The two magazines have been edited in time by some of the most outstanding authors of children's literature in Hindi. At present, Jai Prakash Bharathi, a prominent writer, is the editor. Modern trends can be best studied through the contents of these magazines, which because of their fine management are widely read by children. The traditional story is more popular than the modern story because it has more to offer in form and content. A concession to modern trends is the adventure story with a flavor of science, as in *Come, Let's Go to the Moon,* which has proved very successful. The portrayal of true tales of bravery, humorous verse, and short original pieces that are brief but telling appear more regularly these days. Science fiction, though rare, is of good quality. A book for children on "Oceanography and Space Travel" has won the UNESCO Award.

Unfortunately, publishers have been reluctant to translate even the most outstanding books in Hindi into regional languages and vice versa.

This limits overall readership because only a small section reads the literature of any particular region. Lack of interest and a patronizing attitude on the part of institutions and individuals are held responsible for the present low quality and quantity of children's books. Once again, young writers stick to traditional folk tales; only the established writer has the privilege of exploring new ground and experimenting with new styles.

Despite these drawbacks, children's literature in Hindi remains widely read. Children's writers in Hindi have a better standing and recognition than those in most regional languages. A few of the more popular authors are Anand Prakash Jain, Jai Prakash Bharti, Vishnu Prabhakar, Yog Raj Thani, and Ved Mitra. Sohan Lal Devadi, Nirankar Dev Sevak, and Dr Sri Prasad are some of the poets who have written lively and exciting verse for children.

Children's literature in English is still very new, a product of the last twenty years. Of the large and well-known organizations interested in children's literature in English the most active and noncommercial agencies are the Children's Book Trust, National Book Trust, and Southern Languages Book Trust. The Children's Book Trust aims at providing good children's literature at a reasonable price for all age groups. The founder and moving force behind this organization is Shankar, who has devoted himself to raising standards in children's literature. The Children's Book Trust houses the only inclusive international library for children in the capital—the most up-to-date and well-stocked library for children in the entire country. Improving the reading habits of children is one way of insuring higher publishing standards within the country. A child exposed to the best reading selections from countries all over the world is bound to demand a higher standard from contemporary writers of children's literature.

The Children's Book Trust has had great influence in the children's publishing industry since it is one of the few large organizations devoted solely to the promotion of higher reading standards. Books published range from classics, folk anthologies, tales from the epics, and translations into regional languages of newer titles like *Man in Khaki, Balloon Travel,* and *What Shall I Be?* which follow the more modern trends of children's literature in form and content. Books from the Children's Book Trust are marked by their excellent production. Books are well conceived, effectively illustrated, and attractively designed.

The National Book Trust, a government organization, is also dedicated to producing good reading material for children. Apart from textbooks, supplementary reading material is also published. Themes predominant in National Book Trust publications are India's cultural heritage, folk tales and festivals, and selections from great Indian authors. National integration appears to be the supplementary objective in the choice of subjects and titles.

A selection of juvenile literature can be made on an ad hoc basis from publishing houses like the Lalvani Brothers, India Book House, Echo, Somiaya Publications, and Thomson Press. Many smaller presses print elementary readers which are colorful and well produced. Publication of occasional children's books by those who cater exclusively to adults is only a recent phenomenon. The sales proceeds have probably been enough to encourage a wider representation of children's books within the framework of their organizations. In 1969 the Federation of Publishers and the Booksellers Association of India formed a Central Publishing Exchange Unit to encourage publishers in different Indian languages to produce high-quality children's books at lower prices by sharing the cost of artwork and plates.

A recent trend in publishing houses clearly demonstrates a drawing away from themes of fantasy to a more "realistic" approach. Current demand is for exciting adventure stories for children over ten. A recent effort to involve Indian authors in producing something on these lines has resulted in the publication of adventure stories for children with Indian background and themes, among them *The Hidden Pool* by Ruskin Bond and *Goddess of the River* by Sarojini Sinha. Writing an absorbing story relevant to present-day themes is still in an infantile stage of development. Poetry and prose for children under five and large picture books that tell a story in themselves are only now appearing. Conspicuous by their absence are science fiction and well-integrated and meaningful books for teenagers. Such contemporary themes as poverty, communal harmony, and personal adjustments are either not dealt with at all or in such a superficial manner as to make the effort irrelevant. For most readers this gap between a world of fantasy, wonder, and adventure and the adult one of problems and conflicts is left unbridged. For them it is a straight jump into the adult world of fiction writers where social problems are the ingredients of every plot and used with abandon in every theme and story. Such a marked absence of children's literature dealing with contemporary social topics also reflects a tendency on the part of most parents, teachers, and adults generally to shield a child from the harsher, harder aspects of life and prolong a more romanticized conception.

However, it must be admitted that for such a recent movement, children's literature in English has made good progress. An outstanding achievement is the attention given to production, which makes English the only language in the country which has produced handsome, well-printed, and beautifully illustrated books.

When compared with the worldwide boom in children's literature, India's contribution is meagre. In fact, we as a people have not long been associated with the production of children's books as a special field. Judging from the limited material available, in the form of catalogs, annual book lists, stray articles in magazines, isolated seminars, programs and discourses of publishers and writers, one comes to the conclusion that children's literature remains neglected even now. Current children's literature can boast of few prolific or popular authors, but it is mainly because of the interest of a few persons and organizations that such literature exists on any scale at all. There are no special institutes or research or training centers in this field. Publishers display marked prejudice against the unestablished writer, who rarely finds encouragement. But to be a good adult fiction writer is not the best warrant of success in writing for children.

The contemporary scene, as far as overall production and publication is concerned, remains uninspiring. Economics, I am obliged to point out, plays a central role in the functioning of children's literature as a vital cultural manifestation. The dearth of well-produced children's books can be attributed to high costs of production. The publisher cannot afford the kind of paper and material used abroad, nor is he willing to risk a large investment in a field not yet established as a paying concern. Furthermore, such expenses would necessarily raise the price of books which the consumer, in turn, is hard pressed to afford.

As far as illustration of children's books is concerned, there are a number of young competent artists but illustrated books of merit are few. Once again, high costs of production restrict the availability of beautifully produced picture books.

Harnessing television and radio as a method of intensifying interest in children's literature is yet to develop in India. Children's books offer good material for development into plays, stories, songs, ballads, puppet-plays, and children's films of which there is a marked paucity in India.

There is evidence of awakening interest in children's literature—in finding higher criteria for children's reading material and literary criticism and in forming a guild for children's books to provide guidance to parents and teachers in the selection of books. Such trends may help to bring it on par with children's literature in other countries. It is unfortunate, however, that in this, the "century of the child," the Indian child is still to come into his own.

The Current State of
Children's Literature in Canada*

Leonard R. Mendelsohn

Even a capsule summary of the Canadian dilemma reveals the precarious state of children's literature in Canada. Because Canada's fortunes have been for so long all too closely linked with those of the United States, the distinctiveness of the country has lingered in eclipse. This shading of the Canadian world may be witnessed in the benign disregard of things Canadian not only within the United States but even in Canada itself, as the inhabitants hire cables to link themselves to American television, adopt textbooks composed in the United States, purchase 90 percent of their books from British and American concerns, and are in general content to be steady beneficiaries of American media. In recent years, however, Canadian writers, artists, and academics have joined a growing number of dissidents in protesting the country's image as the innocuous neighbor to the north, and they have engaged in an effort, often a painfully self-conscious exercise, to isolate and describe salient features of the Canadian national character. While there is general agreement that such an entity does exist, and while there are numerous suggestions as to its composition, the compleat Canadian, or even a recognizable composite, eludes all speculation. It is not even possible to say "as Canadian as the flag," for the Maple Leaf is of quite recent vintage and has yet to achieve universal endorsement. Confederation of the provinces was accomplished slightly more than a century ago, a period too brief to supply a substantial body of indigenous literature which might reflect the national character in a natural, unstrained manner. Paradoxically, however, as it becomes increasingly evident that the Canadian character resists definition, the intuition waxes stronger that there is in fact something there. Certainly there is some logic behind such intuitive processes, for how else could an image or an idea remain unsatisfying if it were not measured against some archetype?

While the search for definition continues, the Canadian writer finds himself in the predicament of determining how and what to write for an audience with a possibly chimerical common denominator. If he chooses to delimit a specific group and to address himself primarily to a single segment of the Canadian population, he further diminishes an already limited readership, since the total number of Canadians barely exceeds

*Presented at the MLA Seminar on Children's Literature, 1974.

the population of California. It is, moreover, economically more feasible to cater to a California market, which is more compact both in character and in area. Consider for example that the distance from Montreal to Vancouver is greater than the mileage from Montreal to Mexico City. The Trans-Canada highway, which spans the breadth but hardly penetrates the length of the country, extends for more than 5,000 miles, and within this vast and generally sparsely settled territory are markedly diverse groups of people. Unlike the melting pot to the south, Canada is a country of insoluble minorities, a circumstance somewhat euphorically labeled a mosaic. Whatever term one wishes to adopt, it is perhaps a telling Canadian characteristic that virtually every group is either a minority or else behaves like one. Even French Canadians conduct themselves as a beleaguered handful right within the Province of Quebec, where they form a hefty 85 percent of the population. Thus to write for Canadians may well be an exercise in futility, since whatever any sustained inquiry into the national character may yield, it is unlikely to uncover any nationwide literary preference. It is more probable that a book directed to Californians would find favor in Connecticut than it is that a work seizing the fancies of Montrealers would find enthusiastic reception in Halifax or in Ontario. In short, Canadian readership for any literary venture is economically insignificant. In publishing circles the Canadian reading public is generally considered little more than a spillover for an American or a British endeavor, an added profit after the home trade has been exhausted. Faced with such obstacles it should not be surprising to find that most Canadian publishers offer little incentive to native authors, except those whose reputations might generate sales across the border. Viewed realistically, many Canadian publishers might more appropriately be called jobbers, since they are principally engaged in merchandising the overplus of British and U. S. presses.

As might be expected, the vicissitudes of Canadian publishing are mirrored in its children's literature. Accordingly, the number of children's books appearing in any given year is smaller than would be anticipated for a literate, relatively affluent nation of twenty-two million. Counting reprints, my list includes slightly more than sixty Canadian children's books in English since 1970—an average of about twelve books per year. And I have been quite liberal in employing the term "children's," including as I did several nostalgia items which were without doubt principally directed at adults. I have been equally lenient in accepting as Canadian any book written by a Canadian author or any book about a Canadian subject, even though some of them were conceived and edited in the United States or in England. I have included as well offprints of vanity presses, omitting only textbooks and other items of a purely pedagogical nature. Admittedly my list is not definitive, but I dismally suspect that it reasonably approaches completeness.

Crisis, however, is the stuff that letters thrive on. Under such unpromising conditions, creativity and excellence become requisite for both publisher and author, and a number of Canadian enterprises in children's books have responded imaginatively to the challenge of survival. Virtually emblematic of heroic promise in the face of adversity is Tundra Books, a Montreal-based outfit so small that it can afford to produce no more than four or five books annually. On this miniscule scale it becomes essential that each volume attain the quality and recognition which would expand tenuous marketing horizons. May Ebbitt Cutler, editor of Tundra and herself award-winning author of *I Once Knew an Indian Woman,* devised a formula for providing effective children's books, a formula as remarkable for its simplicity as for its sensibility and results. She began with the premise that the image is preeminent. Image always precedes articulation, verbal facility as it were deriving from a clearly conceived visual impression. The movement from image to articulation not only approximates the natural process of thought, but it also obviates the often unfortunate opposition of text and illustration. Further, when the text itself is an outgrowth of a specific image, it is less likely that a reader will find that pictorial representation competes with his own privately rendered picture. A gratifying by-product of the formula lies in its potential for prompting Canadian content while resolving problems of regionalism: for distinctive Canadian themes, if they are to emerge, will derive from well-produced impressions of the landscapes and peoples of Canada, their seasons, festivities, rituals, and moods. Once such indisputably Canadian images are before us, the text follows as an appropriate response to a concrete visual reality. Thus May Cutler began her search for quality children's literature, not by combing stacks of manuscripts and then matching the chosen with an illustrator, but by commissioning the talented Canadian artist William Kurelek to produce a collection of twenty paintings based on the theme of winter in the prairies.

The result, entitled *A Prairie Boy's Winter,* is accompanied by a text supplied by the artist, the combination a striking confirmation of the Cutler thesis that a firm visual impression will prompt a narrative which accommodates and amplifies pictorial details. Kurelek's drawings are indeed evocative, virtually demanding some form of verbal participation. The individual prints display themes of wonder in the middle of a wasteland, inventiveness in the face of isolation, and the sportive imagination opposing a wearying monotony of routine. Throughout there are various shapes—circles, triangles, and squares—simultaneously suggestive of no exit and of infinite artistic possibility. The hockey rink and the pinwheel, devised by the children for wintertime delight, symbolize as well the confines of the harsh surroundings. Yet the human spirit endures, perhaps in part as a result of this ceaseless dialogue with the environment, which, however cruel, incessantly demands response. This same kind of dialogue is carried on between the paintings and the text. The first painting, The Coming of Winter, is a suitable example of this interplay.

Here the grayish-blue sky dominates almost three quarters of the canvas. There are no clouds, as the tint by itself suffices to convey an ominous mood. Everywhere the fullness of space imposes itself, dwarfing the nine figures of children who are little more than enclothed stick figures distinguishable for each other only through their relative sizes, their postures, and the color of their clothing. Separating the children from the endless expanse, a line of white poplars bereft of foliage exposes about a dozen deserted crows' nests, while a few splotches of white in the horizon and the overall barrenness reinforce the theme of winter's imminent arrival. Dotting the sky are several score of black wings, apparently in exodus. One child points to the sky, perhaps first articulating the obvious and then lapsing into his commentary. Almost as if to supply this muted voice the narrative commences, at first overlapping with the picture by restating its images, and then breaking out on its own:

> It was chilly. The skies hung heavy and gray as William, his brother John and his sister Winnie, joined other children on the highway schoolbound.
> The crows had been loitering around in great flocks quarrelling, cawing and raiding farmers' cornfields. Now they were finally leaving. They flew south every fall about this time to escape the harsh prairie winter. In the cow pasture the leaves had fallen from the white poplars and the oaks, leaving the crows' nests bare in the high branches.
> It would be months before one of these noisy black birds came flapping back over the pasture bush to announce the end of winter.

The simple text, a polished recollection retrieved from childhood, shows not only expansion of details but also a sense of the dramatic. The crows are not simply symbols of impending winter, but are native denizens chattering in the cornfields, competing with the farmers, and, perhaps as well, suggestive of pesky children whose departure brings at once sighs of relief and tears of desolation. The sameness of the prairie landscape is offset by suggestions of perpetual movement, the motion of the

Snowdrift Fun, from William Kurelek, *A Prairie Boy's Winter*. Reproduced by permission of Tundra Books, Montreal. Published in the United States by Houghton Mifflin Company of Boston.

"The wind had swept the snow . . . from across two miles of open fields. The bush broke the force of the wind and the snow settled in its twigs and branches where it lay loosely packed.

"The drifts were so high the children could make two-story apartments by honeycombing the snow with tunnels and caves."

The Coming of Winter, from William Kurelek, *A Prairie Boy's Winter*. Reproduced by permission of Tundra Books, Montreal. Published in the United States by Houghton Mifflin Company of Boston.

crows southward, of the children schoolward; the inevitable cycle of the seasons with their fierce activity and transformations pulls everything onto a stage whose space cries out to be filled.

A Prairie Boy's Winter was selected by the *New York Times* as one of the ten best illustrated books of 1973. Awards constitute more than encouragement, since prominent recognition carries with it library adoptions within the United States, a sales boost critically necessary to Canadian publications, particularly since nationwide library purchases in Canada contribute but meagre financial support. Unfortunately, however, endorsement within the United States is rare for Canadian books. The governing body of the National Book Award withdrew Kurelek from further consideration when their query to Houghton Mifflin uncovered his Canadian citizenship. Kurelek has, nonetheless, carved out a considerable audience in the United States, and his succeeding volume, *Lumberjack,* was equally successful, with the *Times* choosing it as one of the ten best illustrated books of 1974. *Lumberjack,* containing twenty-five paintings depicting the author's apprenticeship in logging camps in northern Ontario and Quebec, abounds in the same naive realism characteristic of *A Prairie Boy's Winter.*

The image-dominated text provides another gallery of delights in Carlo Italiano's *Sleighs of My Childhood.* In this compelling collection a child's gleeful fascination with winter's masterstrokes in Montreal surpasses any nostalgic grip on the irretrievable. This unrestrained joy uncovers artistic charm right in the teeth of the season's threatened isolation. For mobility and communication men invented sleighs, and colorful ones at that. The variety of wintertime conveyances provided a distinctive personality for their owners and for the city streets as well. There is the green milk delivery sleigh; the primitive red of the vegetable vendor's, replete with smokestack to keep his stock from freezing; a sleek black box for the nuns making their yuletide rounds; and the chip wagon poised upon runners, about which Italiano muses:

> No matter what ingredients and love our mothers used, their
> French-fried potatoes never tasted as good as the chipman's.
> While the whistle on the roof blew and the windows fogged up,
> the chipman shook the basket of his deep fryer, turned the valves,
> and dispensed happiness.

The Canadian landscape can be the source of appealing sounds as well as of inspiring sights, as is shown in two volumes of children's poetry by Dennis Lee, winner of the Governor General's Award. In both *Alligator Pie* for younger children and *Nicholas Knock* for the slightly older set, even prosaic Toronto takes on a Mother Goose glow. The poet makes his intentions explicit in an epilogue. For years he put his children to bed with English nursery rhymes, poems which despite their manifold merits were of another land and another era. Convinced that the contemporary world and the homeland, the familiar sights and sounds, were also the substance of poetry—but finding no products from these resources—he sat down to compose his own. As his rhymes demonstrate, place names like Chicoutimi, Témiscaming, Montmagny, and Michipicoten Bay reverberate with poetic possibilities, and certainly such inviting sound and picture combinations as Red Deer, Corner Brook, Medicine Hat, and Winnipeg have a lot going for them. One could only wonder what Kit Marlowe might have done with a Canadian atlas in hand. Dennis Lee has studied his Mother Goose well, and it shows as he produces in catchy rhymes the hallucinating effects of caricature, repeatedly revealing the exotic implications of the immediately familiar. The Ookpik, that curious looking arctic owl, appears throughout the poems, perhaps as a leitmotif of the Canadian character. We see him, but what is he? Dennis Lee proclaims:

> The Ookpik is nothing but hair,
> If you shave him, he isn't there.

It could be that this playful couplet contains hints about the Canadian character, as well as warnings for those searching for it. Dissection and study are not possible without formaldehyde, which renders the subject lifeless and unreal. Likewise, Canadian content will never be discovered by shaving away the externals and embalming the residue.

A quiet but pleasant triumph of the interplay between image and text may be seen in *Mary of Mile 18,* winner of the 1972 Gold Medal, Canadian equivalent of the Newbery Award. Anne Blades, for one year an elementary school teacher in a Mennonite community eighteen miles to the east of mile 73 along the Alaska highway, found the faces of the children and the stark beauty of the surroundings crying out for a narrative. Her paintings contrast the harshness of subarctic life with the intimacy of the family. Like the pictures, the story is simple but satisfying, perhaps in this way capturing the lifestyle of these gentle but hardy people. The following year Anne Blades served in a school on an Indian reserve at Stuart Lake in the British Columbia wilderness. Her desire to provide these isolated school children with a book about themselves led to *A Boy of Taché,* an understated account of the heroism of an Indian lad on a trapping expedition. The two volumes show that regionalism may be an asset, at least on the artistic level if not on the economic one, and they demonstrate that good images can make good narratives, even out of the most unpretentious plots.

The formula of beginning with images need not be restricted to portraits of Canadian life. In *Thomasina and the Trout Tree,* by Joan Clark, the artist-centered book brings on a surrealistic feast. The narrative no less than the drawings represents the world as seen on oil-bloated canvas. City life becomes refracted as colors and experiences collide in a zany though ultimately pleasing pattern. Thomasina, with two cheese and cherry sandwiches tucked in the back pockets of her jeans, goes in search of an object about which she knows nothing except that it is a work of art and that it is called the trout tree. In her wanderings she encounters the Great Vincent, a recognizable British artisan, who, in the words of the dust jacket, "rolls abstract expressionistic paintings for his goat to eat and nearly kills the poor animal by being careless about his choice of colors." Later she meets "the park policeman who has turned his lost and found department into a pop art billboard, because he likes art that changes every day," and then the lady sculptor who never knows what she is creating until she finishes, but who never completes anything. The book is a refreshing exemplar of the fact that a book may be markedly Canadian through technique and other subtle hints, not only through blatantly imprinting the country of origin on each page.

Montreal artist Elizabeth Cleaver, whose flaming colors literally engulf text and all, and whose art work has been deservedly acclaimed in *The Wind Has Wings, How Summer Came to Canada,* and *The Mountain Goats of Temlaham* (all highly successful volumes of the late sixties), has produced both narrative and drawings for *The Miraculous Hind,* a book not about Canada at all, but a retelling of the mythic origins of Hungary. The volume is of oversized width to permit the artist the expansive scope required by her distinctive style. Often it is necessary to gaze intently into the artwork in order to discover the very letters of the text, another fulfilling variation of what might well be a hallmark of the better Canadian children's books—if not of children's books everywhere —the preeminence of the image, and its narrative-provoking potential.

And Hungary is not the only old country celebrated artistically and thematically in the past year. *The Farmer's Year,* with scenes composed by seven different Canadian-Polish artists and with a collaborative effort in the text as well, proposes to recapture the rural seasons in Poland. Such volumes reflect the vividness with which not only customs but the details of the countries of origin remain alive within Canadian groups.

No discussion of Canadian children's literature could ignore the Eskimos, a people who apparently have dominated the international image of Canada. Several volumes of the seventies are especially appealing. Pitseolak's *Pictures of My Life* recounts the personal and artistic experiences of an accomplished Cape Dorset artist. The text, culled from tape recorded interviews, is in both English and Eskimo and features Pitseolak's own illustrations. Father Maurice Metayer has edited and translated traditional legends of the Copper Eskimos in *Tales from the Igloo*. These brief legends uncover the Eskimo's world view, which is surprisingly expansive in a people whose existence is forever marginal. The Eskimo can be playful and proud, cruel and compassionate, and if these stories approximate the manner of narration, consummate story-tellers as well. The volume is suggestively illustrated in traditional Eskimo style by a native artist. Ronald Melzack's *Raven Creator of the World* recounts both the mythic past and the historical though long-vanished early days of the Eskimos. Raven is alternately if not at once the god figure and the quintessential Eskimo. He has created the world, but he is in desperate need of his creations, and his omnipotence is tempered by his weakness in longing for them. Melzack's *The Day Tuk Became a Hunter,* a justly popular collection of Eskimo stories, has been reprinted in 1971.

The Canadian Indian also commands a considerable share of ink, but unlike the portrayal of the Eskimo, the Indian takes on a kind of literary individualism which marks him more in the line of the hero of a novelistic tradition than as a creature of the Canadian landscape. The portrait can be appealing and it can also lead onto the outskirts of satire as with Claude Aubry's Maha Maha the Second, monarch of the Yellow Ants, in *King of the Thousand Islands,* who, becoming bored with uninterrupted peace, prosperity, loyalty, and devotion, searches out extraordinary means of diversion and ultimately sacrifices himself and his nation for what turns out to be a toothless old woman. Aubry's more recent hero, Agouhanna, in a book by the same name, is endowed with traits decidedly smacking of the 1960's, though the story is set in mercifully more primitive times. Agouhanna, literally brave among braves, son of an Iroquois chief, clings unabashedly to his mother's apron strings, loathes the sight of blood and the killing of animals, and with no more shame than a conscientious objector devises means of bypassing the successive ordeals which are the tribe's traditional gateway to manhood. He is neither misanthrope nor loner as he knows how to win the few friends he desires. Loyal to our age, Agouhanna eschews work, and "the only skills he had were thinking and dreaming." Little Doe, ultimately his bride, is on the other hand more successful than any upstart brave at palming burning coals, a trial devised only for aspirants to warrior-hood. She asks, "Why are we all destined for the most degrading work just because we're females? It's all ridiculous and stupid." Similarly, James Houston in *Ghost Paddle* embroiders portraits of historical Indians with a modernist flare. Hooits (Grizzly Bear) becomes a peacenik as the book progresses from preoccupation with tribal warfare to a reverence for shrewd diplomacy. James Houston, in keeping with a noticeable Canadian trend, derived his inspiration from specific visual impressions, in this case from the legendary Indian carvers of the Northwest coast of Canada. Appropriately, Houston serves as his own illustrator. He has also recently published *Wolf Run: A Caribou Eskimo Tale,* drawing on his experience of twelve years living among the Eskimos. His award winning Eskimo books, unlike the Indian volumes, attempt to reflect Eskimo life without recourse to modernism. The supreme nonconformist Indian is the subject of a modern fairy tale by A. P. Campbell—*Kaki-Wahoo: The Little Indian Who Walked on His Head.* True to our decade, Kaki-Wahoo never condescends to tread on his feet, learning only that he should not attempt to impose his predilections upon others.

The most balanced portrayal of the traditional though unconventional Indian is Madame Dey, unassuming, accepting, though redoubtable heroine of Ebbitt Cutler's *I Once Knew an Indian Woman,* reprinted by Houghton Mifflin in 1973 after stagnating on Canadian shelves since its initial appearance in Canada in 1967 under the title *The Last Noble Savage.* Living almost in poverty, though with style and vigor, Madame Dey assumes the decency of the community. When a young boy, a stranger to the town, dies suddenly, no one including the village priest attends to the body. She carries the corpse to her home, washes the clothing, and places the body upon her candle-decked kitchen table until the parents can arrive to provide for burial. There is no saccharine in the tale of Madame Dey, only a delicate understanding of the primitive, uncorrupted and undeterred by a life of distasteful encounters with the English and French Canadian communities.

In the interests of space, I have had to omit a major component of children's literature in Canada, those books dealing with historical themes. At least passing reference should be made to William Toye, editor at the Oxford University Press in Toronto, who has produced several distinguished volumes in this area, most recently *Cartier Discovers the St. Lawrence.* The voyageur and the tall tale combine intriguingly in *Jolly Jean-Pierre* by Lyn Cook, a major Canadian writer of children's books, and Mary Davies. In keeping with the prominence of images, the book displays brightly colored drawings which modulate the abstract and the authentic. It is another bilingual volume with the English text, terse though appealing, charmingly reproducing the French Canadian accent, and it is unquestionably one of the best children's books of the past year.

It would be unfortunate not to mention the resurgence of the works of Lucy Maud Montgomery, whose *Anne of Green Gables* is probably the best-known Canadian children's book. The popularity of *Anne* has endured, and the novel has now been translated into thirty-six languages and has been adapted into a long-run stage presentation, as well as into two film versions. Almost a dozen of her other books have been reprinted in the past decade, the last two years witnessing the reappearance of *Anne's House of Dreams* (originally published in 1922); *A Tangled Web* (1931); *Rilla of Ingleside* (1920); *Rainbow Valley* (1923); *Emily of New Moon* (1925); *Anne of Windy Poplars* (1936); and *Anne of Ingleside* (1939). All these books have been printed in paperback as part of the Canadian Favourites Series published by McClelland and Steward. This same Favourites Series has also reissued *Beautiful Joe* by Marshall Saunders. Pierre Berton's appearance in the children's hour is less fortunate. *The Secret World of Og,* a bland imitation of C. S. Lewis' Chronicles of Narnia, has nonetheless enjoyed success in sales, relying on Berton's deserved reputation as author of Canadian novel epics. The five Berton children and their family pets are central characters in the book, and the reissue is illustrated by daughter Patsy.

As if to show that the young Canadian is much on the mind of writers and artists, the past year has witnessed the first Canadian children's annual. Though the idea was lifted from a British model, the contents are of decidedly Canadian vintage. Edited by Robert F. Nielsen, with a cover by William Kurelek, and called *Canadian Children's Annual, 1975,* it contains contributions by fifty Canadian writers and artists. Perhaps the consolidated endeavours of these Canadians and the anticipation of the new year show a determined and vigorous challenge to the sustained dilemmas confronting the writer of Canadian children's literature. In the meantime the word from Canada is almost an embodiment of the landscape, sparsely settled, but rich, varied and fully worth exploiting.

A PARTIAL BIBLIOGRAPHY OF CANADIAN CHILDREN'S BOOKS APPEARING IN PRINT SINCE 1970

Aubry, Claude. *Agouhanna.* Translated from the French by Harvey Swados. Illustrated by Julie Dinchloe. Toronto: Doubleday Canada Limited, 1972.
Barclay, Isabel. *The Story of Canada.* Rexdale, Ontario: John Wiley and Sons

Canada Limited, 1974. (Originally published in 1964 as *O Canada!*)

Barkhouse, Joyce C. *George Dawson: The Little Giant.* Toronto and Vancouver: Clarke, Irwin and Company Limited, 1974.

Berton, Pierre. *The Secret World of Og.* Illustrated by Patsy Berton. Toronto: McClelland and Stewart Limited, 1974. (Originally published in 1961 with illustrations by William Winter.)

Blades, Ann. *A Boy of Taché.* Montreal and Plattsburgh, New York: Tundra Books, 1973.

―――. *Mary of Mile 18.* Montreal and Plattsburgh, New York: Tundra Books, 1971.

Bowsfield, Hartwell. *Louis Riel: The Rebel and the Hero.* Toronto: Oxford University Press, 1971.

Campbell, A. P. *Albert the Talking Rooster.* Ottawa: The Borealis Press, 1974.

―――. *Kaki-Wahoo: The Little Indian Boy Who Walked on His Head.* Ottawa: The Borealis Press, 1973.

Clark, Joan. *Thomasina and the Trout Tree.* Pictures by Ingeborg Hiscox. Montreal and Plattsburgh, New York: Tundra Books, 1971.

Cleaver, Elizabeth. *The Miraculous Hind.* Montreal: Holt, Rinehart and Winston of Canada Limited, 1973.

Cook, Lyn, and Mary Davies. *Jolly Jean-Pierre.* Bilingual edition with French adaptation by Micheline St. Cyr. Toronto: Burns and MacEachern Limited, 1973.

Cooper, Gordon. *Hester's Summer.* Illustrated by Robin Jacques. London: Oxford University Press, 1974.

Cutler, Ebbitt. *I Once Knew an Indian Woman.* Illustrated by Bruce Johnson. Boston: Houghton Mifflin Company, 1973. (Originally published in 1967 as *The Last Noble Savage.*)

Cutt, W. Towrie. *Message from Arkmae.* Toronto: Collins, 1972.

―――. *On the Trail of Long Tom.* Toronto: Collins, 1970.

―――. *Seven for the Sea.* Toronto: Collins, 1973.

de Roussan, Jacques. *Beyond the Sun.* Bilingual text, French and English. Montreal: Tundra Books, 1972.

Downie, Mary Alice and John. *Honor Bound.* Toronto: Oxford University Press, 1971.

Engel, Marian. *Adventures at Moon Bay Towers.* Toronto and Vancouver: Clarke, Irwin and Company, Limited, 1974.

Eustace, Mary. *Piney, The Talking Christmas Tree.* Illustrations by Manolo Corvera. Scarborough, Ontario: McGraw Hill Ryerson, 1974.

Harris, Christie. *Secret in the Stlalakum Wild.* Illustrated by Douglas Tait. Toronto: McClelland and Stewart Limited, 1972.

Hazzard, Russ (editor). *It's Not Always a Game / Un Eté D'Illusions.* A collection of poetry and prose by young Canadians. Montreal: Content Press, 1973.

Hill, Kay. *More Glooscap Stories: Legends of the Wabanaki Indians.* New York: Dodd, Mead and Company, 1970.

Houston, James. *Ghost Paddle: A Northwest Coast Indian Tale.* Illustrations by the author. Don Mills, Ontario: Longman Canada Limited, 1972.

_____. *Wolf Run: A Caribou Eskimo Tale.* Illustrations by the author. Don Mills, Ontario: Longman Canada Limited, 1971.

Italiano, Carlo. *The Sleighs of My Childhood.* Illustrations by the author. French text by René Chicoine. Montreal and Plattsburgh, New York: Tundra Books, 1972.

Kurelek, William. *Lumberjack.* Illustrations by the author. Montreal: Tundra Books and Boston: Houghton Mifflin Company, 1974.

_____. *A Prairie Boy's Winter.* Illustrations by the author. Montreal: Tundra Books and Boston: Houghton Mifflin Company, 1973.

Langford, Cameron. *The Winter of the Fisher.* Toronto: The MacMillan Company of Canada Limited, 1971.

Lee, Dennis. *Alligator Pie.* Pictures by Frank Newfeld. Toronto: The Macmillan Company of Canada Limited, 1972.

_____. *Nicholas Knock and Other People.* Illustrations by Frank Newfeld. Toronto: The MacMillan Company of Canada Limited, 1974.

MacKenzie, Jean. *River of Stars.* Illustrations by Tom McNealy. Toronto and Montreal: McClelland and Stewart Limited, 1971.

MacMillan, Cyrus. *Canadian Wonder Tales.* Illustrated by Elizabeth Cleaver. Toronto and Vancouver: Clarke, Irwin and Company Limited, 1974. (Originally published in 1918.)

McLaughlin, Lorrie. *Shogmoc Sam.* Illustrated by Randy Jones. Toronto: The Macmillan Company of Canada Limited, 1970.

Melzack, Ronald. *Raven Creator of the World.* Illustrated by Laszlo Gal. Toronto and Montreal: McClelland and Stewart Limited, 1970.

_____. *The Day Tuk Became a Hunter and Other Eskimo Stories.* Illustrated by Carol Jones. Toronto: McClelland and Stewart Limited, 1971. (Originally published in 1967.)

Metayer, Maurice (editor and translator). *Tales from the Igloo.* Illustrated by Agnes Nanogak. Edmonton, Alberta: Hurtig Publishers, 1972.

Montgomery, Lucy Maud. *Anne's House of Dreams.* Toronto: McClelland and Stewart Limited, 1972. (Originally published in 1922.)

_____. *Anne of Ingleside.* Toronto: McClelland and Stewart Limited, 1972. (Originally published in 1939.)

_____. *Anne of Windy Poplars.* Toronto: McClelland and Stewart Limited, 1973. (Originally published in 1936.)

_____. *Emily of New Moon.* Toronto: McClelland and Stewart Limited, 1973. (Originally published in 1925.)

_____. *Rainbow Valley.* Toronto: McClelland and Stewart Limited, 1974. (Originally published in 1923.)

_____. *Rilla of Ingleside.* Toronto: McClelland and Stewart Limited, 1973. (Originally published in 1920.)

_____. *A Tangled Web.* Toronto: McClelland and Stewart Limited, 1972. (Originally published in 1931.)

Nichols, Ruth. *The Marrow of the World.* Illustrated by Trina Schart. New York: Atheneum (Macmillan), 1972.

Nielsen, Robert F. (editor). *Canadian Children's Annual, 1975.* Hamilton, Ontario: Potlatch Publishers, 1974.

Pitseolak. *Pictures Out of My Life.* Edited from tape recorded interviews by Dorothy Eber. Montreal: Design Collaborative Books in association with Oxford University Press, Toronto, 1971.

Quinton, Leslie. *The Lucky Coin and Other Folk Tales Canadians Tell.* Toronto: McClelland and Stewart Limited, 1972.

Richards, Jack. *Johann's Gift to Christmas.* Illustrated by Len Norris. Vancouver: J. J. Douglas Limited, 1972.

Roch, Ernest (editor). *The Farmer's Year.* Seven different illustrators. Toronto: Signum Press Limited, 1973.

Rokeby-Thomas, Anna E. *Ningiyuk's Igloo World.* Pictures by James N. Howard. Chicago: Moody Press, 1972.

St. John, Judith. *Where Saints Have Trod.* Toronto: Oxford University Press, 1974.

Tait, Herbert. *Redwulf the Outlander.* Toronto and Vancouver: Clarke, Irwin and Company Limited, 1972.

Takashima, Shizuye. *A Child in Prison Camp.* Montreal and Plattsburgh, New York: Tundra Books, 1971.

Toye, William. *Cartier Discovers the St. Lawrence.* Illustrated by Laszlo Gal. Toronto: Oxford University Press, 1970.

Widell, Helene. *The Black Wolf of River Bend.* New York: Farrar, Straus and Giroux, 1971.

Young, Chip. *The Boy Who Came with Cartier.* Illustrated by John Marden. Toronto and Vancouver: Clarke, Irwin and Company Limited, 1974.

———. *Honky the Christmas Goose.* Illustrated by Louise Shepherd. Toronto and Vancouver: Clarke, Irwin and Company Limited, 1972.

———. *The Little Hen of Huronia.* Illustrations by Christiane Duchesne. Toronto and Vancouver: Clarke, Irwin and Company Limited, 1971.

———. *The Rose of Ba Ziz.* Illustrated by Tom Mortensen. Toronto and Vancouver: Clarke, Irwin and Company Limited, 1972.

Young, Delbert A. *The Ghost Ship.* Illustrated by William Taylor. Toronto and Vancouver: Clarke, Irwin and Company Limited, 1972.

Childhood's Pattern

The Parting of the Ways*

Gillian Avery

This book has arisen out of one that I wrote nine years ago. *Nineteenth Century Children* was published in 1965, when a new interest in the history of children's reading was beginning, but comparatively little had yet appeared in print. Since then the whole aspect has changed. Children's books now have their own niche in the study of English and of education. Journals are devoted to them; for a graduate to produce a thesis on Ballantyne or Mrs. Molesworth is regarded as in no way eccentric, and the ancient university of Oxford has even gone so far as to include the subject on its lecture list. To repeat my trite remarks on the better-known nineteenth-century authors would be, in the light of the present interest taken in them, superfluous to say the least, though there was a stage when I would have liked the chance to correct some of the errors of fact and of judgment that I had made.

But in spite of the avalanche of words that has been poured out during the last ten years, the great work that Harvey Darton wrote as long ago as 1932—*Children's Books in England*—does still remain the best study. Only he has had the knowledge, the judgment and the detachment to stand back and take a long, cool look at the whole landscape without getting lost in the trees. He provided literary assessment and bibliographic details—all part of the subject—but his real interest in children's books was because they represent "a minor chapter in the history of English social life," not because they play a great role in English literature.

"Literature," in the sense that they deserve serious and weighty literary discussion, they are not—except for a small handful. But what they do mirror is a constantly shifting moral pattern. What in any given age do adults want of children? What are their values? What are the virtues they are striving to inculcate, the vices they are trying to tread down? Do they rate learning above godliness, truth-telling above obedience; do they encourage or suppress imagination? Examine children's books in this light and even the dreariest becomes rewarding.

---

*The preface and first chapter of *Childhood's Pattern,* published in August 1975 by Brockhampton Press, Leicester LE1 7QS, England. the extract appears here by kind permission of author and publisher. Nine subsequent chapters examine the ethos of books reflecting, among others, the Rational Child, the Evangelical Child, the Innocents, the Schoolgirl, and the child's heroes.

This is what, in the present study, I am attempting—having made a faint beginning nine years ago. The giants stand above this scrutiny. Lewis Carroll, Lear, *The Just-So Stories, The Wind in the Willows, The Hobbit, Tom's Midnight Garden,* cannot be treated in this way. They are in any case works of fantasy and imagination, a subject which lies outside my province and which I do not try to include.

I have given the dates 1770 to 1950 as marking the limits of the study, but it is in fact the middle years that have received most attention. Before the nineteenth century the publishers were not properly under way. After 1910 or so the moralists and educationalists temporarily lost interest in juvenile reading and some thirty years or so of comparatively undirected commercial production followed. No new patterns emerged, only extensions of those formed at the beginning of the century. Of this period I have given only a slight indication. Since 1950 there has been a renaissance, far too recent to assess, but one which will present great interest to future chroniclers. Not only is the output formidable, in quantity and quality, but the educational experts are once again fully involved, as certain as ever they were in the days of Richard Lovell Edgeworth and Mrs. Trimmer and all their successors that their generation is uniquely equipped to form the child mind. . . .

"Damn them! I mean the cursed Barbauld Crew, those Blights and Blasts of all that is Human in man and child," wrote Lamb to Coleridge in 1802. He had been to Newbery's bookshop to try to buy some children's books, and had found that the new educational reading had banished all the old classics that he knew, and that "Mrs. Barbauld and Mrs. Trimmer's nonsense lay about in piles." It was hard to find even a copy of Goody Two-Shoes.

"Is there no possibility of averting this sore evil? Think what you would have been now, if instead of being fed with Tales and old wives' fables in childhood, you had been crammed with geography and natural history?"

There never has been an age which did not mourn the good old days, and hardly anybody who could make an objective assessment of the state of things in his childhood. This is particularly true of our first books. There are certain details that we seize on, cherish and perhaps add to over the years, and completely forget the longueurs of the rest. The story of Margery Meanwell, alias Goody Two-Shoes, the trotting tutoress, is a very moral tale indeed. It exemplifies, according to an edition of c. 1830 (it was first published by Newbery in 1765) "the good consequences of early attention to learning and virtue," which in Margery's case is rewarded by her being made a village schoolmistress and later by marrying a country squire.

There is not much of the stuff of childhood in it, certainly less than in *Lessons for Children,* which Mrs. Barbauld wrote in 1778 for her nephew, or even in that meaty, if fundamentally serious hotch-potch of information which she and her brother compiled in the 1790's under the title *Evenings at Home.* The first, in spite of its forbidding title, is a loving account of the small things in a small child's life, written in words that he would understand. As for the second—most children would be able to skip over the items on Cruciform Plants and Metals, and make for the autobiography of Grimalkin the Cat, and the story of Phaeton Junior which begins:

> *Ye heroes of the upper form,*
> *Who long for whip and reins,*
> *Come listen to a dismal tale*
> *Set forth in dismal strains.*

What Lamb was lamenting was the new professional seriousness that had overtaken the juvenile book-trade. But instead of kicking the modest and diffident Mrs. Barbauld, he would have done better to have damned Mrs. Trimmer and her *Guardian of Education,* which had started up that year and was busy ferreting out hitherto undetected jacobinism and subversion and corruption in all his old favourites. Or the whole climate of education opinion—Richard Lovell Edgeworth, Thomas Day and other disciples of the Rousseau school of thought; or Hannah More who spoke for the evangelicals—who had persuaded the public that works of the imagination could only stunt the growth of the child's mind, and that his leisure reading should be used to absorb knowledge and to improve his nature.

Lamb, born in 1775, had been out of petticoats and in the blue gown and yellow stockings of a Christ's Hospital scholar by the time *Sandford and Merton* appeared. In his infancy the juvenile book trade did not take itself very seriously. Its output consisted of a cheerful medley of old tales from the chapbooks, and lively new ones which stated how good children were rewarded and naughty ones were punished with frightful fates calculated to satisfy the most bloodthirsty infant mind. And there were alphabets and spelling books and rhymes, all gaily if crudely coloured.

Those middle years of the eighteenth century had seen the beginnings of the trade. Mrs. Trimmer attributed its rise to the influence of Locke. Before his time there had been little to wheedle children into learning; then suddenly the publishers realised what money was to be made out of them. "The youthful mind, which was formerly sick from inanition, is now in danger of a plethora," Hannah More was to make one of the characters in *Coelebs in Search of a Wife* complain.

Mrs. Trimmer, too, was as churlish about the little books that had
delighted her childhood: Mother Goose and Aesop and Gay's fables.
Born in 1741, she was a whole generation older than Lamb, but she had
enjoyed that Georgian flowering. She was in fact three years old when
John Newbery, having moved from Reading to London with a stock of
patent medicines and a fairish number of books for adults, set up business
at the sign of the Bible and Crown, and published *A Little Pretty Pocket
Book*

> intended for the Instruction and Amusement of Little Master
> Tommy and Pretty Miss Polly, with an agreeable Letter to read
> from Jack the Giant Killer, as also a Ball and a Pincushion, the
> use of which will infallibly make Tommy a good Boy, and Polly a
> good Girl.

Harvey Darton has described this little collection of rhymes and pictures
of children at their games as a key publication. It may not have been the
first attempt to amuse the young reader, but it was the beginning of
extended activity to do so, and the opening of forty years of amusement
for children, before a new school of thought put such books under an
interdict.

When we look at these little books, probably only in reproduction on
the pages of Tuer and Leonard de Vries for they are now of great rarity,
we get the impression of a comfortable earthy society where humor was
simple and ways were insensitive. The stories had morals, but they were
of a very obvious and materialistic sort. The good boy in the *Little Pretty
Pocket Book* is shown riding in a coach and six; the good girl gets given
a fine gold watch. It is the moral world of the fairy story. There is no
difficulty about being good, you just have to be diligent; and no doubt
about being rewarded for it. Any child can understand this.

It is this common touch that marks the children's book in those
happy-go-lucky years in the middle of the eighteenth century. The children of the poor man, if their father could spare them the ha'pence
(and always provided of course that they knew their letters) might
enjoy the story of Tommy Trip and his dog Jouler from Newbery's
A Pretty Book of Pictures just as much as Charles Lamb in the Inner
Temple.

> As he rides through the town [Tommy Trip] frequently stops at
> the doors to know how the little children do within, and if they
> are good and learn their books he then leaves an Apple, an
> Orange or a Plumb-cake at the door, and away he gallops again—
> *tantivy, tantivy, tantivy.*

No obscurity of language or sentiment there, nothing that would not be equally enjoyed in cottage or in drawing-room, or that makes it more suitable for one class than for another.

Up to about 1780 there was a single culture so far as children were concerned. The ideal child was the industrious child. Dick Whittington was a favorite hero. So was Giles Gingerbread, who learned his letters by eating them, because they were made of gingerbread. His father tells him: "Why, Sir Toby was poor once, yes, as poor as thee, Giles: do not be disheartened, boy, only when you climb, climb in a proper manner."

Then there was *King Pippin,* the story of Peter Pippin, son of Gaffer Pippin, a poor laboring man, who goes out to work when he is six, and is seen by Lady Bountiful crying because he has no money to buy a book. She sends him to Mr. Teachum's school, where the boys do not resent him as a jumped-up clod but buy him a fine cap, ornamented with white feathers, and engraved with letters of gold, "Peter Pippin, King of the Good Boys." His companions go out birdsnesting and for their sins are variously drowned or devoured by monstrous bears (in other chapbook versions these are lions). King Pippin, surviving, goes from strength to strength; he is sent out to the West Indies to manage a plantation, weds the owner's daughter, inherits the plantation, and at length is made governor of the island.

A successor of Goody Two-Shoes was Primrose Prettyface (published under the title of *The renowned history of Primrose Prettyface* by J. Marshall & Co. about 1783), "who, by her sweetness of temper, and love of learning, was raised from being the daughter of a poor cottager, to great riches, and the dignity of lady of the manor." When she goes into service with Squire Homestead and his family it is little Jemmy Homestead who is the wrongdoer and the liar, not virtuous Primrose whom he so falsely accuses.

Stories then did not hesitate to extol the poor boy, and to set the rich one in an unfavorable light beside him, or to allow the well-born to learn from the humble. In Catnach's version of *Nurse Lovechild's Legacy* (an eighteenth-century chapbook originally):

> Tom Trueby was a good and sensible boy, who neither played the truant nor kept company with naughty children. He did not like tossing up nor chuck farthing, because he thought it might lead him to love gaming when he was grown up; but he liked very well to play at ball or top, and most particularly at marbles, at which he was very clever, never cheated, and played so well that he used to teach the neighbouring children. And here you see him instructing Master Manly, a Baronet's son in the place, as he did

in matters of more consequence, and behaved so well towards him, that he was his friend all his lifetime.

But once the book trade, urged forward by the teacher and the moralist and the conscientious parent, began to take the child mind seriously, a new chasm opened between the prosperous home and the cottage. It was the mind and the person of the child of the educated classes that the book trade bestirred itself to improve according to the best modern theories: that was where the money lay. The ribald crudity of the chapbooks (or at any rate of some of them) became an abomination in the eyes of a more fastidious age; so, to a lesser extent, did anything for children that lacked a pronounced educational purpose. And when the serious-minded decided that the poor child too should be improved, the two classes had so drawn away from each other that a completely new cottage literature had to be provided. It would be decades before class distinction in children's reading vanished and it was reckoned that the same book could serve both worlds.

Even in 1887, when Charlotte Yonge published her advice on the choice of reward books and the equipping of parish libraries *(What Books to Give and What to Lend),* she included a section which she called "drawing-room stories." By then the children in the board schools and parish schools and those who were being educated at home by governesses and mammas might meet on common ground with, say, *The Water Babies* on the one hand, and *Little Meg's Children* on the other. But there were still whole areas where the literary style or a background completely remote from their experience or knowledge put books beyond the range of cottage children. Miss Yonge was well aware of this difficulty; she had read scores of books aloud to her classes at Otterbourne school, and knew just what held their attention and what would send their eyes and their minds wandering.

To a certain extent the old ways lingered. There still were enough parents uninfected by the modern cult of the rational and the learned child, or too lethargic to keep up with the new prestige names, who went on buying the sort of books they had had in their childhood. John Harris, the successor of Newbery, catered for this public in the early years of the nineteenth century. It was he who published *Little Rhymes for Little Folks* (1823) with its delicately tinted pictures of children both of the gentle and the humble sort playing in gilded salons or on cottage doorsteps: *The Talking Bird, or Dame Trudge and her Parrot* (1806) in the Mother Hubbard tradition, and the dangerously subversive *The Courtship and Marriage of Jerry and Kitty* (1814), an "elegant engraving" and a rhyme per page, which finishes

> *And Jerry was sick of his sweet little Wife*
> *Jerry alone, Jerry alone*
> *Jerry was sick of his dear little Wife*
> *And wish'd he alone could be.*
> *So he told her the Sea was not very deep*
> *And popp'd her in when she went up to peep.*
> *Oh! fye Mr Leary, where is your deary?*
> *Just gone a bathing said he.*

To this example of boisterous humor (though this is not the adjective Mrs. Trimmer would have used) we might add two other relics of an age when jokes of the rough sort were perfectly acceptable; both of them untouched by the new sensibility that had come into fashion. *The Little Boys Laughingstock, or New Figures of Fun* (Hodgson & Co., 1822) pairs grotesque handcolored copperplates with rhymes to match. There is a tight-laced dandy, a one-legged black man, a bandy-legged "dandazette," all for rude little boys to laugh at.

The same rude little boys undoubtedly would have enjoyed *Monsieur Tonson* (Juvenile Library, 41 Skinner Street, 1808), which records the exploits of Tom King, an actor and notorious prankster, who solemnly presents himself each night at the house of an inoffensive French couple in Soho, asking for a mythical Mr. Thompson. There is a triumphant conclusion.

> *At length King's wild perplexing plan*
> *The Frenchman so did goad,*
> *That the poor persecuted man*
> *Soon shifted his abode.*

But this sort of "unimproved" coarseness is rare. Marching side by side with the new children's literature which provided for the informed, sensible being that the up-to-date parent wished his child to be, are plenty of moral tales with an earthy directness, that seem to stem from the old-style Newbery tradition, even though they are perhaps told with a simpering elegance of style that belongs to the end of the century.

There is the Awful Warning story, where bad conduct meets with immediate and violent physical results, of the sort that seems to us now who have been brought up on Belloc's *Cautionary Tales,* to be a parody of itself. Naughty disobedient boys lose an eye or a limb or their bowels, or blow up their fathers with fireworks so that they are orphaned and obliged to become chimney sweeps instead of going to a genteel boarding school. Even Mrs. Trimmer, that arbiter of all that was good and proper, wrote a fable of this sort among others in *Easy Lessons.* Julia Sandford will persist in eating the ends of her thread. It unrolls itself in her stomach "and got a-bout her bow-els, and ti-ed them to-ge-ther in pla-ces." She dies of course.

All the moralizing in this simple-minded literature has a materialistic approach. It goes with the industry theme that was so common in the early books. Work hard enough and you will ride in your own coach. The classic tale of the idle and the industrious apprentice appears in many forms. In *Juvenile Philosophy* (Vernor and Hood, 1801), Mrs. Wilson even manages to cure her son Thomas of his idle habits by showing him Hogarth's engravings on the subject. And in *A Step to Fortune* (a two-penny booklet published without any date by G. Thompson and J. Evans), George Graceful, who is so diligent in learning the history of England and the rules of grammar, rises to the giddy heights of a partner-ship with a rich West India merchant and residence in Jamaica.

An extreme example of the conflation of virtue and self-interest occurs in the tale of *A Mother's Affection* in *The Youth's Cabinet* (D. Omer Smith, n.d.). Snellgrave, "a man truly commendable for his humanity, was the captain of an English vessel engaged in the African slave trade." He manages to bribe an African chief with the gift of blue beads to yield him a little boy he specially covets. This proves to be the child of a woman already on the slave ship, and she is so overwhelmed with grati-tude that she persuades the other captives to be submissive and obedient and give him an easy passage home. "This historical fact . . . will serve to confirm a truth which cannot be too often repeated, and that is, that virtuous actions are always conducive to personal interest."

Conversely, materialistic arguments are used to counter wrongdoing. The social disadvantages are stressed. Take the approach to falsehood in *Early Impressions* (J. Hatchard & Son, 1828), a book distinguished by its attractive lithographs by Denis Dighton. James habitually lies to his protector and is dismissed from his service. "Falsehoods are very soon detected. . . . We must therefore take great care to avoid [the habit] if we wish to be believed and respected by others."

In the same spirit is the condemnation of thieving in *The Half-Holiday Taskbook* (Hodgson & Co., n.d.), whose anonymous author (he signed the preface "J.N.") recommended that his trite little reflections should be committed to memory on half-holidays. He pointed out what a draw-back stealing was. "If thieves could but see how foolish they look when detected, they would be ashamed to commit so wicked and degrading a crime."

J.N. contents himself by showing loss of face; most of his contempo-raries would triumphantly have sent their thief to the gallows. "I think, my dear," says the father to the mother in Dorothy Kilner's *Life and*

Perambulation of a Mouse, after rebuking his children for small deceits, "I have heard you mention a person whom you were acquainted with when a girl, who at last was hanged for stealing, I think, was not she?" "No," says the mother casually, "she was not hanged, she was transported for one-and-twenty years . . . but she died before that time was out as many of them do.

Different consequences, perhaps, but the spirit is the same. Certainly there is no mention of sin, the first word that the evangelicals would have used. "These entertaining authors seldom ground their stories on any intimation that human nature is corrupt; that the young reader is helpless and wants assistance; that he is guilty and wants pardon," wrote Hannah More in *Coelebs*.

Be punctual and diligent, obedient and dutiful, do not lie or thieve or blow up your sister, beware of mad dogs and gaming, and you will live to be a successful sugar planter and to give your rivals a handsome funeral. This in essence seems to be the uncomplicated and cheerful message of the old-style late Georgian book. It was a message that various schools of thought found lacking.

Reviews

Children's Verse

Four Styles

A. Harris Fairbanks

Where the Sidewalk Ends, by Shel Silverstein. Illustrated by the author. (Harper and Row, $7.95.)
Let's Marry Said the Cherry and Other Nonsense Poems, by N. M. Bodecker. Illustrated by the author. (Atheneum, $4.95.)
That Was Summer, by Marci Ridlon. Illustrated by Mia Carpenter. (Follett, $3.50.)
The Way Things Are and Other Poems, by Myra Cohn Livingston. Illustrated by Jenni Oliver. (Atheneum, $4.95.)

N. M. Bodecker's *Let's Marry Said the Cherry* is a slim volume of high-quality nonsense verse. Mr. Bodecker's forte is playing inventively with words within the bounds of demanding nonsense formulas. While the title poem is based on the simple "Cock Robin" formula, others are more complex and original. "If I Were an Elephant," for example, employs stanza pairs in which the second stanza offers a comic definition for an alternative meaning of the noun that concludes the first stanza:

> If I were an elephant,
> I would love my trunk.
> If I were a junk man,
> I would love my junk.
>
> *You don't know what a junk is?*
> *It's an ancient Chinese craft*
> *that's not quite like a clipper*
> *and not quite like a raft.*

The most engaging aspect of *Let's Marry* is that one is constantly coming upon a new poem written according to one of two nonsense formulas. Seven of the thirty-three poems are descriptions of imaginary islands. The cleverest is "The Island of Yarrow":

> The island of Yarrow
> was long, low, and narrow,
> too long to hoe
> and too slim to harrow.
> They tried with a plow,
> but the sea filled the narrow
> deep furrow that once
> was the island of Yarrow.

165

The other recurrent type, which appears nine times, is the nonsense portrait of such a figure as

> Sitter Bitter
> (baby-sitter
> Violet Amanda Bitter)

who took her duties literally and sat *on* babies, knitting and drinking tea as she worked. Each poem of this type ends with a section beginning "When they said . . ." or the like, followed by a description of the subject's response:

> When they cried:
> "AMANDA BITTER!
> Most outrageous baby-sitter
> BITTER! You get off that knee!"
> She inquired:
> "Want some tea?"

Mr. Bodecker's poems are almost subtle (if the term can be applied to nonsense verse) in their dependency on nuance and the arch turn of phrase. His black-and-white drawings are equally elegant, detailed, and controlled; the lines are crisp, resembling those of an engraver, and frequently appear to have been drawn with a straightedge and compass.

Shel Silverstein's *Where the Sidewalk Ends* could hardly be more different in character. The poems are raucous and zany, and the drawings sprawl delightfully across the page. In at least nine instances, poem and illustration are so interdependent that the child—or adult, for that matter—has the pleasure of making connections and sharing a joke with the poet. For instance, in "The Loser," a boy has lost his head—literally. He can't look for it since his eyes are in it, can't call to it because his mouth is in it, and so on, so he guesses he will "sit down on this rock" and rest for a minute. Illustration: he is sitting on his lost head. Again, "Melinda Mae" begins on a two-page spread showing a little girl with a fork sitting at a table occupied, and overflowed, by a whale. Text:

> Have you heard of tiny Melinda Mae,
> Who ate a monstrous whale?
> She thought she could,
> She said she would,
> So she started in right at the tail.
> And everyone said, "You're much too small,"
> But that didn't bother Melinda at all.
> She took little bites and she chewed very slow,
> Just like a good girl should . . .

(Turn to the next two-page spread)

> . . . And in eighty-nine years she ate that whale
> Because she said she would!

(Illustration: same chair, same table, but Melinda Mae is eighty-nine years older and the whale is reduced to curlicues of rib.)

Silverstein has gifts rarely found in children's poets, most particularly the gift of direct communication with the roguish, playful, and uncivilized tendencies of healthy children. In many of the poems he establishes a tone of delicious complicity with the child's disobedient, naughty, asocial, or even wicked impulses. "For Sale" is the chant of a boy auctioning off his "crying and spying young sister." A more typical example is "My Hobby":

> When you spit from the twenty-sixth floor,
> And it floats on the breeze to the ground,
> Does it fall upon hats
> Or on white Persian cats
> Or on heads, with a pitty-pat sound?
> I used to think life was a bore,
> But I don't feel that way anymore,
> As I count up the hits,
> As I smile as I sit,
> As I spit from the twenty-sixth floor.

Silverstein has no patience with moralizing, either parental or literary. One poem argues that either Ma or God must be wrong, since

> God gave us fingers—Ma says, "Use your hanky."
> God gave us puddles—Ma says, "Don't splash."

"The Little Blue Engine," after three stanzas of apparent fidelity to the narrative and tone of "The Little Engine That Could," concludes:

> He was almost there, when—CRASH! SMASH! BASH!
> He slid down and mashed into engine hash
> On the rocks below . . . which goes to show
> If the track is tough and the hill is rough,
> THINKING you can just ain't enough.

"The Land of Happy" is directed against the kind of children's verse that Silverstein does *not* write:

> Have you been to The Land of Happy,
> Where everyone's happy all day,
> Where they joke and they sing
> Of the happiest things,

> And everything's jolly and gay?
> There's no one unhappy in Happy,
> There's laughter and smiles galore.
> I have been to The Land of Happy—
> What a bore!

Bodecker and Silverstein follow the mainstream of children's verse in their reliance on humor, rollicking rhythms, and pouncing rhyme. Myra Cohn Livingston, in about half the poems in *The Way Things Are and Other Poems,* tries to do without meter and rhyme, and in some of them without humor also. Well, why not write free verse on serious themes for children?

Unfortunately, Ms. Livingston's poems are so flat and diffuse that they do not provide a fair test for this question. In her title poem she undertakes the forbidding challenge of telling children "The Way Things Are":

> It's today,
>   This road,
>   This knowing the road is there.
>   A few brambles,
>   A few tangles,
>   A few scratches,
>   A rough stone against your toe,
>   But still, you've got to go
>   And take it.
>   Fast, sometimes,
>   Or slow,
>   But go—
>   everywhere.
>   anywhere
>   You need
>   to go.

The main problem with this poem, aside from its sententiousness, is that once the hackneyed metaphor of the road of life is introduced, everything else follows predictably. "A few brambles" leads inevitably to "A few tangles"; "Fast, sometimes," to "Or slow"; "everywhere" to "anywhere." Secondly, the poem lacks that vital coalescence of what is said with the way it is said that should justify its being presented as poetry at all. For instance, the necessity that the child should push on despite brambles and tangles is never made concrete, but instead comes across in a series of lifeless lines such as "But still you've got to go." Free verse, in surrendering rhyme and stanza as even the weakest excuses for a line's existence, incurs the obligation to make every line and every word in it self-justifying. It cannot admit a line of conjunctions, flabby verbs, and spiritless qualifiers that fail to exploit either the imagistic, connotative, or polysemantic potentialities of language. The Imagists and other early proponents of free verse realized that the only point in abandoning traditional rhythms was to allow the poem to discover its own: "A new cadence means a new idea." They discovered early that except in the long line of Whitman or Ginsburg, free verse rhythms were deadened by the steady coincidence between line and syntactic unit that characterizes Ms. Livingston's poems.

The fact that Ms. Livingston cannot write effective free verse suitable for children does not prove that it cannot be done; indeed, William Carlos Williams' well known "Poem" ("As the cat . . .") is a conclusive counterexample. Yet the task poses difficulties. For one thing, while verse strongly measured, accented, and rhymed is an aural form, with its lines and stanzas perceptible to the ear alone, free verse is a visual form. Consider this line-group from Pound's "The Return":

> See, they return; ah, see the tentative
> Movements, and the slow feet,
> The trouble in the pace and the uncertain
> Wavering!

For these lines to have full impact, the reader must sense the effect of the line break between "tentative" and "Movements," and between "uncertain" and "Wavering." He must also sense the first line as a whole, so that the tension between the three strong pauses and the impetus of the line is perceptible. The ability to appreciate verse techniques of this sort demands sophistication and perhaps even education, while the appreciation of rhyme and regular accentuation is visceral and present in the child even before he understands the meaning of the words.

We must also consider that traditional children's verse depends so heavily on wit not because children have low tastes or because they are incapable of serious thought and emotion, but because wit provides a way of charging language with meanings—of giving the verbal medium that independent interest essential to poetry—without demanding the extensive vocabulary or awareness of connotative nuance that come only with age and experience.

Marci Ridlon's *That Was Summer* draws many—though by no means all—of its themes and images from the city. The book includes some nonsense verse, skip-rope rhymes, and a charming urban counting rhyme:

> Ten cars parked in a parking lot.
> Some can run and some cannot.
> Number one is out of gas
> Number two has broken glass . . . [etc.].

Many of Ms. Ridlon's poems explore moods and impulses distinctive of childhood: the frustration of being excluded from adult conversations, the urge to run away, anger at being ignored, night fears, and so forth. Sometimes these are handled with humorous exaggeration or wit:

> What did you do?
> Where did you go?
> Why weren't you back
> An *hour* ago?
>
> How come your shirt's
> Ripped on the sleeve?
> Why are you wet?
> When did you leave?
>   (from "Questions")

Even in poems that enter with complete sympathy into troublesome childhood moods, some light touch of humor or the resurgence of a more mature perspective keeps the poems from seeming to endorse self-pity, as in this concluding stanza of a poem called "Angry," about a child who has crawled behind the front stairs in resentment at being rebuffed and ignored:

> After I've been there awhile
> And find that I can almost smile,
> I brush me off and count to ten
> And try to start the day again.

Let's Marry Said the Cherry is not directed chiefly towards children, unless it is on the assumption, probably false, that children have a livelier appreciation of nonsense than adults. The other three volumes all make some attempt to adopt the child's perspective, explore his values seriously or comically, and offer him vicarious ventilation of his impulses. Each of these three volumes includes a poem on the child's attitudes toward a new baby, and in each case the poem serves to illustrate the psychological depth, general emotional character, and level of technical competency of the volume from which it is taken.

First, Ms. Ridlon's "My Brother":

> My brother's worth about two cents,
> As far as I can see.

I simply cannot understand
Why they would want a "he."

He spends a good part of his day
Asleep inside the crib,
And when he eats, he has to wear
A stupid baby bib.

He cannot walk and cannot talk
And cannot throw a ball.
In fact, he can't do anything—
He's just no fun at all.

It would have been more sensible,
As far as I can see,
Instead of getting one like him
To get one just like me.

This poem formulates the specific grounds of the child's resentment: jealousy at the deflection of parental attention, compounded by a sense of injured merit. The child reading this poem has the pleasure of seeing his perfectly reasonable gripe skillfully and sympathetically defined; at the same time, the last stanza presents with understanding and gentle humor the egotistical premise on which the child's case rests.

Ms. Livingston's "New Baby" has less psychological insight, the child's basis for resentment now being the baby's freedom from responsibility. In her short lines, where compression is essential and where the surprise level must be maintained, we have only a humorless and unimaginative catalogue of the most obvious obligations of the older child:

Whoever's the new baby around here
    has it o.k.
Just crying and eating and sleeping all day.
No schoolwork.
No chores.
No trash to empty.
No slamming doors.
No nothing to do but lie around and play.

From the second line on, this poem, like the title poem quoted earlier, is completely predictable. After "schoolwork" we expect "chores"; after "chores," emptying the trash. True, the line "No slamming doors" is a surprise, but only because it makes no sense in context. How is a baby free of "slamming doors" in a way that the older sibling is not? I am forced to conclude that in a poem where the rhyme is obscured by chaotic rhythms anyhow, Ms. Livingston has managed to trap herself into a rhyme-forced line.

Shel Silverstein, as we have already seen, has his own forthright style of writing for children. No gentle and sympathetic explorations of the child's destructive impulses for him:

DREADFUL

Someone ate the baby,
It's rather sad to say.
Someone ate the baby
So she won't be out to play.
   We'll never hear her whiney cry
   Or have to feel if she is dry.
   We'll never hear her asking "Why?"
   Someone ate the baby.

Someone ate the baby.
It's absolutely clear
Someone ate the baby
'Cause the baby isn't here.
   We'll give away her toys and clothes.
   We'll never have to wipe her nose.
   Dad says, "That's the way it goes."
   Someone ate the baby.

Someone ate the baby.
What a frightful thing to eat!
Someone ate the baby
Though she wasn't very sweet.
   It was a heartless thing to do.
   The policemen haven't got a clue.
   I simply can't imagine who
   Would go and (burp) eat the baby.

Mapping Numinous Ground

Wayne Dodd

The Spring on the Mountain, by Judy Allen. 153 pp. (Farrar, Straus, & Giroux. $4.95.)

Sweetwater, by Laurence Yep. Pictures by Julia Noonan. Ages 10 and up. 201 pp. (Harper & Row. $5.50.)

Stag Boy, by William Rayner. 160 pp. Ages 12 and up. (Harcourt, Brace, Jovanovich. $4.25.)

A Wind in the Door, by Madeleine L'Engle. 211 pp. (Farrar, Straus, & Giroux. $4.95.)

Mysticism, magic, a sense of the supernatural—it's in the air nowadays, from astrology to Zen, from exorcism to witches. It should not be surprising, therefore, that writers of books for children are incorporating this interest into their work, or even launching out onto it as the true sea, to be explored and experienced. There is, of course, nothing new about the presence of the wonderful in children's books. And a serious concern for the numinous was as strong in George MacDonald as it was to be later in C. S. Lewis. What is perhaps noteworthy is the number of works that now offer to map this territory, of which these four books are examples.

Fantasy/science fiction has always seemed to be at least a second-cousin to the authentically visionary. The very spring of its conception would appear to be a dissatisfaction with the merely ordinary, with the generally verifiable, the mundane. In short, it has, at its best, a yearning for more, for "other." Laurence Yep's *Sweetwater* reflects and embodies that yearning. And at moments the feeling for it is truly present in the bitter-sweet tone of the book, as these future descendants of the human residents of earth struggle to perpetuate a dying way of life and its system of values on another planet, which has for generations been their home. Nostalgia, loss, regret, even the sense of the largeness, the vastness of life (human and nonhuman) in which they participate—these emotions anchor this writing in the firm substance of loss-longing that is involved in the quest for the unknown.

But *Sweetwater* shares a major problem of fantasy/science fiction whenever it leaves the familiar terrain of this world, earth. It has to introduce the reader to another literal world. It has to convince him of its physical presence. It's a difficult task, particularly if the setting is to be not only another world, but even a change from a dry-land existence to a life on and in the water. Yep almost succeeds in making this existence come fully alive, but the life remains somehow alien, for all its sympathetic beauty. And that fact may well keep readers from going back to this book a second time, to relive the experience. Still, *Sweetwater* does have the energies of authentic emotions, and that is a considerable strength.

Madeleine L'Engle's new book, *A Wind in the Door,* also attempts to get to the spiritual by way of fantasy/science fiction. But she also takes other routes as well: namely both the "dragon" road and that familiar street that runs through the unnoticed gap in the everyday and into the beyond. The result is that, in terms of wonder, we get nowhere. Mrs. L'Engle really can't make up her mind whether she wants the reader to be involved in the realistic dimension of her story (which is rendered with superfluous and unselective detail) or to be caught up in the discovery of the "other" in our lives. The idea for this story is a promising one: the discovery (by the children) of the presence, in the strange illness of one little boy, of a whole universe of struggle between good and evil, order and chaos, integration and disintegration. This is the same territory C. S. Lewis worked, both in the chronicles of Narnia and in the Perelandra series for adults. The difference is that genuine wonder is never present in *A Wind in the Door.* The problem appears to be one of writing, primarily. For not only is there a confusion of routes (lack of commitment?) but also the spiritual (galactic) dimension, once moved into, is simply too confusingly vague and obscure to win acceptance. In addition, the treatment of the realistic point of departure is too charmingly eccentric, even, finally, clichéd—that is, cliché ideas of charmingly eccentric people. Moreover, *A Wind in the Door* shares what appears to be the burden of all fantasy/science fiction: only the idea really interests the writer.

Judy Allen, in *The Spring on the Mountain,* and William Rayner, in *Stag Boy,* take a more single road into the beyond. Theirs is the world of the familiar, more English story, in which we start with a summer (or autumn) vacation in an atmospherically potent remote country cottage and move, steadily and inevitably, into an experience of the mysterious. But though the beginnings are similar and the destinations, in a very loose sense, the same, their ways of going are very different.

The Spring on the Mountain employs many of the devices of the more mundane mystery story to entertain and engage us on our journey. And the old-fashioned adventure combines with some of the waystops of the holiday romance to forward this story through what seems, after all, unthreatening enough country. To an extent, therefore, this unusual combination of narrative ingredients reinforces the strangeness of the encounter with the "other" when it is finally made, atop a mountain on a familiar English countryside. For a time, at least, the reader seems close to an authentic sense of wonder, a sense that other meanings, other powers, quite simply do exist. But the trail of mystery/adventure-story clues and questions continues to stretch both forward and backward, so that a feeling of contrivance is perhaps a bit too strong for it to last.

William Rayner's course is quite different. It takes us very quickly into a sudden and utterly mysterious experience of the temporary transformation (through some sort of totemic power) of an adolescent boy into a powerful stag. From that point on, the author moves the reader steadily deeper into this experience (no explanation, no apology), at times fearful, at times joyful, and into the living involvement the boy makes and must deal with in this personal focus of natural and supernatural, modern and primitive, commonplace and magical. It is a gripping story, and there are moments when wonder is surely present.

Family Relationships and the Growing-up Task in Four Recent Novels for Adolescents

Eleanore Braun Luckey

A Family Failing, by Honor Arundel. (Thomas Nelson, Inc., $4.25.)
They'll Never Make a Movie Starring Me, by Alice Bach. (Harper & Row, $4.95.)
Remove Protective Coating a Little at a Time, by John Donovan. (Harper & Row, $3.95.)
The Summer Before, by Patrica Windsor. (Harper & Row, $4.95.)

Adolescence should be seen as a segment of continuing development which ordinarily links a dependent, family-dominated period of human life with an independent, responsible-for-self, ready-for-life kind of experience. The chief task of the adolescent years is stepping away from parents and looking at them more as people and less as "keepers." This involves not only looking back into the childhood years but peering speculatively into the future when "I will be grown up." It is a period of experimentation, of making decisions, some of which are "right" ones, of making commitments, of experiencing new people and places, of dreaming and converting dreams into reality and being able to tell which is which.

One of the most important developmental tasks of adolescence is to learn how people "are" with one another and how one is him/herself with others. Basic to this understanding is one's adolescent perception of one's own family and one's role in it.

One criterion, then, for "good" reading for the teen years would be how well the literature helps the reader assess his or her family situation: its patterns of interaction and communication, and especially the relationship of the adolescent to other family members. What are the subtle familial influences that either encourage or inhibit the teenager in the task of cutting free of parental authority and assuming responsibility for his own life? The story that helps the adolescent discover these strands might well be judged a "good" one, and by that standard two of the reviewed books are top rate.

In *A Family Failing,* Arundel has portrayed through amazingly real-life conversations the changing relationships, over a period of time, of husband and wife, mother and daughter, father and daughter, mother and son, father and son, sister and brother. Each person is both an individual and a family member with his own peculiar ties to every other member. The basic concept that one's feeling about others and one's behavior toward them is determined by how one feels about oneself is beautifully demonstrated in the father's rising resentment of his son as his own self-esteem falls. The importance of one's sense of identity as based in one's profession is emphasized by the crumbling of the stable, happy husband-wife relationship when father loses his job and mother succeeds at hers. The most vivid and empathically portrayed relationship is that between the daughter, who is the first-person storyteller, and her father.

The story is written with crisp, down-to-earth language—most of it in direct-quotation dialogue that reveals the character and feeling of the participants. It is an honest presentation of a family as it falls apart— its unhappiness, its saving graces, and, very poignantly, its pain in separation.

The Summer Before shares many of the same literary virtues: it is a sensitively written, honest book that leaves no doubt in the reader's mind about the reality of its characters. But because the theme is centered more on the narrator herself and less on the family, and because its action revolves around the accidental death of a loved youth rather than the break-up of a family, the familial relationships are less vividly portrayed. Young people who have not had emotional breakdowns that require psychiatric care and hospitalization, who have not run away to join a commune or who have not been in automobile accidents, will have more difficulty in identifying with Apple Alex Sandy Alexandra, but they will have little trouble in recognizing the feelings she has toward her parents —impatience, disdain, love, admiration, fear, anger—the gamut.

Death and the guilt of feeling "it was my fault" are heavy concepts for even adults to deal with, and a teenaged reader would have to do some stretching to cope with the depth of the book; yet its story flows so well and its language is so clear that one enters into the story as if it were one's own. Sandy's growing-up process is different from most, yet it has aspects familiar to all.

They'll Never Make a Movie Starring Me falls far short of helping the teenager discover much about family relationships or even self in the process of growing-up. Parental relationships are shallow, stereotypical, and not presented with insight. Alice is the only child of pampering, "impossible" parents who are apparently quite good at game-playing— as is Alice herself. The book introduces two sexual themes, lesbianism and contraceptive measures, but does not deal with either of them. It is as if the author dared not do more than mention "having a crush on" a senior girl and the word "diaphram." This "touch it and drop it" game is the same one the parents in the book play, and teenaged readers will not miss seeing through it.

Donovan's *Remove Protective Coating a Little at a Time,* unlike the other three books reviewed, has a male for its main character—Harry, aged fourteen, the child of parents who are barely in their thirties. We are told in the third paragraph of the book that "Harry's dad slipped it to his mother that glorious night, on the beach in front of the hotel, and she got pregnant with Harry." Other sexual episodes of mutual masturbation and unsuccessfully trying to make it with a camp girl at thirteen are reported with the same lack of delicacy, which may be the author's intent to define the male attitude toward sex.

The primary relationship in the book is that between Harry and Amelia, a seventy-two year old female derelict whom he meets in the park and visits in her condemned apartment house hideaway. This is a relationship that is far more fantasy than probability. There is, however, an interesting contrast depicted in the honesty and straightforwardness of Harry's relationship with Amelia and his relationship with what seems to be mere cardboard caricatures of Bud and Toots, his parents. One gains almost no feeling of what goes on between Bud, a professionally successful, pal-like father, and Harry; between Harry and Toots, the emotionally disturbed and depressed mother, nothing much at all goes on. The protective covering of all the characters is so thick that it is hardly worth the reading; one is left to wonder if perhaps this is not what the author is cynically saying about adolescents, families, people, dogs, and life itself.

The three books with women authors have much more in common than any of them has with Donovan's book. They definitely appeal to female readers and have a good deal to say about where young women are today. They each deal to some extent with the question of premarital intercourse; two of them deal very realistically with communal living and the relationships that may exist in communes. All strive to be open and nonjudgmental with regard to sexual values. All portray the difficulties of becoming free of one's parents and becoming one's own woman. However, it is hard to reconcile the characteristics of the mother-role models with the hoped-for characteristics of the adolescent girl who is becoming an adult female. Far from glorifying wifery or motherhood, the authors each have depicted mothers as nagging, complaining, not understanding, possessive and manipulative, weak or silly even in success. Except for Arundel, the authors are much less definitive about fathers: they are also less derogatory. Fathers are generally more sensible, less talkative, less emotional, stronger in character and good judgment, or if they are not these things and are barely something more than a zero, they still have all these attributes as potentials. The social transition from the traditional family to the liberated female that today's adolescent girl expects to become is not easily portrayed; it is apparently even more difficult to portray an insightful, mature woman who has freely chosen to be a wife and mother and who fulfills these roles well.

Photography as Children's Literature

Ted Wolner

The Eye of Conscience: *Photographers and Social Change,* edited by
Milton Meltzer and Bernard Cole. (Follett, $6.95.)
Looking at Architecture, by Roberta M. Paine. (Lothrop, Lee & She-
pard, $6.95.)

For children, magical associations may easily attach themselves to the
camera, to the process of freezing and preserving on film a moment in
time. The camera mysteriously catches images inside it; by a leap of the
imagination, it may also seize something of the essence of what is photographed. The primitive's fear that the camera will rob him of his spiritual
being, that the act of photography is itself deviltry, is akin to the child's
fascination with a dark box that in one click captures light and form. The
camera inspires awe because it seems to imply the use of surreptitious
power. It is the conceit that the people photographed, even while posing
in conscious knowledge of the camera's presence, do not know that
something is being taken from them.

Like all magic that enchants, photography is surrounded by ritual,
adding to a child's unarticulated sense of the power of the camera.
Focusing, testing for light exposure, and opening the shutter for an
instant are all limited, rigidly defined actions which produce magical
results seemingly out of proportion to the effort expended. The necessary
element of taboo attending all ritual is present in the prohibition against
exposing film to light. The liquid alchemy of the darkroom further
deepens the mystery of the camera, and accords greater power to both
photographer and photograph. The transubstantiation of film occurs at
the moment of its immersion in a chemical bath; white development
paper is miraculously consecrated to produce an image.

Photographs themselves play host to a child's curiosity, recording
strange moments and new happenings. The visual presentation of a
reality beyond the child's immediate experience, its transportation from
there to the child through the medium of the photograph, must play
upon his sense of wonder. Unlike most cartoons, which employ imaginary characters in a completely self-contained fantasy world, photographs invite the child to ask questions about the incomplete reality they
present. Cartoons may induce excitement and exclamation but their
narrative closure denies questions. The story a photograph tells, by
contrast, is only implicit in its image; the story consists of the answers

to the questions the child asks as his curiosity moves him to fill in the narrative gaps that a photograph suggests but does not reveal.

Such considerations are especially true of the documentary photograph. It places limitations on the extent to which the formal elements of composition can be emphasized. These elements—of line sharpness, focus, filtering, framing, mood, and the modulation of shadow—cannot be self-consciously displayed in photo documentation. They must be disciplined, limited, and given direction by the documentary intent, made to serve social and political ends. The statement of suffering or victimization must be direct, must be the controlling element in the photograph's composition. It is this directness, the photo's legibility as drama and history, that makes this kind of photography particularly attractive to children. For it focuses on people and hints at a larger story, encouraging questions that will complete the narrative suggested by the image.

The Eye of Conscience, a book of documentary photographs, is not written and edited expressly for children. But on the above grounds, and for other reasons as well, it may have an immense appeal for them. Many of the photographs in the book are of children. Among them are Dorothea Lange's Depression waifs and Jacob Riis' Lower East Side: its overcrowded, gaslit classrooms in condemned schools, its homeless boys sleeping on stoops, curled into one another like animals. And there are Lewis Hine's haunting child miners, illegally exploited for their labor, dressed like little men in jackets and gloves too big for them, their faces blank and stained with coal dust, their bodies and wills broken at age ten.

In these photos, children can see not reflections but *refractions* of themselves, for the photographed children are victims, orphans of social inequality. The photos may bring a child to sense his own relative impotence in a world where the balance of power lies with adults, his own helpless innocence before a potentially exploitative environment.

The book also taps a child's psychic life in less bleak ways. In the brief biographies preceding each photographer's work, the editors' prose and vocabulary are deliberately simplified in order to convey the social outrage and serious intent of the photographers: their hope that a visual documentation of suffering—more powerful, accessible, and immediate in impact than a purely verbal record—would yield reform. This stylistic posture unnecessarily romanticizes them, but it seems apt for children because it transforms the photographers' lives into stories of heroes who tried to do right:

> [Jacob Riis'] unrelenting struggle wiped out the horror of
> Mulberry Bend, brought light to dark hallways, cleaner water to

tenement taps, desks to schoolrooms, settlement houses to slums, and improved conditions to factories. The camera was only the tool a humane man needed to express the misery and squalor he found in the slums.

The biographies, then, call upon a child's desire for a moral universe of Manichean simplicity—absolute evil pitted against absolute good. Because the photographers are presented as heroes, they appeal to a child's relatively untested powers of trust, to his will to believe in supermen, to his comparatively uncurbed sense of omnipotence.

In related fashion, the photographers' lives appeal to children on the level of sheer adventure. Here the photographers become moral swashbucklers abroad in dangerous territory. To take his photographs of the Civil War, Timothy O'Sullivan risked his life "amidst the excitement, the rapid movements and the smoke of the battlefield." Lewis Hine, also at great peril, hid his camera in a lunchpail and passed himself off as a fire inspector to get inside textile mills exploiting child labor. When Jacob Riis first came to the United States, he bought "the biggest revolver he could find. He strapped it outside his coat and paraded up Broadway, ready for the buffaloes and Indians he'd read about." Later, as a reporter, he witnessed street fights and gang warfare and photographed ominous locales like Bandits' Roost. Other newsmen called him the "boss reporter" and "The Dutchman." Landlords hated him because he exposed their practice "of jamming fifteen people into one or two rooms." For children, the text and the photos in combination are morality made animate with the photographer as romantic hero in a drama of man and magical machine against evil.

Several of the photographers' lives reflect in some measure their subjects' experience of suffering. O'Sullivan and his family were forced to flee the Irish potato famine of 1841. Dorthea Lange was lame from birth; she said it "formed me, guided me, instructed me, helped me, and humiliated me. . . . My lameness as a child and my acceptance, finally, of my lameness truly opened gates for me." Riis in his early poverty was forced to mine coal, cut timber, harvest ice, sell furniture, peddle flatirons, shiver in doorways, and sleep in stinking vagrants' rooms at police stations before he landed a respectable reporter's position at the *New York Tribune.* These experiences of the photographers add to the power of their photographs, enhance a child's understanding of the suffering they portray, and enlarge his sense of the photographers' conviction and the rightness of their course of action.

The victims in the photographs of O'Sullivan, Riis, Hine, and Lange are, of course, anonymous as individuals. Their collective pain is not; in retrospect, it is at least partly redeemed and dignified because it forms an integral part of crucial historical periods—the Civil War, the immigrant movement to American cities, the Great Depression, the decades of child labor and attempts at unionization.

Fung Lam's photographs of physically handicapped children differ markedly. The world of the handicapped child is an entirely private and hidden one, unconnected to events in the larger society. Because their stigmata are visible, undeniable, and permanent, we are tempted to deny them *any* future or responsibility in our rush to pity them; we may make victims of them when they are not. Lam's achievement is that his beautifully rendered photos break through this overlay of pity which hinders us from seeing handicapped children as human. He relieves us of the insistent victimization in the work of the other photographers. His photos are moments in the everyday life of the handicapped child: crippled children laughing together, hanging out on a porch, taking a first swimming lesson. Lam's photos are quietly lyrical, mute celebrations of ordinary life removed from history and the passage of time.

If Lam's photos fall outside history's compass, the other photographs in this book, because of their power as images, skew history by inflating the role of the photographer as an agent of social change. The editors in their text aggressively promote this distortion. Their viewpoint is uncritical, and they make no effort to set the documentarists in the perspective of other variables that led to reform. This further concentrates the power of the photographs, granting the photographers an Olympian presence in the flow of events.

But it is precisely this exaggeration that gives a child purchase on the notion of history itself. A child ten or eleven years old can see in the photographs other children of undeniably different social circumstances from his own. His curiosity stimulated and his feelings aroused, he can turn to the text or talk to someone who can help him fill in the gaps in the photographs' unclosed narrative. Perhaps, then, he senses the possibility of change. Because social arrangements are different for him, he may even sense that they could have been different for the photographed children, had people cared and acted sooner.

The photographs are thus subversive of comparatively linear, fact-oriented textbook history. For they provide a tactile link from the child-reader's present to the child-victim's past. The photographs join them in their common humanity through a demonstration, however vicarious, of their shared vulnerability before the threat of victimization. Paradoxically, through the example of the photographers' lives, they embrace a wider faith in the power of men to act.

A child's relation to architectural images, to photographs of buildings rather than people, is necessarily more abstract. His anthropomorphic imagination and fantasy-life make it difficult to identify with images of structures. He needs a conceptual framework derived from his experience to engage the information such a photograph presents.

Without this framework, a book on architecture intended for children faces serious problems. Photographs of great architecture, however striking, are already at one remove from a child's reality, unless the photograph is of a building for which the child has first-hand experience. (Here the photo calls up the visual sensations the child garnered while looking at and moving around and through the building.) Photos of the Parthenon, or any other architectural monument from a different time and culture, place the child at a second remove. The text itself pushes him still further away, asking him to absorb details about building structure and design with which he may have had no contact. The book may be designed as a learning experience, but a child's movement through it will be forced, not organic.

Roberta M. Paine's *Looking at Architecture* fails because of these and other problems. The book attempts to introduce eight to twelve year olds to the history and appreciation of architecture. It chronologically presents architectural masterpieces from different historical periods and cultures—Egyptian tomb architecture, Sumerian ziggurats, the Parthenon, the Pantheon, the Gothic cathedral, Mayan and Aztec cities, Versailles, the Crystal Palace, the skyscraper, Habitat. Each building or architectural genre is treated in a chapter of photos and prints, accompanied by a text explaining the central design ideas of each, its structural innovations, the building materials used, and the architect's dependence upon the patron who commissions the building.

The author has long experience at the Metropolitan Museum of Art lecturing on architecture to children. Her lectures and the exhibits she has created for them may be considerably more interesting than this book, for there she can exploit the real resources of the Museum, and the children can see the architecture through her. *Looking at Architecture* probably derives from her lectures. But without the intermediaries of her person and the Museum, the book becomes too formal and didactic. The static tone and content of its text do little to arouse or excite the child, and effectively suffocate any curiosity that the photographs may inspire. This is Paine on classical architecture:

> Classical is a term that means of the first class or of the highest rank. The word classic, or classical, is used to describe both the

architecture and the civilization of fifth-century Greece. Often, too, "classical" is used loosely to describe the culture of the Greeks and Romans.

The book is addressed to the "young reader," an offensive phrase because it implies that children at this age are merely a smaller version of an adult reader. Or worse, it implies that there is a rigidly prescribed set of needs and abilities uniquely characteristic of eight to twelve year olds to which this book has scrupulously tried to adhere.

These notions, reinforced by the book's format and layout, assume horrible things about family life and education. The book generates a picture of the child as Little Scholar, the parents or teachers as Learned Tutors. The book is given to Little Scholar and he is instructed to walk softly to his study, sit erectly in his chair in front of a desk that is too big for him, and read and absorb. After an hour or so, Little Scholar emerges from his mini-library prepared to talk about flying buttresses and *oculae*. Learned Tutor feeds him some more information about structure and possibly treats him to some notions of architectural style, smiles proudly at Little Scholar's mastery, and thinks Little Scholar may just make it to Columbia's History of Art and Architecture Program. At worst, he will be a competent archivist. Very precociously, Little Scholar becomes an old wart.

The book's most objectionable assumption is that architecture is to be found only in large-scale, monumental buildings, not in the built environment familiar to the child. Why not help instruct him in the more prosaic architecture he already knows? Or, if children like erector sets, linked logs, doll houses, and plastic bricks, why not teach them about architecture through three-dimensional puzzles whose pieces match in scale and function the structural and design components of particularly skillfull, arresting, and innovative buildings? A child could then erect the Pantheon and Chartres himself. Or why not give a child another type of three-dimensional puzzle whose pieces would permit the design of, say, seven or eight different houses?

Buildings, stones, steel frames, and pyramids are not exciting to a child if there is no way he can tangibly identify with buildings through their function or form. To appreciate and understand architecture, he must experience it. The built environment, for most children, is unimportant by itself; it exists only as a convenient shell for function. A child's view of architecture tends to be materialistic and static, not dramatic or symbolic of social values; architecture does not seem to be what it really is: a proscenium for a collective cultural experience. Great architecture in photographs tends to appear deceptively inanimate and permanent. The buildings become mere gross formations on the ground, pure form and structure unrelated to everyday life. To comprehend architecture in its distinct phases of design, construction, and cultural expression requires a conceptual knowledge that is difficult to communicate to children in print and photograph.

The documentary photographs of O'Sullivan, Riis, Hine, Lange, and Lam are, of course, nonspatial, nondimensional in their impact. Because these photos are themselves peopled with children, the past resurrected in them activates a child's own storehouse of emotional experience. While no children in this country are victims of a widespread exploitation of child labor, or of a sweeping economic depression, most children do have some experience that is registered in in their own psyches as victimization. In other subtle but powerful ways as well, these photos stimulate a fundamentally literary act, inviting a child to penetrate time and history through an imaginative identification with the photographed children, at once so alike and so dissimilar to children of our own time.

Academic Wonderlands

Edward F. Guiliano

The Philosopher's Alice, introduction and notes by Peter Heath. **Alice's Adventures in Wonderland & Through the Looking-Glass,** by Lewis Carroll with illustrations by John Tenniel. (St. Martin's Press, $10.00.)
Lewis Carroll: *Une vie,* by Jean Gattégno. (Paris: Editions du Seuil, 1974.) Translation forthcoming: Lewis Carroll: *A Life* (Thomas Y. Crowell, Feb. 1976).
Play, Games, and Sport: *The Literary Works of Lewis Carroll,* by Kathleen Blake. (Cornell University Press, 1974, $8.75.)

The literary works of Lewis Carroll have never fallen into disfavor among academicians, or anyone else for that matter. On the contrary, in recent years Carroll's works have enjoyed new popularity on university campuses. They are now regularly found on required reading lists for courses from children's literature and Victorian literature to linguistics and philosophy. This widespread academic emergence is partially responsible for (and further verified by) the increasing number of critical articles on Carroll that appear annually in our leading scholarly journals. Clearly deserving credit as a key contribution to this growth is Martin Gardner's *Annotated Alice,* first published in 1960, which has both opened and entered many doors. Also the times—that is the general social milieu of the late sixties and early seventies—were, and still are, ripe for Carroll's version of sense. In 1974 the publication of three books on Carroll by university professors reflects this increased popularity.

Peter Heath, Professor of Philosophy at the University of Virginia, has produced a second-generation annotated edition of the *Alices* which is keyed upon aspects of logic, philosophy, and the study of language. As Heath affirms in his introduction, and demonstrates through his annotations, the *Alice* books "are works of unsleeping rationality, whose frolics are governed throughout, not by a formal theory of any kind, but by close attention to logical principles, and sometimes by a surprising insight into abstract questions of philosophy."

Perhaps the best way to provide a sense of the book, glibly dubbed on its dust jacket as "The Thinking Man's Guide to a Misunderstood Nursery Classic," is to reproduce a representative annotation. Remember the Duck's interruption of the "driest thing" the Mouse knew? The Duck asks *what* the Archbishop of Canterbury found and the Mouse replies *it.* Well:

The Duck is a sort of illogical positivist. The word *it* has meaning for him only by standing for some concrete, verifiable, and usually edible object of experience. Holding such a view requires either the dismissal of many ordinary expressions as unintelligible, or a peopling of the world with anonymous agencies, responsible for raining, snowing, and so forth, and with equally mystifying items of the kind supposed here (for another example, see p. 170). Descartes' famous "I think, therefore I am" has sometimes been amended by purists to the more noncommittal "it thinks in me." But if thereby condemned to accepting a faceless demon that does Descartes' thinking for him, most people would find the remedy worse than the disease, and would sooner have Descartes back again, or, failing that, a better account of the word *it*.

The Mouse, unsurprisingly, ducks the issue. Historians generally do. (Sutherland, pp. 172–73; Shibles, p. 18; Baker [4], p. 707.)

The references at the end are to writers who have alluded to the passage under discussion. Complete documentation appears in an appendix consisting of two bibliographies—a select bibliography of commentators and a select list of philosophical authors who quote or allude to Alice. The latter is a new and valuable listing of fifty writers provided as partial evidence that philosophers are among the most habitual quoters of Alice.

The Philosopher's Alice with its annotations, appendix, and introduction is particularly valuable, as all annotated editions are to some degree, as a reference book. Heath has thoroughly researched, assimilated, pondered, and presented (with considerable wit and charm) information that previously had been difficult to come by.

The introduction, which attempts to touch all bases, contains yet another interesting comparison of Edward Lear and Carroll. Regrettably, the typeface in this part of the book is very small—an obvious concession to costs which also accounts for the book's clumsy size (6½ ″ by 9½ ″). Heath rightly points out that "Carroll's fame as a nonsense-writer is by now so firmly established that it is probably too late to persuade anyone that, apart from a few isolated instances such as the *Jabberwock* poem, he is not strictly a writer of nonsense at all." The term nonsense is regularly misused to mean anything that fails to make sense. Carroll makes too much sense. His proper genre is the absurd, which rigidly adheres, after it has ceased to be sensible to do so, to "the ordinary conventions of logic, linguistic usage, motive and behavior." At the opposite pole the true nonsense-writer neglects or defies these conventions. "Lear, for the most part, is a true nonsense-writer, who gets his effects by random aberration from a norm he does not respect."

Finally it must be noted that the complexity, the provocativeness, and in many ways the richness of Heath's annotations make them too taxing and tedious to digest in large chunks. However, for the tired reader, or the purist, there is, of course, Carroll's text along with Tenniel's drawings which in this edition are extremely well reproduced. From Heath's annotations one learns that philosophers have a language well in advance of politicians' and media commentators'. Edwin Newman might snicker while reading *The Philosopher's Alice,* but there is a clear sense that Heath has already had that chuckle. Remember the White Rabbit anxiously muttering, "The Duchess? The Duchess? Oh my dear paws? Oh my fur and whiskers! She'll get me executed, as sure as ferrets are ferrets"? That's "an example of the nonvacuous use of a tautology. Anything as sure as this formally necessary truth is presumably as sure as anything can be. Strictly speaking, however, it is also a necessary truth that predictions of the future do not enjoy this degree of certainty. The Rabbit is a victim of a category mistake in equating factual probability with logical truth." Well, speaking strictly, what can you expect from one of the world's foremost authorities on nothing? a man whose entry on *nothing* in *The Encyclopedia of Philosophy* contains the astute observation that "Nobody seems to know how to deal with it."

Lewis Carroll: Une vie (in French; English translation forthcoming) is the result of a French boom in Carroll interest that parallels and often exceeds our own. Jean Gattégno, Professor of English at Paris VIII–Vincennes and a highly regarded Carroll critic and translator, has produced a biography that consists of a series of thirty-seven brief and diverse essays on aspects of Carroll's, or rather Dodgson's, life. Gattégno reasons that we can gradually and subconsciously come to an understanding of Carroll the dual personality and unique author by reading about selected aspects of his life and work. The chapters Gattégno selects are entitled (translated and in the order they are presented): Alice, Money, Stuttering, Celibacy, Christ Church College, Correspondence, Childhood, Family, Little Girls, Illustrators, Games and Inventions, Juvenalia, Liddell, Macmillan, Mathematics, Worldliness, Occultism, Oxford, Father and Mother, Photography, Politics, Priesthood, Professorship, Prudery, Pseudonym, Religion, Rugby, Russia, Health, Sexuality, Theatre, Trains, Tristan da Cunha, Uggug, Victoria, Vivisection, and Zeno of Elea.

Gattégno's information is drawn from the standard Carroll reference sources, most of which were published from 1945 to 1955 and which are currently unavailable to the French-reading public. It is regrettable that he did not take advantage of the great quantity of still unpublished Carroll material available to advance our knowledge of Carroll significantly—nor did Gattégno fully utilize recent publications. For instance, the essay on Carroll's health is written without awareness of his suffering fainting spells in later life, although that is reported and thoroughly discussed with the question of possible epilepsy (probably not) by Morton Cohen and Roger Lancelyn Green.[1] This omission is more significant than it may appear at first to be. Carroll was preoccupied, to the point of obsession, with loss of consciousness and death. Allusions to fainting, fits, and death appear throughout his work (e.g., going out "just like a candle" in *Looking-Glass* and "softly and suddenly vanishing away" in *Snark*). An accurate assessment of Carroll's health may shed some light on the nature of his imagination, genius, and on the works themselves.

While the Gattégno book may be a disappointment for well-read Carroll scholars, his approach does succeed in cleverly eliciting a sense of the complex life behind the pseudonym. It should satisfy general readers and especially the eager French audience for whom it is intended. Moreover, when the English version appears it should earn a spot on any Carroll bookshelf for conveniently bringing together material into unified essays, much of which was previously only available through book hopping and tedious index crawling.

The centrality of a play and game impulse in Carroll's work is obvious even to the most casual adult reader of the *Alice* books. All Carroll's literary works are filled with puzzles, games, anagrams, playful parodies and riddles, logical queries, and an overall sense of a game-like contest with his reader. Dodgson loved and invented puzzles and games and was particularly well–acquainted with backgammon and chess. (Chess, of course, figures prominently in the design of *Through the Looking-Glass.*) It follows as no surprise that the play aspect of Carroll's art has continually interested Carroll scholars, notably Elizabeth Sewell and more recently Roger Henkle, and has developed into a distinct area of Carroll scholarship. Kathleen Blake's *Play, Games, and Sport: The Literary Works of Lewis Carroll* is the first published book-length investigation of this area.

Professor Blake, who teaches English at the University of Washington, specifically investigates Carroll's literary presentation of a psychic impulse, that of play. Her approach, psychological though not psychoanalytical, is programatic and her theory, developmental. "The play impulse," she writes, "underlies games and sport, which are its further and later manifestations." Her investigation starts with a psychological model of play and follows the progression from play, including a discussion of *A Tangled Tale,* to games, with an interpretation of the *Alices* in the light of both play and games, to sport, with readings of *Sylvie and*

Bruno, Sylvie and Bruno Concluded, and a brief discussion of *The Hunting of the Snark.* Her approaches, theories, and conclusions are all new and different.

The model, her theory of play, aims at making "a new kind of sense of what Carroll wrote." It is derived from Schiller, Spencer, Freud, Groos, Erikson, Piaget, Huizinga, Ehrmann, Callois, and Von Newman, and can be epitomized as follows: "Play—spontaneous, disinterested, nonutilitarian—is characterized by a fundamental urge to mastery through incorporation of experience to the ego rather than by adjustment or accommodation of the ego to experience. Less dryly, if more roughly, the difference is between eating up life—for the pleasure, not the hunger —and being digested by it." When it takes two to play and one will win, play becomes a game and subsequently when the game becomes so unbalanced that one is playing and the other being played, with the winner a foregone conclusion, we have sport. For Carroll this means the hunt—sport in the sense of cat chasing mouse. Carroll endorses the innocence of play and games and desires human activity to be better formalized and bound by game constraints so as to combat aggressiveness. The innocence of play and games is a problem for him, according to Blake, if after all they are related to sport. "Carroll treats sport as the ultimate manifestation of an amoral and self-aggrandizing strain in play and games. He almost always conceives of the more harmless forms of play as aggressively goal-oriented and competitive: the goal is the triumph of one by means of the defeat of the other. This may be acceptable, up to a point innocent (as long as the rules hold and both sides are willing), but the same cannot be said for triumph via infliction of pain and death, as in the sport of hunting."

Blake's methodical readings of Carroll's work are by no means exhaustive. She looks at play primarily through the card game, the croquet match, the chess board, and the hunt. Rather than being a definitive statement of the play impulse in Carroll, the book is more akin to a formal and provocative opening statement. Indeed, critics will be disagreeing with Ms. Blake's beliefs for years to come. I remain unconvinced by her sophisticated theory. Simpler notions of escape and probing for alternative adult life-styles similar to play are fundamentally more readily acceptable explanations of this impulse in Carroll's work. Yet Ms. Blake's intent is not so much to convince the reader of her theory as to provide a useful model with which to approach the works. To this end she is somewhat more successful. Still, the narrowness of her chosen approach leads Ms. Blake to conclusions that repeatedly violate the essential spirit and nature of the works she discusses. The book is valuable for reporting and assimilating an awesome amount of diverse information. It is a work whose copious footnotes often prove as valuable as the text itself. It is not a book that reads easily. The footnotes are diverting and the opening chapter tends to require such hard work that in her introduction Ms. Blake offers her readers encouragement to wade through it.

The book's final chapter, "A Victorian Gospel of Amusement," stands quite apart from what precedes it. It is a cultural study of how Victorians played and what they thought of it, drawing evidence from the toy industry, the sports associations, and the journals of the day. Though it is justifiably included as providing a context for Carroll, I can recommend this chapter independent of the rest of the work. Characteristically well researched and documented, it is a valuable study of an important dimension of Victorian life—an aspect seemingly alien to the popular notion of "Victorianism" and thus often neglected.

NOTE

1. In "Lewis Carroll's Loss of Consciousness," *Bulletin of the New York Public Library,* LXXIII (1969), 25–64, and also in a comprehensive review, "The Illnesses of Lewis Carroll," *The Practitioner,* CIX (August 1972), 230–39, by Dr. Selwyn Goodacre, a British physician.

A Miscellany

Wonderful Wizard Marvelous Land, by Raylyn Moore. Preface by Ray Bradbury. (Bowling Green University Popular Press, $9.95 cloth, $4.50 paper.)

The publication of *Wonderful Wizard Marvelous Land* is a sign of the increasing attention scholars in children's literature are giving L. Frank Baum and his Oz books. Mrs. Moore's book, despite some serious flaws, is one of the most important Baum studies to appear.

Mrs. Moore analyzes Baum's Oz stories as they relate to the counterculture of the 1960s, as they were influenced by Baum's life, and in terms of their mythic significance. Unfortunately, much of what she says is undercut by frequent factual errors. These errors range from minor (Baum's famous magnified insect, H. M. Wogglebug, T. E., becomes T. E. Wogglebug, H. M., on page 21) to major (the plot of *The Lost Princess of Oz* is attributed to *The Magic of Oz* on page 104). Sometimes Mrs. Moore creates doubt when none is called for. For instance, she says on page 170, shortly after she uses *Rinkitink in Oz* (1916) as an example of Baum's later Oz books, that "some sources say that it was an earlier story pulled into the series with minor rewriting." That *Rinkitink* was written around 1905 has been known since 1961, when Russell P. MacFall reported it in *To Please a Child* (p. 198). The book is mentioned as *King Rinkitink* in a contract of 28 June 1906 between Baum and his publisher (in fairness to Mrs. Moore, I should mention that this contract has not yet been published). Again, Mrs. Moore is the only Baum scholar who remains uncertain that *The Royal Book of Oz* (1921), which was published under Baum's name and "enlarged and edited" by Baum's successor Ruth Plumly Thompson, is entirely Miss Thompson's work. Another unpublished contract exists stating that Miss Thompson was to write an Oz book to be published under Baum's name, but if Mrs. Moore is unaware of this contract, surely she could have asked Miss Thompson herself. Miss Thompson, who now lives in Malvern, Pennsylvania, has given assurance that she used no Baum notes in writing the book and that crediting it to Baum was a publisher's gimmick to ease the transition between the two authors. Mrs. Moore makes a serious error when she suggests on page 186 that there is "reason to believe much of the final writing" of Baum's posthumous *Glinda of Oz* (1920) "was done by Ruth Plumly Thompson." There is no justification at all for this statement, which Mrs. Moore is the first to make (but I fear not the last, since it appears in a major scholarly work). As MacFall states in *To Please a Child* (p. 236), the original *longhand* manuscript of *Glinda* survives in the possession of Baum's granddaughter. Peter E. Hanff of the Bancroft Library has examined the manuscript and informs me that it is entirely in Baum's holograph and is the book as it was published. Though Mrs. Moore frequently cites *The Baum Bugle*, I suspect that most of the factual problems in her study could have been avoided if she had had access to a complete file of that journal. Most of the errors are minor (there are many I have not mentioned), but readers should check every fact in *Wonderful Wizard Marvelous Land* by more reliable sources.

Mrs. Moore's interpretations, however, make up for her factual problems. Her interpretation of Baum's life is the most astute and sensitive yet to appear, and her comparisons of Baum's fantasies with myths and mythic devices from several cultures comprise a major contribution to Baum criticism. Her comments are admittedly suggestive rather than conclusive; hopefully, Mrs. Moore and other Baum critics will build on her important suggestions. Occasionally Mrs. Moore does not present adequate evidence for her judgments. She condemns, for example, Baum's magazine stories as generally "little better than [his] adult novels" (p. 72) on the basis of only four of over twenty such stories; she does not discuss at all his excellent "Animal Fairy Tales," nine short fantasies which appeared in *The Delineator* during 1905. For her opinion that Baum's later (post-1913) Oz books are, on the whole, poor, she presents as her major evidence the cutenesses of Dorothy and other Baum heroines (a regrettable trait fully developed in 1907 in *Ozma of Oz*, a book which Mrs. Moore justly praises), Baum's overuse of "the 'strange race' for purposes of satire" (which, as Mrs. Moore says, reached its peak in 1910 in *The Emerald City of Oz*, a book she admires), elements which she doesn't care for in *Rinkitink in Oz* (which was written around 1905), and the fact that villains get more menacing as the series goes on.

Despite its problems, *Wonderful Wizard Marvelous Land* is an important book about a major writer of American fantasies. While it must be used with caution, it belongs in every library supporting the study of children's literature.

—David L. Greene

M. C. Higgins, the Great, by Virginia Hamilton. (Macmillan, $6.95.)

This prize-winning book by the author of *The Planet of Junior Brown*
is a composite of rich interwoven themes, strengthened by vivid characterization and a deep sense of place.

M. C. Higgins is a thirteen-year-old boy who lives with his family on
the slope of a mountain near the Ohio River. The mountain is called
Sarah's Mountain after M. C.'s great-grandmother, who escaped from
slavery and came to settle there. His family loves the mountain, but now
their home is endangered by a sliding heap of subsoil abandoned by strip
miners on the mountain top. M. C. has nightmares about this danger,
but his father will not face it because nothing would cause him to leave
the burial place of his ancestors.

Much of the story revolves around M. C.'s emotional tension as his
love for the mountain conflicts with his belief that the family must
leave its home. Further, his friendship with Ben Killburn is thwarted
by his family's superstitious dread of the Killburns, whom they consider "witchy." In the end M. C. saves his home by building a wall to
stem the onslaught of the threatening "spoil heap." The wall is made of
dirt, reinforced by rusty fenders and other car parts and, finally, by the
very burial stones of his ancestors, with their markings still visible.
And it is an itinerant young girl who helps him to see the folly of the
local superstitions and gives him a larger vision of the world. She tells
him to "find out what there's to see. What there's to know, just to be
knowing."

There is magic in this book. Virginia Hamilton's style is mesmerizing,
a combination of such poetic expressions as the description of a sunrise
as "a brilliant gash ripped across the summit of Hall Mountain" and of
such quaint mountain expressions as the remark Banina, M. C.'s lovely
mother, makes about the mountain. She says it "must be what Sunday
people call God Almighty. . . . High enough for heaven and older than
anybody ever lived."

The symbols this author uses are also unique. M.C.'s forty-foot steel
pole, his prize for swimming the Ohio River (the feat which he thinks
gives him the right to the title "M. C. Higgins, the Great"), is unusual
and significant, but its purpose is not quite clear. When M. C. climbs the
pole and makes it move in "a slow, sweeping arc," he seems to have
visionary glimpses of the past: "As if past were present. . . . He sensed
Sarah moving through undergrowth up the mountainside. . . . As if he
were a ghost, waiting, and she, the living." Again, the pole seems to be
the pivot around which the whole story turns. Banina calls it "the marker
for all of the dead," and, indeed, the bones of the ancestors are actually

buried around the pole. Finally, it is the gravestones themselves, encased
in the wall, that seem to be the cement that connects the living present
to the past.

It is impossible to do justice to this many-faceted book. The beauty of
the writing, the poetic imagery, the characters, each unique yet completely believable, and the original themes all make the reading of this
book an unforgettable experience, and mark Virginia Hamilton as one
of the most important of today's writers for children.

—*Carol Vassallo*

Bread and Honey, by Ivan Southall. (Penguin Books Australia, 1970;
Puffin Books, 1972.)

Reviewing an Australian novel published five years ago offers an occasion to comment upon the speed with which sexual mores have changed
in children's literature. Its author, Ivan Southall, is the three-time winner
of the Australian Children's Book of the Year Award and was the first
Australian to win the English Carnegie Award for his contribution to
children's literature. *Bread and Honey* concerns a motherless thirteen-
year-old boy who lives in a small Australian town and who is obsessively
fond of rolling around naked in the wet grass behind his house. The
author intimates that this has something to do with his burgeoning
sexuality, but American kids in 1975 would simply say, "He does it for
kicks."

Mick Cameron's alienation is somehow related to a larger conflict of
moral values than the furious disapproval his intermittent nudity pro-
vokes in the family next door. He is in conflict about the big Anzac
parade honoring dead war heroes which is going on in the town, and he
is also suffering the symptoms of the flu. Fearful and embarassed because
of his inappropriate dress, he seeks refuge from the public eye on the
beach below the town. There he meets nine-year-old Margaret—winsome, provocative, and literary. She *also* likes to take her clothes off. In
a stand-off fight with the town bully, who impugns his honor and hers,
Mick attains his manhood, comes to a new appreciation of his Gran, and
perceives that taking off one's clothing in public is simply Not Done.

Throughout the book, Southall suggests that there is a relationship
between dying for one's country and the chivalric defense of helpless
females, and there certainly is, even though Mick never does come to
grips with it, nor does the plot. The parade above the town and the
encounter below it remain two separate activities.

The quality of Southall's writing is fine enough to carry even the skeptical reader through the long, feverish episode on the shingle, yet much of Mick's crisis could have been eliminated by a nice change of clothing and a big box of Kleenex.

In sum, the marvel and terror of the bodily changes which take charge of the adolescent, regardless of gender, time, or culture, are circumvented by the story, and the sensitivity of the author lavished instead upon the affirmation of some rather outmoded social precepts. On the other hand, the book would probably be banned in Kentucky.

—Feenie Ziner

Arrow to the Sun, by Gerald McDermott. (Viking, $6.95.)
Songs of the Chippewa, by John Bierhorst. Pictures by Joe Servello. (Farrar, Straus, and Giroux, $5.95.)
Earth Namer, by Marjory Bernstein and Janet Kobrin. Illustrated by Ed Heffernan. (Charles Scribner's Sons, $4.95.)
Baldur and the Mistletoe, by Margaret Hodges. Illustrated by Gerry Hoover. (Little, Brown, $5.95.)

McDermott's *Arrow to the Sun* is a graphic production of exceptional power and beauty. The geometrical design-motifs are unmistakably derived from Southwest Indian patterns and are highly stylized, but their abstract qualities have been personalized and come across as vital and dramatic. The narrative, based on a Pueblo Indian myth, is terse and straightforward, employing a vocabulary that, for the most part, is within the range of most schoolchildren, though not preschoolers. The story is about a boy conceived by an earthly maiden from a spark of life from the Lord of the Sun. The boy, ostracized because he has no father, goes in search of his progenitor. Standing at last in the presence of his divine father, the boy has to prove himself by undergoing a series of trials, which are essentially rites of initiation, though they are not so designated. Having survived lions, serpents, bees, and lightning, the youth is acknowledged by his solar father and, "filled with the power of the sun," returns to earth. His return to the pueblo is celebrated by the people in a Dance of Life.

. This allegory of Pueblo initiation rites seems to be intended as much for adults as for children. I say this because the fine drawings—in themselves a *tour de force*—are highly sophisticated. The author-illustrator has integrated the illustrative and decorative elements of his art-work, eliminating everything circumstantial and concrete; that is, strictly speaking, everything that is inessential. For this reason, *Arrow to the Sun,* at least in its visual aspect, may prove to be less accessible to children than to adults. As far as the story is concerned, the difficulty lies in another direction. The narrative is not communicated within a cultural-historical frame of reference. The result is that even the adult reader is not in a position to grasp the significance of the allegory; still less is he likely to relate the myth to actual initiation rites as performed by Pueblo Indians to this very day. The emotional impact of these rites on Pueblo boys and girls and their function of symbolically incorporating the children into the adult community are not treated. Hence, we have a book which is perhaps too sophisticated pictorially for children, but with a narrative that is too simple and too incomplete for adults. These criticisms aside—they apply to many children's books today—*Arrow to the Sun* is a beautiful book, one that sets a very high standard for graphic productions in its field.

Bierhorst and Servello's *Songs of the Chippewa* consists of songs adapted from the collections of Frances Densmore and Henry Rowe Schoolcraft and arranged for piano and guitar. The book achieves a perfect unity of mood with its brief, gentle lyrics and the fine pictures by Joe Servello. The mood is one of harmony between man and nature and between young and old. The pictures show scenes of domestic Indian life, mostly at dusk or at night: animals glimpsed in the forest, a mother with her infant, parents playing with their baby under the trees, the fears and dreams of Indian children. The lyrics usually consist of only a handful of words, either in English translation, or in the language of the Chippewa, or even in nonsense syllables.

This is a special purpose book: the musical scores obviously are intended to be played and sung. The pictures correspond in content to the short lyrics, but only approximately; in fact, the illustrations can stand by themselves simply as charming vignettes of man living in nature, and still in a state of innocence. Based on ethnographic materials gathered over fifty years ago on the western shores of the Great Lakes, the book is a romantic evocation of a timeless past. Indian life is depicted as it might have been lived before the coming of the white man, or, indeed, before the birth of human strife. Without doubt, the lullabies and other songs are intended for very young children, and with one or two exceptions they are soothing. The parent or teacher who wishes to use Indian lore to communicate the idea of Eden will be highly pleased with *Songs of the Chippewa.* For others, the romantic treatment of Indian life, even for the benefit of small children, will appear to be too sweet to be truly nourishing.

Earth Namer, a legend of the Maidu Indians of northern California, is a creation-myth that closely resembles the Bible account. It tells how "Earth Namer," evidently in human form, descended from the sky to join Turtle on his raft. With the help of some mud scraped up from the bottom of the sea by Turtle, Earth Namer proceeded to create dry land, the sun, moon, and stars, trees and plants, animals and birds, and finally the first man and woman. He then climbed back up into the sky and was never seen again.

Without speculating on the origins of this myth, it is clear that its potential appeal to children rests in its simplicity and understated humor no less than in the charm of its anthropomorphism. The drawings by Ed Heffernan are very simple, playful cartoons, which have the effect of reducing the act of creation to a rather modest operation. But it is necessary to enter into the spirit of the legend, which recognizes the equality of all living creatures, and views the creation of the world as a low-keyed cooperative venture between men and animals. The appeal of the book, as of the legend from which it is derived, is, after all, that it is unassuming, and children will surely find it entertaining for this very reason.

Baldur and the Mistletoe is a sensitive account of Baldur's death, beautifully illustrated, and faithful to the Norse myth in its essential details. This book can be read with pleasure by adults as well as school-children. Margaret Hodges has attempted to give the sacred myth a human dimension, emphasizing the grief of Baldur's parents, and the human loss involved in the malicious destruction of the shining god by his nemesis, Loki. Gerry Hoover's illustrations convey the cosmic scope of the myth, and his depictions of frozen Hel, with its dead spirits, are reminiscent of Goya's etchings. The rocky landscapes are especially striking and original.

Taken by itself, the myth of Baldur is no doubt sufficiently dramatic to engage the reader's interest, whether young or old. In the opinion of this reviewer, however, something of value would have been gained by relating the myth to its associated ritual of seasonal renewal. It is important for children to understand that myths are more than entertaining stories, and that in many instances they reflect the vital concerns of archaic man. This fuller understanding is possible only if the myth is presented in its proper context of magical beliefs and ritual enactments. No doubt, the myth of Baldur can stand on its own, like many other myths whose contents are essentially dramatic. Indeed, as everyone knows, tragic drama is an outgrowth of sacred myth and its associated mimesis. But I think we owe it to children to let them know the human significance of myths—lest they imagine that we have outgrown our need for them.

—Leo Schneiderman

The Perilous Gard, by Elizabeth Marie Pope. Drawings by Richard Cuffari. (Houghton Mifflin, $5.95.)

Ellen and the Queen, by Gillian Avery. With illustrations by Krystyna Turska. (Thomas Nelson, $4.95.)

A Dance to Still Music, by Barbara Corcoran. Illustrated by Charles Robinson. (Follett, $6.95.)

Troublemaker, by Lynn Hall. Illustrated by Joseph Cellini. (Follett, $4.95.)

Grandpa's Maria, by Hans-Eric Hellberg. Translated from the Swedish by Patricia Crampton. Illustrated by Joan Sandin. (William Morrow, $4.95.)

It Must Have Been McNutt, by Jeffrey Leech and Glenn Edward Sadler. Illustrated by Kathy Kushe and David Hastings. (G. L. Publications, $2.50.)

In the early part of the present century Ellen Key expressed her concern at the great proliferation of books, many of which were lifeless and dull, by recommending that there should be a "general crusade against all children's books and freedom for the young to read the great literature" (*The Century of the Child,* 1909). With the latter part of her statement few would quarrel. Ellen Key felt, as do many who are concerned about literary quality, that the great tidal wave of publication throws up too much chaff, too little wheat. Children's literature in any age, however, furnishes an important key to its social history. Literature of earlier times informs us that our forbears wished their children to behave in a certain way. Indeed, the models of conduct urged upon the children of our ancestors could rival that of saints of the Middle Ages. Today the literature is less obviously didactic, less humorless. Even so, like Wordsworth in his *Prelude* we sometimes cry:

Oh! give us once again the Wishing Cap
Of Fortunatus, and the Invisible Coat
of Jack the Giant-Killer, Robin Hood,
And Sabra in the Forest with St. George!
The Child whose love is here, at least doth reap
One precious gain, that he forgets himself.

The contemporary world is characterized by political and social ferment, forces which affect its literature. No one can predict with accuracy which books will survive to be returned to again and again with pleasure. The potpourri considered here is offered without prediction. To quote Louise Field, in the past "the works which have taken the most permanent hold are those originated in some powerful mind whether it be the mind of a nation or some distinguished man." In any case it is "the soul of a child" which "acts as a test for true gold" (*The Child and His Book,*

1891). Each of the following works must stand or fail upon that test.

In the twentieth century not too many people believe in fairy folk or demons but occasionally a story about them is so well-written, so successfully presented that the reader can scarce fail to identify with the beliefs of another time, another place. Elizabeth Pope's *The Perilous Gard* is that kind of story. This second novel, like her first, is a mystery, a suspensful tale of derring-do. It is carefully researched, carefully written—its purpose sheer entertainment through historical perspective. The plot is tight, the action swift, the characters believably real. In short, *The Perilous Gard* possesses a spell-binding quality that refuses readers the temptation to read pages or chapters out of sequence.

Set in mid-sixteenth-century England with Queen Mary on the throne and Elizabeth soon to succeed her, this story is essentially that of Kate Sutton, the young protagonist unjustly sent by Queen Mary to Elvenwood Hall, a remote castle believed by superstitious country folk to be associated with heathen magic. At Elvenwood, Kate is caught up in a series of events so frightening and otherworldly as to break the spirit or damage the sanity of even the strong. Not so with the clever and spirited Kate. Indeed from the very outset a powerful story is unfolding, a story through which Elizabeth Pope takes her readers captive, holding them in breathless suspense while her heathen and human characters play out a perilous prose drama. In a chapter appropriately entitled "The Evidence Room" there is one unforgettable scene representative of others presented with equal skill. This scene, between the evil Master John and his young charge Kate, is masterfully written and illustrated. The power of Richard Cuffari's drawing and Elizabeth Pope's words show Master John savoring lush slices from a plump pear while he figuratively slices and quarters Kate. *The Perilous Gard* presents a polished, if frightening panorama of intricate relationships—master with servants, queen with subjects, leaders with followers, brother with brother, sister with sister, good with evil. It's all here in bold yet subtle array.

Ellen and the Queen is in length a slight book, its purpose largely to amuse and entertain. In this it succeeds, as much through the remarkably effective and appealing illustrations of Krystna Turksa as through the warm-humoured spirit of Gillian Avery's text. Together author and artist have created a highly believable nine-year-old Ellen "with fiery red hair and a fiery temper to match it." Ellen's actions and thoughts as revealed through the short episodic segments of plot are equally believable. The story is alive with expectation and surprise. The expected arrival of the New Earl and his family to Winterbourne and the Great House, the expected visit from Queen Victoria, the expected courtesies of the villagers as they prepare to meet the great and the near great are useful contrivances upon which to hang the surprises furnished by Ellen, whose creator maneuvers her in and out of difficulty with skill. Some will feel however, and justifiably, that an otherwise highly satisfactory child's book is weakened by the occasional intrusion of a phrase or a sentence smacking of baby talk. Even in the mouth of a small Victorian child such as little Lucy, a question such as "Won't us ever see her again?" hardly rings true.

Childhood, especially the growing-up years, is sometimes characterized by loneliness and uncertainty, a groping toward being, becoming. The themes of alienation and self-discovery appear with frequency in contemporary fiction. In *A Dance to Still Music* these themes are paramount and handled by Barbara Corcoran with finesse. Key West, Florida, provides the setting for the story of Margaret, a deeply sensitive and intelligent deaf girl of fourteen who lives with her restless and somewhat self-pitying mother, Maggie. The purpose of *A Dance to Still Music* is not ordinary entertainment, certainly not light amusement. This is a haunting story, one with suspenseful plot, undergirded with bold, fast-paced mental actions to which much of the physical is only incidental. The characters are vivid, real, sometimes Steinbeckian. Margaret's special loneliness is acute, and somewhat beyond Maggie's comprehension. The giant steps taken by Margaret in her determination not to impede her mother's future help her to find her own. The love and protectiveness she gives to sustain the life of a wounded deer comes back to fulfill her own life in unsuspected ways, from unsuspected sources. In the hands of a less gifted writer Margaret's story could have been maudlin; instead it is a "dance to still music," a celebration of life. Such a story needs few illustrations. Those conceived and provided by Charles Robinson, however, provide a very correct complementary touch.

Another poignant and moving story of childhood loneliness is that of the protagonist Willis in Lynn Hall's *Troublemaker*. Covering an extremely brief span in the lives of Willis and his younger sister, Mary Lee, who share a small sawmill shack with their irresponsible father, the brief episodes of this story are handled with literary skill and good taste. The theme is always subtle, never intruding. *Troublemaker* is not an instance of author crusading for a cause. Simply put, Ms. Hall asks only that the reader share in the choices, the frustrations, the intense feelings of her young protagonist as he teeters dangerously on a tightrope of circumstance. She is not afraid to show Willie in the raw edges of anger, but she demands one see also his capability for profound tenderness. Witness, for example, his anger when Mary Lee warns she is about to sneeze as Willis positions himself to shoot an old buck deer which has moved slowly into sight. "Willis raised the rifle. Mary Lee sucked in her breath. The buck raised its head. Mary Lee sneezed. The buck bolted. Willis shot, a fraction too late. His fury was too vast to be contained in his thirteen-year-old body. It blanked his mind and blocked his vision. ... When the moment passed, he found himself looking down the sights of his rifle. Centered in the sights was the face of Mary Lee, skin gray, eyes glazed with terror."

Later, and in stark contrast to Willie's propensity for anger, he lovingly helps his sister bury her little dog Peaches. Sharing with sensitive concern his sister's grief and knowing how he would feel if he lost Buster, Willis comforted Mary Lee: "I'll make a marker in woodshop, with her name on it." Mary Lee nodded, and suddenly Willis heard himself say, "Listen, you can have Buster, if you want him." In the final short chapter of *Troublemaker,* Willis is faced with a choice. His creator also is faced with choice: to tell or not tell the reader whether Willis actually gets home to Buster or whether Buster and Willis die simultaneously. Her choice, like the last choice of Willis, is Herculean, giving a final evidence of her skill as a writer. Joseph Cellini's illustrations are superb both in conception and in execution.

Somewhat lighter in texture than either *A Dance to Still Music* or *Troublemaker* is *Grandpa's Maria* by Eric Hellberg, translated into English from the Swedish by Patricia Crampton. Considered one of Sweden's best writers for children, Hellberg has created a happy story. It is clear that he understands the seven-year-old Maria. Her relationships, with older people especially, are natural, warm, trusting. Her grandfather is her very special friend and conversation between them shows no conscious generation gap. Circumstances which could have been used as an excuse for bathos—divorced parents, a mentally sick mother, a slight club-footedness in Maria—these are allowed no reign. The language of *Grandpa's Maria* is simple, direct, suitable; the illustrations by Joan Sandin no less so. If Hellberg's purpose has been simply to depict some happy spontaneity in childhood, he has done well. At the same time he has provided, despite or perhaps because of simplicity in executing the story, some intuitive insights into the intricacies and complexities of human relationships.

"It must have been old what's 'is name, I'm sure that he's the one to blame" for the creation of *It Must Have Been McNutt,* a delightfully light and winsome fantasy and clearly a case of the abilities of its creators to re-enter the stream of happy childhood. The authors, Jeffery Leech and Glenn Sadler, along with two talented illustrators, Kathy Kushe and David Hastings, have produced a highly imaginative retrospective peek into the land of faerie. Flavored with the faerie and folktale legends of Scotland and Ireland which have spilled over into America and cast in a setting to sustain this flavor, *It Must Have Been McNutt* succeeds in establishing the "reality" of "Broonies." The characterizations are superb, believable. Plausible surprises are in store at almost every turn and the story is advanced by strokes of lively anticipation and action. The style is consistently lucid; the language literate and right: "Ah, but the younger ye are, the easier it is to believe, my child," said the little man with a warm smile. "And besides, yer father is away, and if he is a typical grown-up, he may resist such a notion as believing in the likes of me." That four collaborators—two authors and two illustrators—could have succeeded in producing such a lively, entertaining and delightful piece, one of almost perfect textual and pictorial harmony, is within itself a feat fit for the Broonies. Surely they must have helped; otherwise it must have been McNutt.

Not all works produced today will live as great literature, but surely many of them will provide future literary historians, sociologists, anthropologists, economists, linguists, psychologists and others more than enough grist for their research mills. Perhaps one or more of these six will help.

—Charity Chang

An American Ghost, by Chester Aaron. Illustrated by David Gwynne Lemon. Ages 9 to 13. (Harcourt Brace Jovanovitch, $4.95.)

Benson Boy, by Ivan Southall. Illustrated by Ingrid Fetz. Ages 9 to 12. (Macmillan, $4.95.)

Red Pawns, by Leonard Wibberley. Ages 10 to 14. (Farrar, Straus and Giroux, $5.50.)

Stout-Hearted Seven, by Neta Lohnes Frazier. Ages 9 to 12. (Harcourt Brace Jovanovich, $4.95.)

An American Conscience: *Woodrow Wilson's Search for World Peace,* by David Jacobs. With photographs. Ages 10 and above. (Harper & Row, $4.95.)

The Magic Man: *The Life of Robert-Houdin,* by I. G. Edmonds. Ages 10 to 15. (Thomas Nelson, $4.95.)

Snow Bound, by Harry Mazer. Ages 9 to 14. (Delacorte Press, $4.95.)

A Figure of Speech, by Norma Fox Mazer. Ages 10 to 15. (Delacorte Press, $4.95.)

Millie's Boy, by Robert Newton Peck. Ages hard to assign: see review. (Alfred A. Knopf, $4.95.)

A Day No Pigs Would Die, by Robert Newton Peck. Ages 10 to 13. (Alfred A. Knopf, $4.95.)

The present sampling of children's books is by and large an encouraging one. The books vary considerably in subject, appeal, and merit, but in most of them there is evidence that the author takes the child seriously. Some of the books concentrate on traditional adventure, but a few mix into the adventure some psychologizing which not only rings true to childhood in general, but which tries to pinpoint some of the current cultural manifestations of the problems and adventures of growing up. One of the things which the adult reader may stop to ponder in reading some of these books is how specific an introduction to evil the child reader is ready for at various ages.

Benson Boy is an engrossing tale about a young boy who is obliged as a result of accidents to care for his mother as she is having a baby. He is not too clear about where babies come from and he fulfills his responsibility with a mixture of resentment, fear, and bravery. The threats he faces are dark of night, storm, fire, and incomprehensible adult behavior.

There is tension at every moment in the story, the resolution of one crisis introducing the boy hero into another critical situation. It is a natural book to read at one sitting and will probably be read by young readers as unexceptionably plausible. If there is anything in the story which may not sit well with young readers, it will probably be the boy's unnecessarily extensive reflections on his own feelings.

The story brings its hero face to face with such human obstacles as the extreme pigheadedness of his father and the feud between his father and a neighbor over political philosophies. These things are on a par with the mother's child-bearing as far as semi-comprehensibility goes. The story is well calculated to bring young readers up to a frontier of unfamiliarity, but in such a way that the discoveries, or not-quite-discoveries, are exciting without being disturbing. The story gains a certain interest from being set in Australia.

An American Ghost is an adventure that tests its fourteen-year-old hero up to and beyond limits which most fourteen year olds would be familiar with. At least it would seem so if we can assume that most fourteen year olds are not up to duplicating the adventures of Huck Finn.

The central action of the story resembles the action of *Huckleberry Finn* at many points. The young hero's home is washed down river in a flood. He is alone in the house and his voyage brings him into contact with some river hoodlums who are superb bad guys. They are a lot like the murderers in chapter 12 of *Huckleberry Finn,* but the hero of this tale actually *does* fall into their hands. He also falls into a relationship with a flood-stranded mountain lion. These are elements of a good survival story, and indeed this is a good one.

There is a moral element to the story, too, which stands almost apart from the main movement of the story. It is introduced at the beginning of the novel when the boy watches his father gratuitously murder two Indians, one of them a sixteen-year-old boy. The stark horror of the scene almost goes beyond that of the Shepherdson-Grangerford feud or the Boggs-Sherburn incident, but every moral suggestion that the murder of the Indians would provoke has to stay in abeyance until the end of the story, where we find that the boy's adventures have given him a vague respect for life and, presumably, countered the monstrous paternal example. The fact that all recollection of the shocking murders is submerged throughout the story and the fact that the moral illumination about the value of life appears at the end of the story make the message seem a bit too "found."

Red Pawns is one novel in a series about the Treegate family whose members have figured in Leonard Wibberley's other books in adventures in colonial and early federal times. The book is richly laden with historical reference, even with subtle reviews of colonial and revolutionary history. It does the work of a good historical novel in bringing alive the period and its people.

There are little cameos of early American types like the storytelling itinerant merchant (who seems almost made to order to illustrate Kenneth Lynn's description of one) and the former Hessian soldier. There is plenty of lore and the young reader may be sent to the dictionary by words like gudgeon, wain, painter (the rope), fife rail, and makeweight. Idiom of the period is intelligently used ("take his custom elsewhere").

Since diplomacy preceding the war of 1812 is the central action of the novel, there is an excuse for a shift in the action to London, where details of London life, like link boys, beggars, the geography of the city, and the distinction between low church and high church, are treated. The book's hero ends up involved in important dealings with Castelreagh.

Only a part of the book involves the Indians to whom the title refers. They are pawns in the strategy of the War of 1812, but there is important incidental reference to Indians (e.g., a drunken old Indian kept penned up in a coalbin in Springfield, Massachusetts, and exhibited like an animal) at a number of points in the book. The picture of the Indian that emerges is not romanticized. He is represented often enough as threatening, lying, ignorant, and vicious, but none of these charges against him, whether they are true or false, alter the judgment implicit in the narration that the Indian has been the object of massive injustice at the hands of the white man. There is a certain maturity in the moral vision of the story—the oppressed is not obliged to perfect himself before he becomes entitled to justice. This intelligent and underplayed message works well with the recreated historical scenes and the exciting adventures to make a totally commendable children's book.

The subtitle of *Stout-Hearted Seven* tells a good deal of the story: *The True Adventure of the Sager Children Orphaned on the Oregon Trail in 1844.* The author has taken an episode of local history which she was familiar with and narrated it for children with some success.

The cross-country wagon trek of a large family that faces trials and disasters every step of the way (for instance, the death of both parents, but not until mother has given birth to a baby) has the makings of a good story, but the author is not quite up to handling it. There is a soap-opera-ish quality to the staging of the events and there are anachronisms like "you kids." On one point the author could learn a good deal from the author of *Red Pawns:* she neglects the specific names and geography of the places that the wagon train is passing through. Occasionally a concrete reference is made, but for the most part the party seems to be traveling past vague rivers, prairies, and mountains as if it was made up of characters in a medieval romance, not real people in real circumstances. At one point the narration is especially poor: the massacre scene, the most momentous in the book, is so confusingly written that it is difficult to get images of places or to be aware of sequence of events and passages of time.

The authors of *Snow Bound* and *A Figure of Speech* are husband and wife. Their craft must benefit from their relationship, because both of them tell extremely engrossing tales for early adolescents.

Snow Bound, as its subtitle indicates, is a story of raw survival. The two teenagers who are stranded in a blizzard in the most desolate part of New York State contend with the familiar perils from cold, near-starvation, inability to signal rescuers, and despair. These are expertly described, but the real merit of the book is in the representation of the psychology of the two young people. Both are independent and, in different ways and to different degrees, defiant. The boy is bold and impulsive, the girl is intelligent and vexed by what she sees as her stiffness in relating to others. She is the more mature of the two and her eventual responsibility for their rescue alters the thinking of both of them. The relationship that develops between the two of them is sensitively handled, never foolishly romanticized, and will probably be an easy thing for young readers to identify with.

A Figure of Speech is the story of an alliance that develops between teen-age Jenny and her grandfather against the rest of their family—an irascible, autocratic father, a bird-brained, hysterical mother, and a bunch of selfish siblings. There is some incidental action which introduces the girl's best friend and her family—the friend is an only child and no happier with her cool, detached, and tolerant parents than Jenny is with hers.

The fine definition of all characters, the plausibility of the situations and the variety of realistic insights into motivation make this book almost too good to be true. There is no point at which it passes into an area of depiction or explanation that would exceed the experience of a young adolescent. But there is also no point at which the psychological perceptiveness and narrative control would disappoint an adult reader.

It is hard to say whether the story would be more poignant to a young or old reader. The child may read with a strong identification with Jenny as victim; the adult will probably read with appreciation of the exposure of the stupid, attritive family conflicts. The vindication of the old man, which entails Jenny's vindication also, is one of the most pleasing Justice Triumphs plots that could be devised.

Millie's Boy continues the use of the turn of the century southern Vermont setting that Robert Newton Peck introduced in *A Day No Pigs Would Die.* The earlier book was a bit of family history; it described isolated rural life in a residually Shaker community, and delivered a heavy dose of ruralism somewhat on the order of descriptions that Homer Croy might have written years ago, but colored by an overly sentimental examination of the boy narrator's psychology. Even worse was the effort to turn the boy into another Huck Finn by giving him cute ways of expressing his incomprehension of the world. Colorfulness via naiveté has its limits and they are as readily detected by young as by old readers.

Millie's Boy, however, is something else. Time and setting are more or less the same as in *A Day No Pigs Would Die,* but the protagonist is the son of the village whore and the book opens with him being shot and injured by the unseen figure who has just murdered his mother. Definitely a stronger cup of tea.

There is plenty of adventure in the book that is well calculated for young readers: quest of the mother's murderer, escape from ravenous coydogs, near death in a hole in the ice of Lake Champlain, and life with a female country doctor of a Marjorie Main cut.

The main quest of the young hero, however, is not for his mother's murderer, but for his own father. He finds him and learns that he is the most vicious man in the countryside, well known to be an unprosecuted murderer. When the father announces his intention of raping a girl with whom, unknown to him, the son is in love, the father's words do justice to the deed: ". . . it'll draw enough loving out of me to make do all winter. I won't be able to walk without help until the four of March. Neither will she. Because if there is one way I aim to do this Christmas, it's to split that little vix into two even pieces. One in each hand." Two impulses strike the boy—one to knife his father to death, the other to castrate him with telegraph wire.

For whom is this book intended? Is it written on the assumption that innocence ends earlier than we usually think? Or that it ought to? If the book could pass as an adult novel, it could simply be called one. But it isn't. The point of view and the framing of the story clearly indicate that it is a children's book.

There is something else in the book that raises a question about its suitability for young audiences. The raw treatment of sex and the extreme violence in the book may not make it unfit for every young reader. But there are scenes between the hero and Amy, the ward of the country doctor he is living with, which have that peculiar teasing quality of the prurient movie. For example, she sits down on his bed in her nightgown; they have a pillow fight; she gets a feather down the back of her nightgown; he gets it out. Facing sex is mature, but playing with titillation is neither mature nor useful. It is no more commendable in a book for adolescents than in a book that capitalizes on the adolescent fantasies of adults.

The two nonfiction books in this group have little in common. *An American Conscience* is a biography of Woodrow Wilson with emphasis on Wilson's post–World War efforts to establish and to assure American participation in the League of Nations. The book is splendidly written history, comprehensible to young people and even satisfying to the older reader who is looking for basic information on Wilson and the period. The objectivity, sense of proportion, clarity, and grace of the book make it a valuable one for a child to own. There is even a short guide to further reading at the end of the book which will help the adolescent reader whose interest in Wilson and the period is whetted by the book. It will whet many interests.

The Magic Man has an interesting subject in the life of the great French magician, Robert-Houdin, and contains an extensive illustrated explanation of some of Robert-Houdin's best known tricks. It is bound to have some appeal to children. But it is shamefully "written-down." Even children will probably be aware of that. Jacob's life of Wilson is proof that there is no need to abandon maturity to achieve clarity. *The Magic Man* not only contains but seems to be constructed out of what *The New Yorker* calls quotes we doubt ever got quoted. A chain of cunning little scenes quickly cloys. The children will sense this, but the subject of the book will hold their interest.

There is an afterthought to these reflections on this group of books—actually it was a thought constantly present to me as I was reading them. Who can afford these books? The total cost (before sales tax) of the ten is $50.05. The canonical price for a 145-page children's book seems to be $4.95. One has to conclude that children's reading is going to be done largely through schools and libraries, which is too bad. Some of these books a child would want to own: *An American Conscience* and *A Figure of Speech,* for example.

We are familiar with the publishers' arguments, but the access to good books is partly a function of wealth. Edmund Wilson complained about the inaccessibility to students of texts of major authors because of cost. The same is true of children's books. Even libraries find themselves able to buy fewer books today; many good titles are thus altogether out of reach. One of the reasons that my son has so many exquisitely beautiful Ukranian and Lithuanian children's books, published in Moscow, is simply that, even after they are imported, they are quite inexpensive, as little as sixty cents. Something has to be done about the cost of children's books if writing them and reviewing them is not to become an increasingly idle undertaking.

—Tom Heffernan

The Duck of Billingsgate Market, by Feenie Ziner. (Four Winds Press, $5.50.)

The Duck of Billingsgate Market is no doubt a familiar story. It is familiar, however, not because it has the jangle of cliché or the stamp of the derivative, but because its characters are as familiar as our own experience, and its theme as recurrent as love itself. It is also a beautifully written story, simple in style, direct in narration, yet never condescending to a young reader's intelligence. A parent and child can read it together as peers.

The tale is about one Tom Codley, packer of fish, an old and lonely man without family or friend. Tom finds meaning only in his work. Sometimes he likes to imagine himself "a kind of father, helping to feed the people of London." But even his fantasy is not really satisfying, for he cannot summon to mind any "particular faces" which might give meaning to his idea of fatherhood. He desires to love, but the world around him seems a blur, and he is too shy to give it focus. One day, however, he rescues a baby duck as it is about to be drowned by an evil oil slick. The duck, "Ducky Dear" as she is affectionately called, becomes the old man's company and consolation and family. She also gives Tom something to talk about, and suddenly he finds himself communicating with a fellow dockworker and an upstairs neighbor. "Ducky Dear," however, is after all a duck, and the day comes when she flies away from domesticity forever. But the old man has gained much from his experience, and ends with a loyal friend, a cheerful wife, and a happy heart.

What is most impressive about Mrs. Ziner's book is that it is heartwarming without being sentimental. Tom Codley's world maintains its potential for joy—indeed the story is a simple celebration—but the ugliness of this world is not masked, nor are its injustices ignored. Finally, the *Duck of Billingsgate Market* is a moral tale, for the pollution of contemporary life (here represented by the oil-smitten Thames) is something our children must be made to know, lest their youth be spent in illusion, and yield only more of what we now experience today: disillusionment and joylessness.

—Mark Zaitchik

Varia

DISSERTATIONS OF NOTE*

Bethea, Sara Kathryn. *Opera for Children: An Analysis of Selected Works.* University of Kansas, 1971.

A comprehensive and stimulating dissertation which surveys opera production for children in the United States and thoroughly analyzes nineteen operas for children from Mozart through Menotti. Other operas are mentioned. A bibliography of scores and recordings concludes the work. To date, the most extensive study in the field.

Graham, Kenneth L. *An Introductory Study of Evaluation of Plays for Children's Theatre in the United States.* University of Utah, 1947.

Concerned primarily with aesthetic criteria for choosing workable children's plays. Included are seventy-six critical statements about writing plays for children. (See Swortzell below).

Hedges, Ned Samuel. *The Fable and the Fabulous: The Use of Traditional Forms in Children's Literature.* University of Nebraska, 1968.

After giving a thorough definition of hhis terminology, Dr. Hedges analyzes Kipling's *Just So Stories,* Grahame's *The Wind in the Willows,* and Tolkien's *The Hobbit.* He concludes that "(1) the writers of the best children's literature tend to produce stories with relatively complex structures, appealing to readers on a number of levels of interpretation; and (2) good children's literature makes use of those literary conventions common to literature regardless of its audience, among them the devices associated with fable, myth, epic, and romance."

Kingsley, William Harmstead. *Happy Endings, Poetic Justice, and the Depth and Strength of Characterization in American Children's Drama: A Critical Analysis.* University of Pittsburgh, 1964.

Althoug Dr. Kingsley's original audience was theatre-oriented, the information of the dissertation should be of interest to anyone associated with children's literature in general. He gives arguments for and against happy endings in children's plays and summarizes the extensive controversy concerning them that has raged for over thirty years.

Lawson, Cornelia V. *Children's Reasons and Motivations for the Selection of Favorite Books.* University of Arkansas, 1972.

A brief, concise dissertation which catalogues children's, teacher's, and librarian's reasons for selecting children's books and comments on favorite books and the most appealing types of literature.

Shaw, Jean Duncan. *An Historical Survey of Themes Recurrent in Selected Children's Books Published in America since 1850.* Temple University, 1966.

*Information for this listing is drawn from a fothcoming book by Dr. Rachel Fordyce entitled *Children's Theatre and Creative Dramatics: An Annotated Bibliography of Critical Works:* (Boston: G. K. Hall).

213

A historical evaluation of major themes and value judgments in children's
literature; major categories are search for values, problems of growing up,
travel and understanding people in foreign countries, lives of heroes, fairy
tales, and the urge to know. Appendix A gives a concise list of reoccurring
themes collected from textbooks.

Swortzell, Lowell. *Five Plays: A Repertory of Children's Theatre to Be Performed
by and for Children.* 2 vols. New York University, 1963.
In addition to the five scripts, Dr. Swortzell extends Kenneth Graham's criteria for good playwriting by another eighty points. A seminal study of playwriting for children.

White, Mary Lou Usery. *Structural Analysis of Children's Literature: Picture
Storybooks.* Ohio State University, 1972.
The study applies a "structural approach to literary criticism to the analysis
of picture storybooks" in an attempt ot determine whether or not this approach would aid in the teaching of children's literature. The findings and
conclusions, which are extensive, suggest that the approach is successful.

IDEAS AND TOPICS FOR STUDENT WRITING AND RESEARCH

(Continued from *Children's Literature,* Volume III)

Mystical Visions in Children's Books
The Sense of Community in Children's Literature
Fusions of Dancing, Poetry, and Music for Children
French-Canadian Folk Rhymes
Piaget and Seuss
Ecology and Kipling
The Power of Love in Czech Folktales
Exploring *The Secret Garden*
The "Pioneer" Archetype in Children's Books
Values in Eskimo Folktales
The Creative Imagination of Children
Musical Nonsense
The Anansi Tales as Told in Jamaica
Stories for the Extremely Young
Children's Plays Created by Children
Violence in Strewelpeter
French Skip-Rope Rhymes
Biological Outlook of Winnie-the-Pooh
Children's Psychic Powers
Symbolism in Tolkien's *Farmer Giles of Ham*
Children's Literature and the Mentally Retarded
Values in Filipino Folktales
Distorted Backgrounds in Literary Fantasy
The Sleeping Beauty and Children
Characters in Disney Productions of the Classics
Salesmen in Children's Books
Wild Men in Children's Books

The "Lost Children" Theme
Moral and Ethical Attitudes of the Hardy Boys
Language in Winnie-the-Pooh
The Protestant Ethic in Picture Books
Current State of Black Children's Literature
Food and Eating as Reward and Punishment
The Use of Contrast in Children's Stories
Photography and Children's Literature
The Wind in the Willows and the *Bible*
Black Dialect in Children's Stories
Why *Black Beauty* Is Still a "Best Seller"
Black Street Games and Rhymes
Legends of the Delaware Indians in Relation to Children
Change of Size in *Gulliver's Travels*
Kissing Games
God in Cartoon Shows
Mickey Mouse's Evolution and Appeal
Poetry and Human Values—An Anthology for Children
The Unicorn and Children's Literature
Loneliness and Grimm's Tales
Evil in the Forests of Children's Stories
Totems and Children's Stories
Lions in Children's Stories
Fantasy in *The Phantom Tollbooth*
Oral Traditions Involving Children in Appalachia
Trees—Their Symbolic Use in Children's Literature
Aesop and the *Bible*
Ecology in Thornton Burgess' Animal Tales
The Uses of Clothing in Specific Works of Children's Literature
The Frightening Aspects of *Alice* and *Oz*
The Relationship of Piglet and Winnie-the-Pooh
French Medieval Rhymes
The Hero Image in *Farmer Giles of Ham*
Riddles as Children's Literature
Peanuts and Human Problems
The Effect of Sendak's Books on Children
Ghetto Rhymes as a Reflection of Social Change
Sports for Girls in Children's Literature
Jonathon Livingston Seagull as Fable
"Rebellion" in Children's Stories
Horses in Children's Literature
Religious Symbolism in Charles Schultz's Cartoons
Shadow Plays as Literature
Techniques of Story Telling
Symbolic Language of the Deaf and Certain Children's Stories
The Image of the Police in Children's Books
The Dragon's Role in Children's Literature
Revenge in Children's Literature
Figures of Authority in "Our Gang"

Music and the Folktales for Children
Bob Dylan's Songs as Children's Literature
Children's Songs as Literature
Parents as Villains in Children's Literature
Sex Roles in *Grimm's Fairy Tales*
Moral Values in *Charlotte's Web* and *Stuart Little*
Analysis of *Nancy Drew* Series
Socialization Trends from 1901 as Expressed in Children's Books
Crime and Punishment in Children's Literature
Attitudes in Children's Literature toward the Handicapped
Old Age in Children's Literature
Riddles as Children's Literature
Fear in the Grimm Brothers' Fairy Tales
New England Folk Tales as Children's Literature
Symbolism in Dr. Seuss Books
Children's Jokes
Witches and Witchcraft in Fairy Tales
Use of Language in *Uncle Remus*
Sibling Rivalry in Children's Literature
The Microcosm of *Winnie-the-Pooh*
The Bible as Children's Literature
Pop Songs as Children's Literature
North Carolina Ghost Stories and Their Phsycological Significance
Hans Christian Andersen as a Feminist

CONTRIBUTORS AND EDITORS

GILLIAN AVERY is the author of a number of novels set in Victorian England. Her *Nineteenth Century Children: Heroes and Heroines in English Children's Stories, 1780–1900* appeared in 1965.

JAN BAKKER teaches in the English Department of the University of Tennessee, Knoxville.

ALLEN M. BARSTOW was for two years a member of the Centre d'Etudes Supérieures de Civilisation Médiévale in Poitiers, France, and has taught at Lehigh and the University of Connecticut. He is a student of the courtly literature of the eleventh and twelfth centuries particularly interested in heraldry and the rituals of knighthood.

MARCELLA S. BOOTH, a specialist in modern poetry, prepared *From Confucius to Cummings: An Anthology of Poetry* in collaboration with Ezra Pound.

BENNETT A. BROCKMAN has written on medieval literature in *MLQ, Speculum, Medievalia et Humanistica,* and *Medieval Studies.*

FRANCELIA BUTLER is Professor of English at the University of Connecticut. She is currently working on a volume of children's literature of the seventeenth century and a textbook for courses in children's literature.

NANCY CHAMBERS is the editor of *Signal: Approaches to Children's Literature.*

CHARITY CHANG is Assistant University Librarian at the University of Connecticut and children's book reviewer for the Hartford *Courant.*

WAYNE DODD, Professor of English and Director of the Creative Writing Program at Ohio University, edits the *Ohio Review* and teaches a course in children's literature. His novel, *A Time of Huntings,* is published by Seabury Press.

A. HARRIS FAIRBANKS is the author of an article on Coleridge's "Dejection" in *PMLA* (October 1975). His poems have appeared in *Chernozem* and *The Apalachee Quarterly.*

LINDA FELDMEIER is a doctoral candidate in English at the University of Connecticut, where she team teaches the course in children's literature.

RACHEL FORDYCE, Assistant Professor of English at Virginia Polytechnic and State University, Blacksburg, is a specialist in children's theatre.

MARTIN GARDNER, author of over a hundred scientific and critical works, is best known to students of children's literature for his *Annotated Alice* and his introductions to several of L. Frank Baum's *Oz* books. He has also contributed some eighty short stories to *Humpty-Dumpty.*

DAVID L. GREENE, Associate Professor of English at Piedmont College, Demorest, Georgia, was editor of *The Baum Bugle,* 1968–73. He has prepared a forthcoming anthology of Baum fairy tales, *The Purple Dragon and Other Fantasies,* and is currently working on nineteenth-century American children's magazines.

EDWARD GUILIANO teaches in the English department at SUNY–Stony Brook and writes regularly on Victorian literature. He is the editor of a forthcoming book of new essays on Lewis Carroll.

PETER L. HAVHOLM is Assistant Professor of English at the College of Wooster. He is at work on a book using Kipling's prose fiction as an example of literature that demands systematic analysis.

TOM HEFFERNAN is Assistant Professor of English at Adelphi University.

ALETHEA K. HELBIG, Assistant Professor of English at Eastern Michigan University, has published articles in *University of Michigan Papers in Women's Studies* and *Michigan Academician.* She is presently preparing an anthology of children's poems.

NARAYAN KUTTY teaches children's literature at Eastern Connecticut State College. A specialist in modern British literature, he is also interested in the comparative study of Eastern and Western literature for children.

T. C. LAI teaches in the Department of Extramural Studies at The Chinese University of Hong Kong.

ELEANORE BRAUN LUCKEY is Professor of Family and Consumer Studies at the University of Utah.

MERADITH T. MCMUNN is the first candidate for the doctorate in Medieval Studies at the University of Connecticut.

WILLIAM ROBERT MCMUNN holds a Ph.D. from Indiana University and specializes in linguistics and the medieval period.

LEONARD R. MENDELSOHN teaches English at Concordia University, Montreal. He has written on Renaissance drama, Milton, Kafka, and other subjects.

ROSS MILLER teaches American literature at the University of Connecticut. He has been an editor of the *University Review* and *The Metropolitan Review.*

ROSA ANN MOORE is Assistant Professor of English at the University of Tennessee at Chattanooga, where she teaches children's literature.

WILLIAM T. MOYNIHAN, author of a study of Dylan Thomas, is Chairman of the Department of English at the University of Connecticut.

PETER F. NEUMEYER is the author of *The Faithful Fish* and other books for children. He has taught English at Berkeley, Harvard, and Stony Brook, and is currently Chairman of the English Department at the University of West Virginia.

GERALDINE D. POSS teaches English at Brooklyn College. A Spenserian, she also pursues interests in children's literature and creative writing.

MILLA B. RIGGIO teaches English at Trinity College, Hartford.

THOMAS J. ROBERTS is Professor of English at the University of Connecticut, where he teaches science fiction and fantasy.

BARBARA ROSEN, the author of *Witchcraft* (Taplinger, 1971), holds a Ph.D from The Shakespeare Institute, University of Birmingham.

WILLIAM ROSEN is the author of *Shakespeare and the Craft of Tragedy.*

LEO SCHNEIDERMAN is a psychologist with an active interest in literature and myth. He has been a contributor to *The Psychoanalytic Review* and the *Journal for the Scientific Study of Religion.*

WILLIAM E. SHEIDLEY has written on Elizabethan poetry in such scholarly journals as *SEL, JEGP, SP,* and *MLQ.*

KAMAL SHEORAN is on the editorial staff of The Children's Book Trust, Nehru House, New Delhi.

R. LORING TAYLOR, Assistant Professor of English at the University of Connecticut, recently studied and taught in Romania for two years.

P. L. TRAVERS was born in Australia and educated in Ireland. She is the author of *Mary Poppins* and *Friend Monkey.*

CAROL VASSALLO was formerly Associate Professor of Children's Literature at Eastern Connecticut State College.

STEPHEN WILKINSON teaches art at the University of Connecticut.

VIRGINIA L. WOLF is Lecturer in English at the University of Kansas, teaching courses in children's literature. Her publications include "The Root and Measure of Realism" and "The Quest for Growth in Children's Literature."

TED WOLNER is a city planner and a consultant to the Cooper-Hewitt Museum. He has published articles in *Harper's, New York,* and *The Village Voice.*

MARK ZAITCHIK is a doctoral candidate in English at the University of Connecticut. A student of E. L. Wallant, he has taught courses in writing and children's literature.

FEENIE ZINER is Associate Professor of English at the University of Connecticut and a frequent contributor to the *New York Times Book Review.* Among her many books for adults and children is *The Duck of Billingsgate Market,* reviewed in this volume.